THE ENGLISH MALADY

HISTORY OF PSYCHOLOGY SERIES
General Introduction

The historically interesting works reprinted in this series helped to prepare the way for the science of psychology. Most of these books are long forgotten, but their relevance to the field is unmistakable. Many of the writings on mental and moral philosophy, published before the dawn of scientific procedures, have much to commend them to present-day scholars. These books serve as groundwork for a fuller account of the background from which the field emerged, and they should be attractive to students who seek in the past for hints of the future direction that certain types of research can take. Each work will have an Introduction stating the provenance and significance of the book and will add appropriate biographical information.

Robert I. Watson
General Editor

University of New Hampshire

THE ENGLISH MALADY
(1733)

By George Cheyne

A FACSIMILE REPRODUCTION
WITH AN INTRODUCTION BY
ERIC T. CARLSON, M.D.

SCHOLARS' FACSIMILES & REPRINTS
DELMAR, NEW YORK, 1976

Published by
Scholars' Facsimiles & Reprints, Inc.
Delmar, New York 12054

Introduction © 1976
Scholars' Facsimiles & Reprints, Inc.
All rights reserved

Printed in the United States of America

Library of Congress Cataloging in Publication Data

Cheyne, George, 1671-1743.
The English malady (1733).

(History of psychology series)
Reprint of the 1733 ed. printed for G. Risk, Dublin.
Includes bibliographical references.
1. Nervous system—Diseases—Early works to 1800.
I. Title.
RC340.C5   1976   616.8   76-49853
ISBN 0-8201-1281-X

INTRODUCTION

Samuel Johnson, the eighteenth-century writer and wit, had words of high praise both for his former physician, Dr. George Cheyne, and the book Cheyne authored in his 60th year, *The English Malady*. On more than one occasion Johnson recommended that James Boswell, his friend and biographer, read it for his recurrent "black fits." Cheyne's name was known to many Britishers who suffered from nervous or hypochondriacal disorders and was mentioned, among others, by the novelist Henry Fielding, though Cheyne was a friend and partisan of Fielding's literary rival, Samuel Richardson.[1] Cheyne wrote for popular as well as medical audiences and his pungent comments regarding English society inevitably gave his books a broad appeal.

George Cheyne was born in February 1673, in Methlick, a town in northeastern Scotland.[2] His ancestors had long been residents of the Aberdeen area and once were large landowners, but by the time of Cheyne's birth the family holdings were markedly diminished. A quiet and studious child, he received a typical classical education but early developed a special interest in mathematics and the sciences. After graduating from Marischal College, Aberdeen, about 1690, he did not go into the ministry as his parents had hoped but instead became tutor to a John Ker, who was to become the first Duke of Roxburgh. He continued in this post until sometime after 1693, when Dr. Archibald Pitcairne returned from Leyden to launch his career at the newly founded Edinburgh Medical School. Cheyne became his devoted student. Pitcairne belonged to the new school of medical theorists, strong in Italy, who were trying to redefine the bodily functions as though the organism was a machine. As the body seemed composed of tubules and enclosed liquids, these writers applied mathematical and hydraulic knowledge to this model. This appealed to the scientifically and quantatively inclined young Cheyne, who wished to produce a mathematical theory of medicine. When his mentor was attacked for his theory of fevers, Pitcairne urged Cheyne to reply for him. He responded eagerly with his first book in 1701 *(A New Theory of Acute and Slow Continued Fevers)*[3], which he later admitted he wrote in "meer indignation" and which he realized even at the time was "a raw and unexperienced performance." Consequently he only agreed to its publication anonymously. It continued in print for 52 years, however, and later in his life he finally allowed his name to be attached to it. When soon after its publication a Dr. Charles Oliphant criticized the work, Cheyne counterattacked with a 1702 pamphlet[4] for which he apologized in 1724, as it contained "malicious and unmannerly turns, and also false and unjust representations."

The details of Cheyne's medical education are obscure. He was awarded a doctorate of medicine from Aberdeen in September, 1701, at the request of the Edinburgh faculty (because Edinburgh was not yet offering this degree). Armed with his degree and his recent election as a Fellow of the Royal Society, he opened a practice, eventually very successful, in London, and continued his writings. Since he was interested in mathematics and fascinated with certain issues in what became integral calculus, he wrote a book on the subject in 1703 which he later termed a "barren and airy" study.[5] For a time he was moving toward becoming one of a circle of young protégés of Isaac Newton, but he had antagonized Newton by refusing a gift. Cheyne's book further agitated Newton by its criticism of Edmund Halley, but had the value of provoking Newton after a long period of publishing silence to issue the 10-year-old manuscript of *The Optics,* with an appendix devoted to quadratures (fluxions).[6] Attacked also by his fellow countryman, Abraham de Moivre, Cheyne responded bitterly in a pamphlet that he typically later regretted.[7] In 1705, Cheyne organized and wrote up his earlier teachings to the future Duke of Roxburgh as *The Philosophical Principles of Religion: Natural and Revealed.* This book[8] reflected alike his religious inclinations and his scientific interests. He hoped that through it young students would have "the principles of natural religion insensibly installed into them." Like most of his books it went through several editions over 30 years and was praised as far afield as the Massachusetts Bay Colony by Cotton Mather. To later editions Cheyne added a second part to demonstrate that any knowledge of nature is obtained by analogy. In this he included a discussion of psychology based on three kinds of faculties which, "like gravity," strove toward three kinds of objects; these were material things, created spirits, and the "supreme and absolute Infinite." Sense perception, which properly belonged to the first faculty, was a model for all three. He set himself against Spinoza, Hobbes, Locke, and others who he felt regarded the soul as equivalent with merely the rational faculties of man.

After 1720, his writings and interests took a different direction. Prompted by his own ill health as well as the ailments of his patients, he struggled with the problems of cure and, more important, prevention of those diseases designated chronic. He wrote out his ideas for the prevention of acute episodes for a gouty patient. This apparently had circulated in manuscript and, fearing a pirated edition, he published it in 1720.[9] It remained in print until 1753. Cheyne suffered from gout himself, but probably not until after the first appearance of this book. In it he stated a number of themes that would appear repetitiously in all his subsequent volumes—the importance of constituion, the harmful effect of Great Britain's weather, the dangers of excessive diet and drink, and the risk of a scholarly and sedentary life. Four years later he produced his most popular work, *The Essay of Health and Long Life*,[10] but wrote, pessimistically and ironically, that it probably would be his last book. It went through at least 17 printings in several languages and was republished in the United States as late as 1813. Cheyne said the book was for "the sickly and the gentlemen of the learned professions." He poignantly wished in his preface that he had known these rules of health when he was a young man—"it is a common saying, that everyman past forty is either a fool or a physician." Then followed *The English Malady* (1733) and *An Essay on Regimen* (1740)[11] which he thought was his best book but which sold so poorly that he had to purchase the remainder of the first edition himself. As it contained much medical theory on the one hand and a religious emphasis on the other, it did not appeal as vigorously to the general public. His last work, *The Natural Method of Curing* (1742),[12] essentially a handbook of hygiene and therapy, was much more popular. It went through four editions the year it was published and was soon translated into French, Italian and Latin.

It is difficult to reconstruct Cheyne's practice, which varied with changes in his health and locale. He did exhibit a trend toward patients with the more chronic disorders, first at London and later at Bath. Many eminent persons were his patients and some were famous. Along with Johnson, there was the Methodist Reverend John Wesley and his follower, Selina Hastings, the Countess of Huntingdon,[13] the philosopher David Hume, whom he may have treated in an early depression, Richard "Beau" Nash, the arbiter of fashion at Bath, and the writer Alexander Pope.

Cheyne marrried Margaret Middleton (1680?-1752) of Bristol. They had a son and at least two daughters, one of whom, from Cheyne's letters to Richardson who was fond of her, seems to have shared her father's hypochondriacal tendencies. Cheyne died at Bath in his 71st year on 13 April 1743. In his final illness, he was attended by his brother-in-law and by the physician-philosopher, Dr. David Hartley.

In a sense, Cheyne's career and posthumous fame were built on his own problems. All of his later books are in part autobiographical. What were his problems and how did they influence his practice? Since the primary account of his sufferings is detailed in *The English Malady,* only a brief outline need be presented. He was a serious and temperate young child, somewhat predisposed to obesity. (There was a history of corpulence on one side of the family.) Vulnerable to stress, he would respond with diarrhea, salivation, and a tremor of his hands. He was diverted from a careful mode of life on his arrival in London at the age of 29, where he became a frequenter of the coffee houses and taverns. He drank and ate lustily and gained a reputation for conviviality as well as for excessive poundage. A contemporary described him thus: "Dr. Cheyne, a Scotchman, with an immense broad back, taking snuff incessantly out of a ponderous gold box, and thus ever and anon displaying his fat knuckles—a perfect Falstaff, a good portly man and corpulent. Almost as witty as the knight himself, his humor heightened by his northern brogue, his humor mirthful. The most excellent banterer of his time, a faculty he was often called on to exercise, to repel the lampoons made by others upon his extraordinary personal appearance."[14] Extraordinary he must have been, for his weight approached 450 pounds at times. Such corpulence led to ill health—Cheyne became short of breath, listless and lethargic. Headaches and severe lightheadedness came next, followed by increasing anxiety and depression. Giving up his high living friends, he went to Bath initially for treatment but remained to become an annual summertime resident. Bath, only one tenth the size of London, was one of the most famous spas and its mineral springs had been used for centuries. The town entered its "Golden Age" at the time of a visit by Queen Anne early in the 18th century and reached the peak of its popularity during Cheyne's lifetime as a place of assemblage for the social upper classes and their invalids. Given time for contemplation during his therapeutic visit to Bath, Cheyne was for a while much occupied with religion. His ruminations temporarily increased his anxiety, but after he had found peace his religious beliefs remained a steadfast personal support for the remainder of his life.

Although Cheyne used the traditional medical remedies of vomits and purges on himself, he discovered his greatest inspiration from a Dr. Taylor of Croyden, who had cured his own epileptic fits by going on a milk diet. Cheyne visited Taylor personally and, recalling that Thomas Sydenham had recommended such a regimen for hysteria and Archibald Pitcairne had a similar prescription for scurvy, he used it himself with the hoped-for results. Thereafter, although his resolve sometimes waivered, temperance in diet and drink were the mainstays of his therapeutic armamentarium, aided by mineral waters and mild exercise. What he practiced himself he advised also for the increasing number of patients who were "chronical, and especially low and nervous."

Cheyne acknowledged the damage his excesses had done to what he called his "crazy carcass," but he believed inherited constitution to be more important. Abandoning the traditional Galenical humoral temperaments (coleric, sanguine, melancholic, phlegmatic) Cheyne said that constitution was a function of the fibers of the body. Of himself he wrote, "I have been all my life of a spongy, flabby, relaxed habit, of weak nerves."

Individuals of this type had "original weak nerves" and a "scurbutic cachexia" or "scobutico-nervose." When this predisposing constitution was acted upon by deleterious factors in the environment, or from poor personal hygiene, scurvy resulted. The clarification of the nature of scurvy by James Lind and Thomas Trotter was to come later in the century; Cheyne reflected a common definition of it as a kind of general ill health or "bad habit of the body." Scurvy was the cause of all chronic disorders, he said. It caused such disparate illnesses as diabetes, asthma, cancer and "almost all nervous distempers whatsoever." He found scurvy the most common chronic disorder in England. Why should this be so? He believed the answers were to be found in the British climate and the customs of the English people. He spoke of an "English constitution," and then a "British distemper" which was identical with the "English malady." The "inconstancy and inclemency of the seasons," the pernicious northeast winds and the "nitrous and sulphurous smoke" polluting the skies of London all contributed to a high morbidity. Even more important were the errors of diet and the excessive use of alcohol which he felt were reaching epidemic proportions and were spreading from the upper classes to the trades people. Another risk he saw for the upper classes and the studious was the lack of proper exercise —a particular danger to the "rich, lazy and voluptuos."

Whether the causes be social, psychological, or physical they ultimately altered the makeup of the body. When the mechanisms of the body became disrupted from any of these causes, treatment was in order but could be difficult. Cheyne therefore strongly favored anticipation and prevention as the easier course. In doing so he in essence followed the tradition of the so-called six non-naturals. They were a contribution of Galen, but so widely used were they that before Cheyne's time they had been dissociated from Galen's name.[15] Robert Burton, for example, had included them in his extensive review of melancholy. They traditionally included air, food and drink, sleep, exercise, various evacuations, and the human emotions. Most of these fitted well into the growing naturalism that was the legacy of the 17th century. In advocating the proper control of these vital factors, Cheyne especially stressed temperance in eating and drinking. Bluntly he asserted a failure in self-control was really "self-murder." John Wesley commented on the futility of Cheyne's hope than an epicure would accept criticism of eating and drinking.[16] Cheyne also knew what he was asking of his patients—his regimen demanded self-denial, and this the British people did not admire. But he pleaded: "To cut off our days by intemperance, indiscretion, and guilty passions, to live miserably for the sake of gratifying a sweet tooth, or a brutal itch; to die martyrs to our luxury and wantonness, is equally beneath the dignity of human nature, and contrary to the homage we own the Author of our beings."[17] Thus guarded, health made a man dutiful to God and useful to himself and others.

A concern with conditions we now would consider emotional may be found in all Cheyne's books, but it is greatest in *The English Malady*. Although not as popular as some of his other writings, it went through six editions in three years.[18] For all the criticisms that may be directed at this book—and there have been many, ranging from lack of originality through a poor writing style[19]—it is important to the history of behavioral science in three ways. First, in his attention to the solid fibers of the body and to weak nerves, he promoted the trend which increasingly associated mental disorders with the nervous system. Leading figures in this tradition were the contemporary German Friedrich Hoffman and another Scotsman later in the century, William Cullen, who, with an emphasis on neural pathology, introduced the word neurosis to represent the nervous disorders. Second, Cheyne contributed to the literature regarding the minor emotional illnesses which grew during the 17th and 18th centuries and started building rapidly at the end of the 19th. Many of the same "nervous disorders" had been discussed in England a century earlier in Robert Burton's *The Anatomy of Melancholy* and can be followed in the scattered literature on hysteria (fits of the mother, the vapours) and hypochondriases (being hyped, the spleen). In Cheyne's own case may be seen a mixture of depression, anxiety and psychophysiological responses. These types of problems were believed to be increasingly common and were more clearly delineated in medical literature. Thomas Sydenham reported that one-sixth of his patients suffered from nervous disorders.[20] Cheyne raised the figure to one-third and later Thomas Trotter said nervous disorders had displaced fevers as the most common illnesses. Trotter believed that a full two-thirds of his patients had nervous complaints.[21] Further clarification would follow in the literature of the 19th century on dyspepsia, neurasthenia, psychasthenia, and anxiety neuroses.

Finally, Cheyne is noteworthy for his emphasis on cultural factors which contribute to the "English malady." The idea that there might be diseases particularly common to the British Isles had been growing for some time both at home and in foreign commentaries. Gideon Harvey, sometime physician to King Charles II, wrote a book in 1672 on the *Morbus Anglicus* in which he considered various wasting diseases including hypochondriacal melancholy.[22] Shortly before Cheyne's book, Richard Blackmore extended the idea further into the psychiatric area by proposing the disorder of the "English spleen."[23] How Cheyne thought living in England increased the rash of nervous disorders is recounted in this volume. Belief that civilization causes diseases generated scattered commentaries in the 18th century, grew in interest with the passing of the 19th century, and has become an object of research in our day.

ERIC T. CARLSON, M.D.

New York Hospital—Cornell Medical Center
New York, N.Y.

NOTES

1. Charles F. Mullett, editor, *The Letters of Doctor George Cheyne to Samuel Richardson (1733-1743)* (Columbia, Mo.: University of Missouri, 1943).

2. Henry R. Viets, "George Cheyne (1673-1743)," *Bulletin of the History of Medicine* 1949, *23:* 435-452. This article and the one by Mullett, above, are the main sources of biographical information.

3. George Cheyne, *A New Theory of Acute and Slow Continued Fevers,* 4th ed. (London: G. Strahan, 1724).

4. George Cheyne, *Remarks on Two Late Pamphlets Written by D[r.] O[liphant] against Dr. Pitcairn's Dissertations, and the New Theory of Fevers* ([Edinburgh], 1702).

5. George Cheyne, *Fluxionum Methodus Inversa; sive Quantitatum Fluentium Leges Generaliores* (London: J. Matthews and R. Smith, 1703).

6. Bernard I. Cohen, *Franklin and Newton,* Philadelphia: American Philosophical Society, 1956, p. 48. See also: Frank E. Manuel, *A Portrait of Isaac Newton* (Cambridge, Mass.: Harvard University Press, 1968), pp. 274-276.

7. George Cheyne, *Rudimentorum Methodi Fluxionum Inversae Specimina* (London: B. Motte and G. Strahan, 1705).

8. George Cheyne, *Philosophical Principles of Religion: Natural and Revealed,* 2d ed. (London: G. Strahan, 1705).

9. George Cheyne, *An Essay of the True Nature and Due Method of Treating the Gout,* 6th ed. (London: G. Strahan, 1724).

10. George Cheyne, *An Essay on Health and Long Life* (London: G. Strahan and J. Leake, 1724).

11. George Cheyne, *An Essay on Regimen* (London: C. Rivington and J. Leake, 1740).

12. George Cheyne, *The Natural Method of Cureing the Diseases of the Body and the Disorders of the Mind depending on the Body* (London: G. Strahan, 1742).

13. Charles F. Mullett, *The Letters of Dr. George Cheyne to the Countess of Huntingdon* (San Marino, Calif.: Huntington Library, 1940).

14. R.S. Siddall, "George Cheyne, M.D.: Eighteenth-Century Clinician and Medical Author," *Annals of Medical History,* 3d ser., vol. 4 (1942): 95-109.

15. Lelland J. Rather, "The 'Six Things Non-Natural': A Note on the Origins and Fate of a Doctrine and a Phrase," *Clio Medica* 3 (1958): 337-347.

16. Siddall, "George Cheyne," p. 99.

17. Cheyne, *Health,* p. 4.

18. The original publisher G. Straham produced a 6th edition in 1735. There is also a reset and perhaps pirated Dublin edition in 1733.

19. Denis Leigh, *The Historical Development of British Psychiatry* (New York: Pergamon Press, 1961), pp. 22-23. For praise of his style see the anonymous "George Cheyne (1671-1743), Master of Style," *J.A.M.A.* 203 (1958): 516-517.

20. John G. Howells and M. Livia Osborn, "The Incidence of Emotional Disorder in a 17th Century Medical Practice," *Medical History* 14 (1970): 192-198.

21. Thomas Trotter, *A View of the Nervous Temperament,* 2d ed. (London: Edw. Walker for Longman, Hurst, Rees, and Orme, 1807).

22. Godeon Harvey, *Morbus Anglicus, or a Theoretick and Practical Discourse of Consumptions, and Hypochondriack Melancholy* (London: Thackeray, 1672). Cited in Richard Hunter, *Three Hundred Years of Psychiatry, 1535-1860* (London: Oxford University Press, 1963), p. 196.

23. Richard Blackmore, *A Treatise of the Spleen and Vapours: or, Hypocondriacal and Hysterical Affections* (London: Pemberton, 1725).

THE
English Malady:
OR, A
TREATISE
OF
Nervous Diseases of all Kinds,
AS
Spleen, Vapours, Lowness of Spirits, Hypochondriacal, and Hysterical Distempers, &c.

In THREE PARTS.

PART I. Of the Nature and Cause of Nervous Distempers.
PART II. Of the Cure of Nervous Distempers.
PART III. Variety of Cases that illustrate and confirm the Method of Cure.

With the AUTHOR'*s own* CASE *at large.*

———Facilis descensus Averni,
Sed revocare Gradum, superasque evadere ad Auras,
Hic Labor, *hoc* Opus est. *Pauci quos Æquus amavit,*
Jupiter, *aut ardens evexit ad Æthera Virtus*
Dis Geniti potuere——— VIRG.

By *GEORGE CHEYNE*, M. D.
Fellow of the *College of Physicians* at *Edinburgh*, and F. R. S.

LONDON Printed, And *DUBLIN*
Re-printed by S. POWELL, for GEORGE RISK, GEORGE EWING, and WILLIAM SMITH, in *Dame's-street*, Booksellers. M,DCC,XXXIII.

To the Right Honourable the

Lord *BATEMAN*, &c.

Knight of the moſt Honourable Order of the BATH.

My Lord,

Beg leave to preſent to your *Lordſhip* this Treatiſe, which, while in *Manuſcript*, you ſo kindly and warmly deſired to ſee in *Print*. The chief Deſign of theſe Sheets is to recommend to my Fellow Creatures that plain *Diet* which is moſt agreeable to the Purity and Simplicity of uncorrupted *Nature*, and unconquer'd *Reaſon*. Ill would it ſuit, *my Lord*, with ſuch a Deſign to introduce it with a Dedication

DEDICATION.

dication cook'd up to the Height of a *French* or *Italian* Taste. Addresses of this Kind are generally a Sort of *Ragous* and *Olios*, compounded of Ingredients as pernicious to the Mind as such unnatural Meats are to the Body. Servile Flattery, fulsome Compliments, and *bombast Panegyrick* make up the *nauseous* Composition. But I know that your *Lordship*'s Taste is too delicate, and your Judgment too chaste to be able to bear such *Cookery*. Your taking these Sheets into your Patronage will probably be a Post not to be maintained without some Difficulty. *Prejudice*, *Interest*, and *Appetite* are powerful Antagonists, which nothing but good Sense, solid Virtue, and true *Christian* Courage are capable of opposing. Was not your *Lordship* eminently endued with those invaluable Qualities, I should not have been so fond of thrusting this, almost *Orphan-Work* out into the World under your safe Conduct. But your Practice, *my Lord*, has long engaged you on the
Side

DEDICATION.

Side of Temperance, Sobriety, and Virtue, and I hope you will not think it a disagreeable Task to avow and justify those Principles to the Publick, by which you have hitherto been guided so much to your Advantage in private. I dare assert, *my Lord*, that in defending this Cause you will fight under the Banner of Truth: and be the Opposition of Prejudice, Error, or Malice, ever so mighty, I know that Patience and Perseverance will be sufficient to render the Conquest secure. The promoting, according to my best Abilities, the Ease, Health, and Welfare of Mankind in general, and of my fellow-suffering *Valetudinarians* in particular, has been the whole and sole View with which I have once more dared to appear in *Print*. Your Love of the Design will, I hope, make you blind to the Imperfections and Weakness of the Execution. The Protection of such a Work, *my Lord*, is properly yours. Your *Humanity* and *Benevolence* are always engaging you in the Pursuit of the same Ends, tho'

DEDICATION.

by different Means. If you still think, after a mature Revisal of these Papers, that these my poor Endeavours may be useful to the *Publick*, I know you will be their generous Advocate, meerly upon Principle, and even in Opposition to Party. The Continuance of your Approbation will give me a most sincere Pleasure, as your Condescension in permitting me to do my self this *Honour*, will always be esteem'd one of the many Obligations you have so kindly conferred on,

My Lord,

Your Lordship's

Most Obliged, Faithful,

Humble Servant,

Geo. Cheyne.

PREFACE.

I. THE Title *I have chosen for this Treatise, is a* Reproach *universally thrown on this* Island *by Foreigners, and all our Neighbours on the* Continent, *by whom* nervous *Distempers*, Spleen, Vapours, *and* Lowness of Spirits, *are in Derision, called the ENGLISH MALADY. And I wish there were not so good Grounds for this Reflection. The* Moisture *of our* Air, *the* Variableness *of our* Weather, (*from our Situation amidst the* Ocean) *the* Rankness *and* Fertility *of our Soil, the* Richness *and* Heaviness *of our Food, the* Wealth *and* Abundance *of the Inhabitants,* (*from their universal Trade*) *the* Inactivity *and* sedentary Occupations *of the better Sort,* (*among whom this* Evil *mostly rages*) *and the* Humour *of living in great, populous, and consequently unhealthy Towns, have brought forth a* Class *and* Set *of Distempers, with* atrocious *and* frightful Symptoms, *scarce known to our Ancestors, and never rising to such fatal* Heights, *nor afflicting such*

Numbers *in any other known Nation. These nervous Disorders being computed to make almost one third of the Complaints of the People of* Condition *in* England.

II. *This* Work *has lain finish'd by me, as it now appears (at least in the main) these several Years past, and was intended as a* Legacy *and* Dying-Speech, *only to my* Fellow-Sufferers *under these Complaints. And had certainly never appear'd (till its Author had disappear'd) had it not been for the perhaps indiscreet* Zeal *of some of my warmest* Friends, *who (upon the late Frequency and daily Encrease of wanton and uncommon Self-murderers, produc'd mostly by this* Distemper, *and their* blasphemous *and* frantick Apologies *grafted on the Principles of the* Infidels, *and propagated by their* Disciples*) extorted it from me, to try what a little more just and solid* Philosophy, *join'd to a Method of* Cure, *and proper Medicines could do, to put a Stop to so universal a* Lunacy *and* Madness.

III. *Some good-natur'd and ingenious Retainers to the* Profession, *on my Publication of my* Book *of* long Life *and* Health, *proclaim'd every where that I was turn'd mere* Enthusiast, *and resolv'd all Things into* Allegory *and* Analogy, *advis'd People to turn* Monks, *to run into Desarts, and to live on* Roots, Herbs, *and* wild Fruits; *in fine, that I was at Bottom a mere* Leveller, *and for destroying* Order, Ranks *and* Property, *every one's but my own. But that Sneer had
its*

PREFACE.

its Day, and vanish'd into Smoak. Others swore I had eaten my Book, *recanted my* Doctrine *and* System (*as they were pleas'd to term it*) *and was returned again to the* Devil, *the* World, *and the* Flesh. *This Joke I have also stood. I have been slain again and again, both in* Verse *and* Prose; *but I thank GOD I am still alive and well.*

IV. *But to cut off all Occasions of Mistake, and every Handle of Misrepresentation of my Meaning and Intention, as far as in me lies, I here solemnly declare it, as my* Judgment *and* Opinion (*if it be worth the knowing*) *founded on the Experience and Observation of many Years:* 1st. *That the* Diet *and* Manner of Living *of the middling* Rank, *who are but moderate and temperate in* Foods *of the common and natural Product of the Country,* to wit *in* animal Foods *plainly dress'd, and* Liquors *purify'd by* Fermentation *only, without the* Tortures of the Fire, *or without being turned into* Spirits, *is that intended by the Author of Nature for this* Climate *and* Country, *and consequently the most wholesome and fittest in general, for* prolonging Life, *and* preventing Distempers, *that the* Ends of Providence *and the* Conditions of Mortality *will admit.* 2dly, *That no* wise Man, *who is but moderate and temperate in this manner, ought* on any Account *to alter the Kind and Quality of his* Diet, *while his* Health *and* Appetite *are good.* 3dly, *That* no wise Man, *even when he has fallen into, or is threatened with a* Distemper, *ought to change*

change the Quality *of his* Diet, *till he has duly and sufficiently try'd, what* proper Medicines *can do, by the Advice of the most experienced and knowing* Physicians. 4. *That the Changes that are advis'd to be made, ought to be duly and maturely consider'd, and enter'd upon by* Degrees, *whether from a higher to a lower, or from a lower to a higher* Diet. 5. *That strong high* animal Foods, *and* generous defecated spirituous Liquors, *as begetting warm, full, and enliven'd Juices, urging on the Circulation with Force, and the Secretions with Vigour, in young, robust, healthy Constitutions, are fittest and most effectual for mechanical and animal Strength, Force, Action, and Labour: And so absolutely necessary for Handy-crafts, great Fatigue, and military Prowess. But these are not the Matter in Question here, which is about preventing and curing Distempers already brought on, brightening the Faculties, and fitting them for intellectual and sedentary Purposes, and lengthening the natural Life.* 6. *That a* proper *and* specifick Diet *for each* Distemper, *is as necessary to be known and prescrib'd by an honest and faithful* Physician, *as proper and specifick* Medicines; (*for in these two* only, *the very* Essence *of the Science consists, not separately but conjointly*). *And* 7. *That only in those Distempers commonly reckon'd* incureable, *the Reproach of* Physick *and* Physicians, *and which are in their own Nature, either* mortal *or insupportably painful, such as as torturing*, habitual Gouts, *confirm'd* Cancers, *obstinate Venereal Distempers, the* Stone *in the* Kidneys, *or in the* Bladder (*when Lithotomy cannot be administrated*); *a* Pulmonick Phthisis, *a* Nervous Atrophy, *the* Epilepsy, *and the other higher and inconquerable hysterick and hypochondriack Disorders, a settled* Hectick (*from Ulcers*) *an* Elephantiasis *and* Leprosy, *a humorous* Asthma, *a chronical* Diabetes, *an incurable* Scrophula *and a deep* Scurvy. *I say, in these only, and only in these when they are become manifest, have resisted all other common Methods, and the Patients are rather growing worse than better under them, is a* total *and* strict Milk, Seed *and* Vegetable Diet, *proper or to be attempted; and that in other more simple and slight Cases, and even in the first Stages of these mentioned Distempers, a common moderate and temperate animal Diet, and well-chosen Medicines, will be sufficient. Now if after all this, any one is dispos'd to be merry with me, I ought not, I shall not grudge them their Diversion.*

V. *I think truly, a thin, poor, cool, low Diet as improper and unnatural to a robust,* active, strong, healthy Man, *as a gross, full, high Diet, is for a poor, thin, low, valetudinary Creature. For the whole Art of Physick, and the Wisdom of animal Life, consists in adjusting Diet and Medicines to the Habit and the Distempers. For the Diet that wou'd make a Nightingale healthy and gay, wou'd starve and kill a Kite, and*

on

on the contrary: But it is odds if a Free-drinking, or Free-thinking Physician be not as improper to advise a poor weak, low, dying Creature, as a Free-drinking, Free-thinking Casuist is to advise a scrupulous and tender Conscience. Men of all Professions think, write *and* advise themselves, *and their own Characters, and impress their own* Signatures *on every thing they do, say, and advise;* which, I hope, may be an Apology *for Me, if in any thing I have overshot the* Golden Mean, *which, I am pretty certain I have not, to those, who reason and think, and prefer Health, Cheerfulness, and long Life, to a short Life and a merry.*

VI. *After all, I would not have it thought, that I am of Opinion that none ever fail'd or died, who enter'd on a* Milk, Seed, *and* Vegetable Diet *under these mention'd* Distempers. *The noble* Organs *may be spoilt or irretrievably obstructed, which the wisest Physician alive cannot absolutely foreknow; the Time remaining and necessary for a total Cure of such tedious Diseases, may not be sufficient in the common* Duration of Life. *All I affirm therefore, is, that such a Diet in the* mention'd Distempers, *with the usual proper Medicines, duly persisted in, will do the Whole that* Art *can possibly do, or Mortality will admit; and infinitely more than the same Medicines under a* full *and free* Diet of Animal Foods *and* Spirituous Liquors; *and at the very least, will make their*

PREFACE.

their Pains and Sufferings less both in Life *and* Death.

VII. *What I pretend to have done in some Degree in the following Treatise, is, That I hope I have explain'd the Nature and Causes of* Nervous Distempers (*which have hitherto been reckon'd* Witchcraft, Enchantment, Sorcery *and* Possession, *and have been the constant Resource of Ignorance*) *from Principles easy, natural and intelligible, deduc'd from the best and soundest* Natural Philosophy; *and have by the plainest Reasoning, drawn from these* Causes *and this* Philosophy, *a* Method of Cure *and a* Course of Medicines *specifically obviating these Causes, confirm'd by long Experience and repeated Observations, and conformable to the Practice of the ablest and best Writers on these Diseases.*

VIII. *The most material Objection my* ablest Friends *have made to this* Piece *is, That much of it is a Repetition of what I have already said in Print, and some of it but a* lame and imperfect Representation *of what is much better said by others. But as this* Objection *regards only myself and my Reputation as an* Author, *I will suffer it to have its whole Effect. There can be no greater Evidence of the* Truth of Principles, *than their being* simple *and* few, *and readily applicable to solve all the possible Appearances. Nature produces many and various Effects in different Circumstances, from one and the same Cause.* Truth *is simple and one*

one in its Root and Source, but various and manifold in different Situations and Circumstances. And I shall not think it Tautology, *to press and inculcate the same* Methods of Cure, *even in different Distempers, from the same Causes, if it be done from different Views and Considerations.*

IX. *There are two Sorts of Readers I have not the most remote Hopes of convincing or giving Satisfaction to*; viz. the Voluptuous *and* Unthinking. *Those who value Life only for the Sake of* good Eating and Drinking, *and those whose* thinking Faculties *and* Organs *have never been truly* form'd *or duly* cultivated; *neither of* these *will ever bear or can receive any Conviction or Reasoning from such* Principles *as I lay down. But the* Laws of Nature, *and the immutable* Relations of Things, *are too stubborn to bend to such* Gentlemen; *and I should not chuse to study such a Sort of* Particulars, *to learn uncorrupted Nature, its* Laws *and* Order, *no more than I should apply to a* monstrous Production *to learn the* Genius *of a* Tribe, *or a* Species *either of* Vegetables *or* Animals. *Possibly even they themselves may be convinc'd at least in some measure, when their* proper Time *is come; and sooner or later it may come, unless the* Minute Philosophy *prevail, and become the* Standard. *For probably when they begin to feel violent* Pain, *long* Sickness, *habitual* Low Spirits, *or enter upon the* Limits of

both

PREFACE.

both Worlds, *they may be convinced. For, in the main, I believe the Cause of these Distempers here assign'd,* just *and* adequate, *and on the Success of the* Methods of Cure *laid down in general (in Cases where any thing would succeed) I could venture my* Reputation, Fortune *and* Life.

X. *If any of your* Authors *without* Names, *who wound in the Dark;* your Hackney-Scriblers, *who want only to give their* Lucubrations *Sale; your profane and* bold Wits, *who fight behind Jingle and Rhime; your* Philomaths, *who, without Experiment or Observation, want only to shew a way; or your* Pestle-and-Mortar Men, *who have more Time on their Hands than Business, think fit to try their* Parts *on this* Performance; *for their Encouragement, they need only consider the* Author *as gone to his* long Home, *or his Faculties (as they could wish) impair'd or extinct. But if any* Sober *and* Serious *Person, who has* Nature *in* View, *and is in Search of* Truth *only, ready to embrace it on what Side of the Question soever it lies, has any* Difficulties *or* Doubts, *he may find some one or other who may give him all the Satisfaction he can desire; if it be true (as it most certainly is) that where the* Philosopher *ends, there the* Physician *begins. If I could choose, I should name only those for my* Judges, *who to a competent Knowledge of the* Laws of Nature *and* Mechanism, *have join'd an Acquaintance with the best* Natural Philosophy, *the latest* Discoveries *in* Natural History, *and the* Pow-

ers

ers *and* Virtues *of* Medicines, *and had been long conversant in the* Practice *of* Physick *and Attendance on the Sick and* Diseased: *And by their Judgment I should* stand or fall. *But since I have not the most remote Prospect to hope, or the least Vanity to flatter myself, either to prevail on but a very few of the Suffering, Sick and Diseased, or to choose my* Readers *and* Judges, *I must be contented to stand my* Fate, *be it what it will.*

XI. *For how this Work may be received by the* Publick *in general, I think I have no further Concern, than as its bad or good Reception may affect the* Publick, *by disappointing the* Good *it might do, or encouraging the* Evils *it might prevent. I flatter'd myself it might entertain, instruct and direct the* Ingenious Delicate Valetudinarian, *and give at least the unprejudic'd younger* Physician *a different way of thinking in these* Distempers *from the* Common, *which has been the Reverse of my* Doctrine. *I am myself come to that* Time of Life *when* Hopes *and* Fears *ought to be contracted into a very narrow Compass. I have done my* best, *and pursu'd in my own* Case *the same Rules I have given to others, and have at present,* I thank God, *inward* Peace, Health *and* Freedom of Spirits.

Inveni Portum, Spes & Fortuna Valete.

THE

THE CONTENTS.

PART I.

INTRODUCTION   Page 1

CHAP. I.

Of the Sources and Causes of Chronical Distempers in general.

The Causes of Chronical Distempers of three Sorts. 1. A Sizyness or Viscidity in the Fluids. 2. A Sharpness or corrosive Quality in the Fluids. 3. A Laxity or Want of due Tone in the Fibres or Nerves   5
The necessary Effects of such Causes   6

CHAP. II.

Of the general Causes of the Disorders of the Nerves.

1. *Want or Excess of Humidity in the Solids*   7
2. *Concretions of Salts*   8
3. *The Interruption or Interception of the Vibrations of the Nerves by the Viscidity of the Juices*   9
4. *The Weakness or Laxity of their Tone*   ibid.

What Diseases are properly call'd Nervous   10

CHAP. III.

Of the general Division of Nervous Distempers.

All Nervous Cases but the several Steps or Stages of the same Distemper   10
Nervous Distempers of three Kinds, 1. *Such as are attended with a partial or total Loss of Sensation for some Time*   11
   2. *Such as are attended with the Loss of voluntary Motion in any particular Organ or Limb*   12
   3. *Such as are attended with Spasms, Cramps, or Convulsions*   ibid.
Another Distinction of nervous Disorders, into original and acquir'd   13
The Misfortune of original weak Nerves may be the Cause of greater Felicity   14
Persons of original weak Nerves incapable of ever intirely obtaining the same Strength and Vigour with those of strong Fibres   ibid.
Such Persons, if they get over the Meridian of Life, commonly live healthy to a great old Age   15
How nervous Disorders are acquir'd   16

CHAP. IV.

That what is swallowed down and received into the Habit, is the first and chief efficient Cause of all that Mankind suffer in their Bodies.

That Men bring upon themselves all their Miseries 18
That what is receiv'd into the Habit is the Cause of all Diseases, prov'd from the Mechanism of the human Body, and the Laws of the Animal Oeconomy 19

CHAP. V.

Of the surprizing and wonderful Effects of Salts, especially of the volatile, urinous, or animal Salts, upon human Bodies and Constitutions.

Of the great Energy and Activity of Salts in general 24
Of the Cause of their Energy and Activity 26
Of mineral Salt, and the various Changes it suffers by entring into vegetable and animal Substances 27
Why mineral and vegetable Salts have more immediate and sensible Effects than animal Salts 28
Of the Effects of Salts in general upon human Bodies 29
That rich Foods and generous Wines owe their Poignancy and high Taste to the Salts with which they abound 30
That the mentioned Properties of Salts arise only from their Size, Shape, and Attraction of their Particles 32

CHAP. VI.

Of the Frequency of nervous Disorders, in later Years, beyond what they have been obferv'd in former Times.

A vulgar Miftake, in accounting for the Frequency of thefe Diforders in later Years   33
The true Caufe affign'd, viz. 1. *Luxury*   34
    2. *An unactive, fedentary, or ftudious Life*   36
    3. *Living in great and populous Cities*   38
Difeafes introduc'd among the Greeks *and* Romans *by the fame Caufes*   39
That all Difeafes are remotely derived from the fame Principles   ibid.
Nervous Difeafes known in fome Degree to the Ancients   41

CHAP. VII.

Of the true Nature of the Fibres and Nerves.

What is meant by a Fibre, and what are its Properties   42
Of the Structure of the Solids in an animal Body   43
Of the different Sorts of fenfible or compound Fibres   ib.
Of their Nature and Properties   44
Elafticity neceffary in Fibres   45

CHAP. VIII.

Of the Ufe of the Fibres and Nerves, and the Manner and Caufes of Senfation, and of Mufcular Motion.

The intelligent Principle of a different Nature from the organical Machine which contains it   47

How

CONTENTS.

How the Sensations are performed 48
Of the Nature and Cause of Elasticity 50
Of Muscular Motion 51

CHAP. IX.

Of the Existence of animal Spirits, and of their Use to account for animal Motion, and the other animal Functions.

The various Opinions of Writers on this Subject 53
The Objections commonly made against the Existence of animal Spirits 54
The Impossibility of their Existence shewn from other Principles 55
The Absurdity of attempting to account for nervous Diseases by the Existence of animal Spirits 57
Of the various Systems of Fluids 58
Of the Nature of the Brain and Nerves, and the Manner in which their Functions are performed 60

CHAP. X.

Of the Generation, Animation, Nutrition, and Growth of the Solids and Fluids of Animals, and some other Functions of the animal Oeconomy.

That there is a self-active and self-motive Principle in all Animals 62
Of the Generation of Animals 63
That the Organs of an Animal are in Number, in some Sense, infinite, at least indefinite ibid.
Some Propositions containing the Nature, Generation, Nutrition, and other Functions of the animal Oeconomy 64

CHAP. XI.

Of the Signs and Symptoms of a too relaxed, loose, and tender State of Nerves.

Weakness of the Nerves discoverable from the Pulse and Nature of the Circulation   68
    From the Nature and Colour of the Hair   ibid.
    From the Muscles and Colour of the Skin   69
Fatness or Corpulence a Sign of weak Nerves   70
Preternatural Evacuations   ibid.
Coldness in the Extremities of the Body   71
Stammering, Difficulty of Utterance, Deafness, &c.   ibid.
That a Laxity and Want of due Tone and Elasticity in the Solids, produce viscid and sharp Juices, and on the contrary   72

PART II.

CHAP. I.

Of the general Method of Cure of nervous Distempers.

THE first Intention, to thin, dilute, and sweeten the Fluids   78
The second Intention, to break and dissolve the saline Concretions in the small Vessels   ibid.
The third and last Intention, to wind up and contract the Fibres of the whole System   79
That each Intention ought to be pursued separately   80
Of the Time necessary for each Intention   81
Of the various Changes of the Blood under Diseases of all Kinds   ibid.
Of the State of the Blood in nervous Disorders   85

CHAP. II.

Of the Method and Medicines proper for the first Intention.

What Sort of Medicines are fittest to attenuate the Juices 86
The Necessity of beginning with Evacuations ibid.
The Medicines of the first Intention specified 87
Calomel, how to be administred ibid.
Of Æthiops Mineral, Æthiops Antimon. Mercurius Alcalisatus, Præcipitat per se, and Quicksilver, &c. 88

The great Use of all Mercurial Preparations in chronical Cases, and the Preparations proper for each particular Case 90
Of the wild Valerian 94

CHAP. III.

Of the Medicines proper for the second Intention.

The Medicines for the first Intention may be compounded with those for the second 95
Active and volatile Medicines fittest for the second Intention 96
The Medicines for the second Intention specified 97
Of Assa-fœtida ibid.
Of Ammoniacum, Sagapenum, &c. 98

CHAP. IV.

Of the Medicines proper for the third Intention.

The Medicines proper for the third Intention, of the astringent Kind. These Medicines specified 100

Contents.

Of the Jesuits Bark, and its great Efficacy in nervous Cases   100
Of Bitters, chalybeat Medicines, and mineral chalybeat Waters   101

CHAP. V.

Of the Regimen of Diet proper for nervous Distempers.

A proper Regimen of Diet much used by the Antients in the Cure of Diseases; and why it is so little regarded at present   103
That the Foods and Physick proper to the middling Sort in each Country is the best   108
The Benefit of the Loathing and Inappetency that attends Disorders   109
That Diseases are cured by the contrary Methods to those which produced them   110
Of the Qualities of the Food proper in nervous Disorders   111
Of the Quantity of the Food   ibid.
That different Degrees of Temperance are necessary, as the Symptoms are more or less violent   112
What Cases require a total Abstinence from animal Food and fermented Liquors   113
That a total Milk and vegetable Diet is not proper in all Diseases   115
The Advantages of a milk and vegetable Diet above any other, in Cases wherein it is proper, and on the contrary   117
The Causes of these Advantages or Disadvantages   118

CHAP. VI.

Of the Exercise proper for nervous Disorders.

The Necessity of Exercise to Health in general   120

Contents.

The great Use made of Exercise by the Antients in the Cure of Distempers   121
The great Benefit of Exercise confirmed from Reason as well as Experience   123
What Kinds of Exercise are best   125
The Benefit of Amusement   126

CHAP. VII.

Of some of the more immediate and eminent Causes of nervous Disorders.

All nervous Disorders proceed from some glandular Distemper, either scrophulous or scorbutical   127
A vitious Liver or Spleen one of the primary Causes of nervous Disorders   128
Knotted Glands in the Mysentery or Guts another Cause   130
Cutaneous Disorders productive of nervous Distempers   131
Some other Causes assigned.   132

CHAP. VIII.

Of the Spleen, Vapours, Lowness of Spirits, Hysterical or Hypochondriacal Disorders.

The Symptoms of these Disorders, whence to be deduced   133
What Symptoms properly belong to Vapours   134
Of the different Kinds or Degrees of Vapours   135
Of the first Degree of Vapours, and the Symptoms attending it   136
Of the second and third Degrees of Vapours and their Symptoms   137
Of the Difference between acute and chronical Diseases, in their Origin and Production   139
That Vapours are the first Symptoms of all Chronical Diseases   141

CHAP.

CHAP. IX.

Of the Cure of the Symptoms of Vapours, Hysterical and Hypochondriacal Disorders.

Gentle Vomits an effectual Remedy for all the Symptoms 142
Of Restlessness and Inquietude of Spirits 143
Of Lowness not attended with Sickness or Pain 144
Of the frequent Discharge of limpid pale Water by Urine 145
Of the Spitting or Salivation common in nervous Distempers 146
Of some other Symptoms attending Vapours 147
Of transient Disorders of this Kind incident to healthy Persons ibid.

CHAP. X.

Of the nervous Disorders of the Convulsive Tribe, particularly of Hysterical and Hypochondriacal Fits, and those other Paroxysms that attend nervous Disorders.

Of the Nature and Cause of Convulsions in general 150
Of the Cause of Convulsions in nervous Cases ib.
Of Childrens Convulsions, and their Cure 152
Of Convulsions in the Sex. 153
Of nervous Fits in grown Persons 154

CHAP. XI.

Of nervous Fevers, Cholicks, Gouts, Asthmas, Rheumatisms, and other Distempers denominated nervous.

Of the Difference between nervous and inflammatory Disorders	156
Of the Nature and Symptoms of nervous Fevers	157
Of the Cure of nervous Fevers	159
Of the Nature and Symptoms of the nervous Cholick	161
Of the Cure of the nervous Cholick	ibid.
Of nervous Gouts, Rheumatisms, and Asthmas	162

CHAP. XII.

Of the Palsy, St. Vitus's Dance, and other Paralytick Disorders.

Of the Cause and Cure of partial Palsies	164
Of the Nature and Cause of Palsies	165
Of the Cure of Palsies	166
Of St. Vitus's Dance.	167

CHAP. XIII.

Of the Apoplexy and Epilepsy.

Of the Nature and Cause of the Apoplexy in general	168
Of the different Kinds of Apoplexies	169
Of the more common Sort of Apoplexy, and its Cause	170
Of the Cure of Apoplexies	171
Of the Nature of the Epilepsy	172
Of the Cure of the Epilepsy	173

PART III.

CHAP. I.

OF those whose nervous Complaints were cured by Medicine, under a common, tho' temperate Diet. 183

CHAP. II.

Of nervous Cases requiring a mix'd or trimming Regimen of Diet, viz. of tender, young, animal Food, and a little Wine and Water one Day, and the other only Milk, Seeds, and Vegetables 187

CHAP. III.

Of nervous Cases, requiring a strict and total Milk, Seed, and Vegetable Diet 194

CHAP. IV.

The Objections against a Regimen, especially a Milk, Seed, and Vegetable Diet, considered   203
The Case of the Hon. Col. Townshend   209
The Case of the learned and ingenious Dr. Cranstoun, *in a Letter to the Author, at his Desire, in Dr.* Cranstoun's *own Words*   212
The Case of the Author   222
The Conclusion   252

THE
𝕰𝖓𝖌𝖑𝖎𝖘𝖍 𝕸𝖆𝖑𝖆𝖉𝖞:

OR, A

TREATISE

OF

Nervous Diseases of all Kinds,

AS

Spleen, Vapours, Lowness of Spirits, Hypochondriacal and Hysterical Distempers, &c.

In THREE PARTS.

PART I.

Of the Nature and Cause of NERVOUS DISTEMPERS.

———— *Nec te quæsiveris extra.*
Persius.

By *GEORGE CHEYNE*, M.D.
Fellow of the *College of Physicians* at *Edinburg*, and F.R.S.

DUBLIN:
Printed in the Year, MDCCXXXIII.

THE

English Malady.

INTRODUCTION.

THE Spirit of a Man can bear his Infirmities, but a wounded Spirit who can bear? saith a Prophet. As this is a great Truth in the *Intellectual World*, so it may allude to the *Human Machin*, to insinuate, that a Person of sound Health, of strong Spirits, and firm Fibres, may be able to combat, struggle with, and nobly to bear and even brave the Misfortunes, Pains, and Miseries of this mortal Life, when the same Person, broken, and dispirited by Weakness of *Nerves, Vapours, Melancholy*, or *Age*, shall become dejected, oppress'd, peevish, and sunk even below the Weakness of a Greensickness Maid, or a Child.

Of this every one who has liv'd any time in the World may have seen Instances, from the *Hero* to the City Girl. This I have often obferv'd, and reflected on within myfelf, with much Pity of the Folly and Mifery, the Pride and Prefumption of *Human Nature*, which could value, or think to fupport itfelf, upon its own natural Courage and Force. To expect *Fortitude, Patience, Tranquillity*, and *Refignation*, from the moft *Heroick* of the Children of Men, under fuch Circumftances, from their natural Force or Faculties alone, is equally abfurd as to expect to fly without Wings, or walk without Legs; the Strength of the *Nerves, Fibres*, or *Animal Spirits*, (as they are call'd) being the neceffary Inftruments of the former, as thefe Members are of the latter. Different natural Complexions of the *Soul* and *Intellectual* Faculties, and different Improvements from Education, *Philofophy*, or *Religion*, may make fome fmall Odds in the Behaviour of different Perfons under thefe Diforders. But this depends much upon the Degrees of the Diftemper, and the original Frame and make of the Body, even more than can be readily imagin'd, as I have often had undeniable Evidences to conclude. And, of all the Miferies that afflict Human Life, and relate principally to the Body, in this Valley of Tears, I think, *Nervous* Diforders, in their extream and laft Degrees, are the moft deplorable, and, beyond all comparifon, the worft. It was the Obfervation of a learned and judicious *Phyfician*, that he had feen Perfons labouring under the moft exquifite Pains of *Gout, Stone, Cholick, Cancer*, and all the other Diftempers that can tear the human Machin, yet had he obferv'd them all willing to prolong their wretched Being, and fcarce any ready to lay down chearfully the *Load* of *Clay*, (we will except thofe who were fupernaturally fupported) but fuch as labour'd under a conftant, internal Anxiety, meaning thofe moft finking, fuffocating, and ftrangling *Nervous* Diforders; it is truly

INTRODUCTION.

y the only Misery almost, to be dreaded and avoided in Life, if, by any means, it can possibly. Tho' other Evils be Burdens, yet an erected Spirit may bear them, but when the Supports are fallen, and cover the Man with their Ruins, the Desolation is perfect. I greatly suspect, (and have actually seen it in some) that most of those who make away with themselves, are under the Influence of this distracting *Evil*, if it proceeds not sometimes from high Passions arising in Constitutions naturally too sensible, and such are the most readily expos'd to the Insults of these Distempers. Having suffer'd once and again under all the Varieties of the Symptoms of this Disorder, partly from my own Indiscretion, and partly from a gross Habit of Body, and an original State of weak Nerves, and having tried in my own Person almost all the possible Means, Reliefs, or Medicines, that *Physicians, Books of Physick,* or *Philosophy*, could suggest, besides my own Observations on many others, who have come to *this Place* for Relief for these Thirty Years, and being once and again perfectly rescu'd from them by the same Means, it will be a great Satisfaction to me, if I can at least alleviate and mitigate the Sorrows and Miseries of my *Fellow-Sufferers*, by the Experience I have so dearly bought.

Those who are desirous to read the ensuing Treatise only for their Relief and Cure, may pass over those Parts (which may be learned by the Index) that are merely *Philosophical*, and design'd only to gratify their Curiosity, they having no necessary Connection with what is *Directory* or *Practical*.

These need only suppose, that the Human Body is a Machin of an infinite Number and Variety of different Channels and Pipes, filled with various and different Liquors and Fluids, perpetually running, gliding, or creeping forward, or returning

returning backward, in a constant *Circle*, and sending out little Branches and Outlets, to moisten, nourish, and repair the Expences of Living. That the Intelligent Principle, or *Soul*, resides somewhere in the Brain, where all the Nerves, or Instruments of Sensation terminate, like a *Musician* in a finely fram'd and well-tun'd Organ-Case; that these Nerves are like *Keys*, which, being struck on or touch'd, convey the Sound and Harmony to this sentient Principle, or *Musician*.

Or, in a more gross Similitude, the Intelligent Principle is like a Bell in a Steeple, to which there are an infinite Number of Hammers all around it, with Ropes of all lengths, terminating or touching at every Point of the Surface of the Trunk or Case, one of whose Extremities being pull'd or touch'd by any *Body* whatsoever, conveys a measur'd, and proportion'd Impulse or Stroke to the Bell, which gives the proper Sound. These, or such like Similitudes, tho' Lame and Imperfect, are all, I doubt, was ever design'd for the Generality of Mankind in the Knowledge necessary towards HEALTH and LIFE, in such Matters. Those acquainted with the best *Philosophy*, *Natural History*, The *Laws* constantly observ'd by *Bodies* in their Actions, on one another, and the establish'd Relations of things, will, I hope, meet with fuller Satisfaction, if they consider the following Treatise, without Prejudice or Partiality.

CHAP

CHAP. I.

Of the Sources and Causes of Chronicle Distempers in general.

§. I. THE most universal and comprehensive Sources and Causes of Chronical Distempers are, 1*st*. A *Glewiness, Sizyness, Viscidity,* or *Grossness* in the Fluids, either accidental, or acquir'd by those Persons who were born with sound or good condition'd Juices; or original and hereditary, in those who have brought them so dispos'd into the World with them, from the ill State of Health and bad State of Humours of the Parents, which, possibly, *they* might have had transmitted to them from theirs, and so on for many Generations backwards. A rotten and corrupt Tree can produce nothing but bad Fruit, nor can any natural Cause have a better Effect than its Principles, or natural Qualities can produce. 2*dly,* Some Sharpness or corrosive Quality in the Fluids, arising from a *saline* or other destructive Mixture thrown into them, or from some gross Concretions not sufficiently broken and divided by the digestive Powers in the *Alimentary* Tube, retarding or stopping the Circulation in the small Vessels, whereby the stagnant Juices become sharp and corrosive, and the Salts have Time, by their innate attractive Quality, to crystalize or unite in greater

greater Clusters, and exert their destructive Force on the Solids; and this will be still more pernicious and fatal, if the Food is not only in too great a Quantity for the concoctive Powers to break and divide it sufficiently, but is likewise too high, strong, and full of Salts, from which the most terrible Symptoms will ensue. *3dly*, A too great Laxity or Want of due Tone, Elasticity and Force in the *Fibres* in general, or the *Nerves* in particular. There is a due Degree of Strength, Power and Sprynginess requir'd in the Fibres or Solids, not only to make the Juices circulate, and carry on their Motions backwards and forwards in a continual *Rotation* thro' the whole Habit, but also to break, divide, and subtilize them further, that they may be able easily to pass, not only thro' the slender and finer Tubes of the capillary Vessels, but also through the Strainers of the *Glands*, either to throw off those Recrements and grosser Parts, which are not required for the animal Functions, or to separate those Juices which are required for the Preservation of the Individual. These are the most effectual, general and immediate Causes of all Chronical Distempers, of which, when any one is, in any eminent Degree, become habitual, the other two spring up, or follow very soon, and join with it in producing the various Symptoms of these Disorders. Other Specialities and Circumstances may concur with them, but they would have little Effect, if these could be supposed absent or removed.

§. II. The *first* Cause mentioned will obstruct and possibly burst the small and capillary Vessels that carry about the Fluids, producing *Tumours, Swellings*, and *Ulcers*, and will not only tumify and afterwards relax and spoil the whole almost infinite Set of *Glands*, external and internal, but especially those which are properly called *Emunctory* ones, and so stop the Secretions, and fill the Body

Body with vicious and morbid Juices. This Diſtention, Swelling and Hardneſs of the *Glands* and ſmall Veſſels, will likewiſe preſs upon the Nerves, ſtop and intercept their *Vibrations* or *Tremors*, or whatever elſe be their Action, and conſequently ſpoil their natural Functions. The *ſecond* will not only rend, tear and ſpoil the Veſſels, creating acute Pains, and producing corroſive, *Scorbutick* and *Cancerous* Ulcers and Sores, in all Parts of the Body, but will alſo, by twitching and vellicating the *Nerves* or nervous Fibres, produce Convulſions, Spaſms, and all the terrible Symptoms of that Tribe of nervous Diſtempers. The *laſt* mentioned Cauſe will not only weaken and deſtroy voluntary Motion, and the Force and Freedom of the *intellectual* Operations (for the Exerciſe of which, as long as the Union laſts, material Organs and their Soundneſs and Integrity ſeems to be required as well as for the animal Functions) but will alſo retard and weaken the Circulation, ſtop the Perſpiration, and confound and diſorder the Secretions, and all the Functions that belong to either Part of the Compound.

CHAP. II.

Of the General Cauſes of the Diſorders of the Nerves.

§. I. THE Solids, and conſequently the Fibres and *Nerves* whereof, they are woven and complicated, are ſubject to ſeveral Diſorders which may interrupt and entirely ruin their Functions. As, *firſt*, by becoming either too dry, or too moiſt, that is by Want, or Exceſs of Humidity, Moiſture or Nouriſhment to keep their Parts, in a due or proper *Tone* or *Elaſticity*. The *firſt* generally ariſes from a too hot, dry, and as it were corroſive Nouriſhment, which renders them too criſp, over *elastick*, and brittle, and so forces on the Circulation, and sends about the Juices with too great Force, Rapidity, and Violence, instead of that calm and uniform manner, in which the Functions, and Secretions of the animal *Oeconomy*, are naturally perform'd, and that due Balance, which ought, naturally to be between the Solids and the Fluids. And this probably has a great Share in the Production of inflammatory Disorders, high Fevers, and the other acute Distempers of strong Constitutions. The *second* from too great a Quantity of oily and nutritious Juices thrown on them more than the Expences of living require, soaking and relaxing the Solids, renders their Action languid, and has a greater Share in the Productions of slow and cold Diseases.

§. II. *Secondly*, By improper, hard, solid and noxious Particles getting into their Substances, which may gradually alter, spoil and stop their natural Texture and Functions whatever that happen to be, whether *Vibration*, *Intestine Action*, and *Reaction* or *Collision* of their small Parts, or however they act or are acted upon, to convey and propagate the Sensations or Influences of external Bodies, to the Seat of the *intelligent Principle*: For when the Juices are spoil'd, and the Blood declines from its due Fluidity and *Balminess*, the nutritive Juices must necessarily partake of their general Nature, and become crowded and filled with hard, large Concretions, of a different Nature from the genuine and natural Condition of the Blood and Juices, in their healthy State, which whensoever they may arise, or whatever different Qualities they may be endued with; I choose to call by the general Name of *Animal Salts*. The *Nerves* and *Fibres* being thus unnaturally nourished and repair'd, must, in such a State, either entirely stop and bring no Sensation at all to the intelligent Principle, and convey no Action from it to the Muscles

cles and Organs of Animal Motion, or at least false, imperfect and delusory ones; for these Salts, and such like hard, solid, compact and angular Particles, will be more readily insinuated into the tender Threads of the Solids, having a greater Degree of *Attraction* in proportion to their Bulks, than the more rare, soft, and spongy ones.

§. III. *Thirdly,* From the Interruption, Interception and Stoppage of their *Vibrations, Tremors,* and the intestine Action of their component Particles, by the greater Pressure of too viscid Juices in the Blood Vessels, and the other Tubes that contain the animal Juices, surrounding these Fibres or *Nerves:* For it's well known, that a more glutinous and viscid Fluid, circulating in an elastick or distractile Canal, will bulge it up, and press upon its Sides more strongly than a thinner and more rare Fluid one, and so the Sides of the Canal will become more strait and tumified, pressing thereby on the *Nerves,* as if it were a *Wedge* or solid Body, and interrupting their natural Actions. The same is to be concluded from the Tumefaction, Induration, and Swelling of the *Glands,* which being extremely numerous over all the Body, must greatly endamage the *Nervous System.*

§. IV. *Fourthly,* From the natural or acquir'd Weakness and Laxity of their *Tone* and *Elasticity,* whether from a natural or accidental ill Structure or Formation of themselves, or the other Organs of the Body, or from any external Injury received on them: And such is the Case of those who are born of weakly or old Parents, or whose Parents have long labour'd under the *Gout, Scurvy, Elephantiasis, Leprosy, Venerial* or *Nervous* Disorders; those who have had a Contusion on the Head, Back-bone, or any other Part of the Body, where there are the greatest Collection of *Nerves*; and *lastly,* those who have a Hump, or any preternatural

tural Distortion or Excrescence, especially on the Trunk of the Body.

§. V. And tho' all these general Causes, mentioned in the former and this *Chapter*, concur in all chronical and nervous Distempers whatsoever, in some Degree or other, and perhaps some other more minute Circumstances, which are not so readily found out, or much to be regarded, yet Diseases differ and have received their Names by *Physicians*, according as the Symptoms arising from this or that general Cause mentioned, are more evident, numerous or stronger. But these Diseases are chiefly and properly called *Nervous*, whose Symptoms imply that the System of the *Nerves* and their Fibres, are evidently relax'd and broken. The Brevity I intend in this Treatise, will not allow me to detail all the Kinds of Nervous Distempers that have been observ'd and named; they are sufficiently known, or may be learned from Books of *Physick*, and I think may be reduced to the following general Heads.

CHAP. III.

Of the General Division of Nervous Distempers.

§. I. ALL Nervous Distempers whatsoever from Yawning and Stretching, up to a mortal Fit of an Apoplexy, seems to me to be but one continued Disorder, or the several Steps or Degrees of it, arising from a Relaxation or Weakness, and the Want of a sufficient Force and Elasticity in the Solids in general, and the *Nerves* in particular, in Proportion to the Resistance of the Fluids, in order to carry on the Circulation, remove Obstructions, carry off the Recrements, and make the Secretions. In treating of Nervous Distempers, the Disorders of the *Solids* are chiefly what are to be had regard to;

to; yet they rarely or never happen alone (except perhaps in those Nervous Disorders that proceed from acute Diseases, preternatural Evacuations, external Injuries, or a wrong and unnatural Make and Frame) but even in original nervous Distempers there is always some Viscidity or Sharpness attending them from the bad Constitutions of the Parents, from whom they have derived their material Organs. This is evident from the nervous Disorders that attend scrophulous and scorbutick Persons. And from long and constant Observation, I am under a Conviction, that no deep and eminent Degree of nervous Disorders happens to young Persons, but from a manifest or latent scropulous or scorbutick Taint, which implies both Viscidity and Sharpness in the Juices: nor any great Degree to adult Persons, originally sound, but from an acquired scorbutick Habit or *Cachexy*.

§. II. The most natural and general Division of nervous Distempers will therefore be thus. 1*st*, Into those Diseases, that besides their other Symptoms, are attended with a partial or total Loss of Sensation for some Time. This Branch will not only comprehend all those nervous Disorders from Lowness of Spirits, lethargick Dulness, Melancholy and Moping, up to a compleat *Apoplexy*, but also those fainting Fits, so common in Persons of weak Nerves. As a Consequence from this Interruption of Sensation, partial or total, there will necessarily follow a Suspension of voluntary Motion. The intelligent Principle, under this Inability of the *Nervous System* being bereaved of proper Organs to convey its Orders to the Muscles, tho' these last should remain sufficiently fitted for their proper Offices. This Class of nervous Disorders seems chiefly to arise from a *Grossness*, *Glewyness* or *Viscidity* of the animal Juices (letting aside at present the Consideration of their Sharpness and Acrimony, which is never totally absent, when these others are in any

emi-

eminent Degree, especially in our *Northern* Climates) which obstructs the *Glands*, the serious Pipes, and the capillary Blood-vessels, and thereby breaks, interrupts and weakens the Vibrations and Tremors, or whatever else is the Action of the nervous Fibres properly so called.

§. III. *Secondly*, Those nervous Disorders, which are attended with a Loss of voluntary Motion or Shaking in any particular Organ or Limb, or in all the Instruments of voluntary Motion. Such are all those of the paralytick Kind, from an universal *Palsy*, a *Hemiplegia* (or Palsy of half the Body) or of a particular Limb, to a Deadness, Numbness, Weakness, or Coldness upon any of the Parts, external or internal. This Class of Diseases seems to owe its Origin to a Weakness, Imbecility, and Loss of due *Tone* in the Nervous System, or an Interruption of their Vibrations or proper Action, (whatever it be) whereby the Soul is disabled to communicate its *Energy* or Principle of Motion to the Muscular Fibres.

§. IV. Those Nervous Distempers that are attended with *Spasms*, Cramps, Convulsions, or violent Contractions of the Muscles. Of this kind are all of the *Convulsive* Tribe from *Hypochondriacal* and *Hysterical* Fits, or the Convulsions of the *Epileptick* Kind down to Yawning and Stretching. These seem to be produced by some hard-pointed Concretions, saline Particles, or some noxious Acid or acrimonious Steam, Wind, or obstructed Perspiration, lodged in the small Vessels, or upon any Place where there are the greatest Collections of *Nerves*, *viz.* in the Alimentary Tubes, the Cavities of the Brain, the Trunk of the Body, or the Interstices of the Muscles, where twitching, stimulating, and wounding the Nerves, or their *Membranes*, it raises a general Disorder in the whole nervous or sensible Fibres, whence the same is derived upon the whole Muscular System, and there provokes violent

lent Throws, Contractions, Cramps, and Spasms, until tormenting and wearying out the elastick Fibres, at last, by their Strugglings and Efforts, the destructive Matter is discharged or removed: Much in the Manner of that Struggle which we observe from sulphureous, bituminous, vitriolick, and ferrugineous Particles, uniting and fermenting in the Bowels of the Earth, and thereby acquiring such Force, Violence, and Impetuosity, as to make Houses, Palaces, and Cities shake and tremble, overturn Hills and Mountains, and make Rivers, Lakes, and the Sea itself, to boil and heave (till they have forced a Breach and Rupture for their Passage into the Air and Day,) swallowing up all around, and spreading Desolation and Ruin, as far as their Influence can reach. But (to return to my Subject) where the offending Matter is so pent up in such great Quantity, or so violent (as in the violent Hysterick or Epileptick Fits) as quite to overpower the weak and feeble Solids, fainter Strugglings succeed, and the Patient lies almost dead, with few or languid Motions, and sometimes foaming at the Mouth: till the Disease is quite spent, or after a few repeated Struggles, the Contest ends in Death.

§. V. There is another common Division, or rather Distinction of Nervous Disorders, into *original* and *acquir'd*: But these differing only as old Age does from Manhood. I shall just mention them. It is to be supposed (at least, at the most remote Distance of Time) that Mankind were originally made so, as not to differ (in any eminent Degree, at least, below that Standard required for good Health) in their Constitutions. Original Nervous Disorders, therefore, must have had the same Source and Cause with acquir'd ones. The Children, as to their Bodies and bodily Diseases being punished for the Faults, Follies, and Indiscretions of their Parents. The Streams or Outlets must partake of the

the same Qualities with the Spring or Fountain Head. The wise Author of Nature, in the present State of Things, seems to have established Laws and Orders, by which second Causes are to act upon, and influence one another; which Laws, natural and material Bodies constantly observe in their Effects and Productions, and which *He* never seems to violate by any uncommon or supernatural Influence, except for intellectual or moral Purposes; and therefore to govern and direct these Laws, *He* has given to his intelligent Creatures, Understanding and free Will. So that a poor Creature, born subject to Nervous Distempers, has no more Reason to complain, than a Child, whose Father has spent his worldly Fortune, and left him poor, and destitute.

§. VI. It is a Misfortune indeed, to be born with weak Nerves, but if rightly us'd and manag'd, even in the present State of Things, (I meddle no further) it may be the Occasion of greater Felicity: For, at least, it is (or ought to be) a Fence and Security against the Snares and Temptations to which the Robust and Healthy are expos'd, and into which they seldom fail to run; and thereby reduce themselves to the same, or, perhaps, a worse State than those whose Misfortune happen'd to be, the being born thus originally subject to Nervous Disorders. Those who have originally bad Nerves, I shall direct in the best Manner I can afterwards.

§. VII. I shall only here observe two things in regard to them. The *first* is, that they are never to expect the same Force, Strength, Vigour and Activity, nor to be made capable of running into the same Indiscretions or Excess of sensual Pleasures (without suffering presently, or on the Spot) with those of strong Fibres and robust Constitutions. No Art hitherto known, can make an Eagle of a Wren, (for tho' a Wren, by Art and Management, may be made, as it were, a Nightingale,
yet

yet never a Carrion Crow or Kite); but for all the innocent Enjoyments of Life, (at least, for Freedom from Pain and torturing Distempers, for Chearfulness and freedom of Spirits, for intellectual Pleasures, mental Enjoyments, and Length of Days they (considering the Temptations and Miseries of this mortal State) generally have, and may always have, the Advantage of these others. (I always except extreme Degrees of Nervous Diseases.) As for intellectual Pleasures, the Case is without all manner of doubt, (without some notable Error, or in extreme Cases) possibly, because the Organs of these Operations being in their own Nature delicate and fine, when wasted or scrap'd, (by Chronical Diseases not mortal) and thus communicated to their Posterity, these naturally subtil Parts *thus* become more fine and sensible, are hinder'd by the natural Weakness of Children, in their tender Years, to incrassate and grow clumsy, and so are longer preserv'd in their Sensibility and Refinement; at least the Case is generally in fact so, (as I have observ'd in most originally tender Persons well educated and disciplin'd) Infinite Goodness and Power bringing Good out of innocent Evil. (For the common Proverb is just and true, that a *Venice Glass* will last as long, if well look'd after, and even shine more bright, than a more gross and course one.) But to leave these Possibilities, and pass to,

§. VIII. The *second* thing, which is, that those who have originally weak Solids, and have carefully avoided the Excesses and sensual Pleasures which reduce the Robust to that Case, and have follow'd the Directions that may be learn'd, for strengthening their Fibres and preserving them from being overlaid, if they get over the Meridian of Life (or their thirty-fifth or thirty-sixth Year) without any mortal Distemper, have a fair Chance to get into a firm State of Health, Vigour, and Spirits

Fits afterwards, and to hold it on without any Rub (if they be so wise then to keep from Excesses, or immoderate Sensual Pleasures) to a great and *green old Age*, as I have constantly observ'd. So true is the common Observation, that every wise Man has a *Youthhood* once in his Life, if not in his early and tender Years, at least, in his old Age: And this seems not only consistent with the Wisdom of Providence, but the Necessity of Things, and the Order of Nature; for let us suppose that crazy putrified Parents should bring into the World such a Child as I have mentioned, the Parent's Juices, for want of sufficient Time, or proper Means, are not rectified. The Child's, on the contrary, from the Necessity of its low Diet, and the Length of its Nonage, (especially if proper Methods be us'd, and proper Medicines join'd) must necessary become sweeter and purer: And if none of the great Organs be spoil'd so, as gradually to infect the whole (which generally begins to shew itself, when the growth or Unfolding of the Solids comes to its greatest Heighth and Extension, or about the mention'd Period of the Meridian of Life) the Juices then becoming sweet, will, by Degrees have their Effect upon the Solids, so that about the Time when others decline, these, on the contrary, begin to revive and spring; and enjoy that *Youth* which others have surviv'd: And thus Age (which naturally hardens and stiffens the Fibres in others) recompenses the Caution, Care, and Sufferings of their younger Days, by a greater Degree of Strength, more Chearfulness, stronger Spirits, and a greater Length of Days than is common.

§. IX. Those who being born sound and healthy, of a strong Constitution, and a firm State of Nerves, have acquir'd the contrary State, may have brought it on, either, *first*, by *Accidents*, as I have before mention'd, such as a Wound, Bruise, Dislocation, or Fracture, which may introduce Humps, Distortions, &c. and alter the natural good Configurations

of

Division of Nervous Distempers. 17

of the Parts, whose Cure must depend upon the Surgeon's Art, by his endeavouring to reduce these to their original State; to which likewise Remedies may be suggested for the present Relief of the Nervous Distempers thence depending, in the Directions afterwards to be given. *Secondly*, By a bad, corrupt, or a too poor and low Diet, indiscreet Excess of bodily Labour, or having expos'd themselves too much to the Injuries of the Weather, whereby the Juices have been defrauded of that due Proportion of Heat, Nourishment and Balsam, the Fibres become weak and relax'd, the Muscles flabby and flaccid, and lowness of Spirits, Melancholy, and all the Degrees and Complications of Nervous Distempers have ensued. Such are those of the poorer Sort, who are deprived of the due Necessaries and Conveniencies of Life, those who have gone long and dangerous Voyages, who live in Prisons, or travel in Desarts, or those who are confin'd to Monasteries or Hermitages. But as this Country is pretty free from such Cases, and the Remedy is obvious, I need say no more of them. *Thirdly*, By Intemperance, want of due Exercise, rioting in sensual Pleasures, casual excessive Evacuations of any Kind, Fevers and other acute Diseases not duly manag'd, by which the Juices have been made sizy or corrosive, and the due Tone, Spring and Elasticity of the Nerves or Solids relax'd and broken, whereby the true acquir'd Nervous Disorders are produc'd. To restore such to a sound State of Health, and a good Constitution, or at least, to relieve their Symptoms, as far as my poor Abilities can effect, shall be my sincere Endeavour in the following Pages.

CHAP. IV.

That what is swallow'd down, and received into the Habit, is the first and chief efficient Cause of all that Mankind suffer in their Bodies.

§. 1. THO' I think it pretty evident, that this terrestrial Globe, and the State of Things in it, and about it at present, is not design'd merely for a *Paradise of Delights,* and the ultimate End of the intelligent Creatures which inhabit it, and that for one good Reason, that lies within my present Province, to wit, our carrying about us corruptible Bodies, in their own Nature perishable, subject to Accidents, Diseases, and, at last, to Death itself; yet can I never be induced to believe that the omnipotent and infinitely good Author of it, could, out of Choice and Election, or by unavoidable Necessity, much less from Malice or Impotence, have brought some into such a State of Misery, Pain, and Torture, as the most cruel and barbarous Tyrant can scarce be supposed wantonly to inflict, or be delighted with, in his most treacherous Enemies or villainous Slaves: For to such a Heighth of Pain and Torture, and higher if possible, have I seen some brought from mere natural Diseases. No! none but Devils could have such Malice; none but Men themselves, or what is next themselves, I mean their Parents, who were the Instruments or Channels of their Bodies and Constitutions, could have Power or Means to produce such cruel Effects. In itself this Law and Establishment of Nature has infinite Beauty, Wisdom, and Goodness: *viz.* by this progressive and continual Succession from one Root, that the Healthy and Virtuous should thereby be growing continually healthier and happier, and the
Bad

Efficient Cause of all Distempers. 19

Bad continually becoming more miserable and unhealthy, till their Punishment forced them upon Virtue and Temperance; for Virtue and Happiness are literally and really Cause and Effect.

§. II. When I see Milk, Oil, Emulsion, mild watery Fluids, and such like soft Liquors, run through Leathern Tubes or Pipes (for such Animal Veins and Arteries are indeed) for many Years, without wearing or destroying them: And observe, on the other Hand, that Brine, *inflammable* or *urinous* Spirits, *Aqua fortis*, or *Regia*, and the like acrimonious and burning Fluids, corrode, destroy, and consume them in a very short time: When I consider the rending, burning, and tearing Pains and Tortures of the *Gout, Stone, Cholick, Cancer, Rheumatism, Convulsions*, and such like insufferably painful Distempers: When I see the *Crisis* of almost all acute Distempers, happen either by rank and fœtid Sweats, thick, lateritious, and lixivious Sediments in the Urine, black, putrid, and fœtid Dejections, attended with livid and purple Spots, corrosive Ulcers, Impostumes in the Joints or Muscles, or a Gangrene and Mortification in this or that Part of the Body: When I see the sharp, (even to the Taste, as I have often tried) the corroding and burning *Ichor* of scorbutick and scrophulous Sores, fretting, gauling and blistering the adjacent Parts, with the Inflammation, Swelling, Hardness, Scabs, Scurf, Scales, and other loathsome cutaneous Foulnesses, that attend such; the white, gritty, and chalky Matter, the hard, stony, or flinty Concretions, which happen to all those long troubled with severe *Gouts, Gravel, Jaundice,* or *Cholick*: the Obstructions and Hardnesses, the Putrefaction and Mortification that happens in the Bowels, Joints, and Members in some of these Diseases: and the Rottenness in the Bones, Ligaments, and Membranes that happen in others; all the various Train of Pains, Miseries, and Torments * that can afflict any Part of the Compound, and for which there is scarce any Reprieve to be obtain'd, but by swallowing a Kind of Poison (such I take *Opiates* to be, upon taking great Doses, or continuing them for any long time.) When I behold, with Pity, Compassion, and Sorrow, such *Scenes* of Misery and Woe, and see them happen only to the *Rich*, the *Lazy*, the *Luxurious*, and the *Unactive*, those who fare daintily and live voluptuously, those who are furnished with the rarest Delicacies, the richest Foods, and the most generous Wines, such as can provoke the Appetites, Senses and Passions in the most exquisite and voluptuous Manner: to those who leave no Desire or Degree of Appetite unsatisfied, and not to the *Poor*, the *Low*, the *meaner Sort*, those destitute of the Necessaries, Conveniencies, and Pleasures of Life, to the Frugal, Industrious, † the Temperate, the Laborious and the Active: to those inhabiting barren, and uncultivated Countries, Desarts, Forests, under the *Poles* or the *Line*, or to those who are rude and destitute of the *Arts* of Ingenuity and Invention. *I must*, if I am not resolved to resist the strongest Conviction, conclude, that it must be something received into the Body, that can produce such terrible Appearances in it, some flagrant and notable Difference in the *Food*, that so sensibly distinguishes them from these latter. And that it is the miserable *Man* himself that creates his Miseries, and begets his Torture, or, at least, those from whom he has derived his bodily *Organs*.

---

* Vide Plutarch. Symposiac Lib. viii. Cap. ix. Seneca Consol. ad Helviam & Epist. 95.

† *Jesephus* observes, that the *Essenes* [a Kind of Solitaries among the *Jews*] lived commonly to a 100 Years, by Reason of the Simplicity of their Diet, and their regular Life. ——— *Cap.* vii. *De Bello Judaic.*

§. III.

Efficient Cause of all Distempers.

§. III. Both the *End* and *Rule*, the *Design* and *Measure* of Eating and Drinking, could be no other but the Supply of the Waste of *Action* and *Living*. The *Friction* and *Collision* that necessarily follows upon the *Impenetrability* of Matter, the Communication of Motion, and the Impressions of the Bodies that surround us, must necessarily rub off, and wear out some Parts from our bodily Machin. The necessary *Collisions* that are made in our Juices, in breaking and subtilizing their Parts, to render them fit for the Animal *Functions*: the various *Secretions* of what is not proper to be retained, or what is necessary for the Preservation of the Individual, make a continual *Waste* of our Substance. To supply all which, it was absolutely necessary, that a due and equal Proportion of proper Nourishment should be design'd us. There is also established by the Rules of the *Animal OEconomy*, a Ballance between the Force or Elasticity of the Solids, or the moving Organs and Channels, and the Resistance of the Fluids mov'd in them (or rather the first ought a little to exceed the latter.) And whenever any of these *Rules* are long and notably transgress'd by either taking down more than the Supplies of Action and Living require in Quantity, or Things stronger in Nature, and of a greater Resistance in Quality, so that the active and concoctive Powers of the Solids, are not sufficient for them, the Individual must suffer Diseases, Pains, and Miseries, in Proportion to the Greatness of this Overballance.

§. IV. Let us suppose, that a Child is born Sound, Healthy, and Vigorous, (as much as the Conditions of Mortality permit) of Parents Healthy and Sound, and in the full Vigour of their Days, and that this Child has continued thus to the Age of *Puberty*, 'bating the Diseases of Childhood, which generally render the Case better (such as a Rash, Measles, or Small-Pox, which are seldom dangerous in those whose Parents are such as I suppose, or who

who have lived in any sober way.) In the Name of *Wonder* and *Astonishment*, How is it possible that such a Person should come to suffer under such terrible Miseries as I have describ'd, by any other Means, than some notable and obstinate * Error in the Manner or Quantity of what he takes down, or introduces into his Habit. For as such Misery and Tortures are internal and intimate, so must the productive Cause be. A bad, noxious, or poisonous *Air*, the Inclemencies of the *Season* and *Climate*, violent Fatigue, and excessive bodily Labour, Accidents, Wounds, and Bruises, are what Mortality is subject to. But as the Influence and Operation of these Causes is seldom so long continued, as that of the other Causes I have formerly mention'd, so those who are most subject to the unhappy Consequences of such Excesses, are generally well guarded and protected against any Hurt from these mentioned Accidents, which accordingly happen more frequently to those of the lower Rank. It is true indeed, when the same Excesses of those of a high Condition, are join'd to the other Perils and Hardships of the lower Rank now mentioned, it makes the Distress and Pain the greatest of all, and is the proper *Scene* where such *Tragedies* are acted to the utmost Perfection of Misery and Woe. But as such extraordinary Circumstances rarely fall out, they are not properly the subject Matter of what we are chiefly concern'd about. To proceed then, let us suppose such a Person as I have describ'd, rioting and wallowing in Luxury for some considerable Time, his Fibres, Nerves, and Motive Organs being yet firm and unbroken. The most natural Effect of such a Course, will be, to fill the

---

* No body will ever be seiz'd with a Disease, who takes sufficient Care not to fall into Crudities, or Indigestion [*i. e.* that eats no more than he can easily digest.] *Gallen Lib.* 1. *De Cibis Bon. & Mal. Succ.*

Blood

Efficient Cause of all Distempers.

Blood and Juices with an Excess of such oily, sulphureous and inflammatory Particles, as are most readily turn'd into red Globules, which make the fibrous Part of the Blood. Such an inflammatory Blood (the Solids being yet tense and firm) will necessarily be driven about with too great Force and Violence, and forced into the small and capillary Vessels, design'd for the Lymph or thinner Fluids only, and thus inflammatory and *acute* Diseases are produced, with all the Varieties and Degrees of their Symptoms: such as *Fevers* of all Sorts and Kinds, the *Gout, Erysipelas, Rheumatism,* and the like. If these small lymphatick Vessels, by the Force of the Circulation, and the Grossness of the Fluid, driven into them, are broken and torn, then follow *Impostumes, Gangrenes, Mortifications,* and all their Train of Miseries, especially, if, together with these mention'd Conditions, great Store of *animal* or *urinous Salts* are brought together in great Quantities (which never fails under such a Course) and unite and combine in larger Clusters and Concretions, whereby the Solids are corroded, eaten and destroy'd, the natural Functions of the Nerves spoil'd and perverted, and the extreme Degrees of Torture, Malignity, and Duration are added to the other Symptoms of these inflammatory Distempers.

§. V. This will necessarily be the Case in a young robust Body and Constitution, when such Excesses are violent, quick, and long continued, and the Solids have not yet lost their Tone and Vigour, whereby the Individual will be quickly brought into those acute, inflammatory, and violent Distempers; and then, by continued violent Conflicts, Nature, after many Struggles, will either break, divide, and subtilize these numerous, fiery, and inflammatory Globules, and those sharp-pointed, hard, and acrimonious Salts, and drive them out of the Habit by such *Crises* as I have describ'd; and the Constitution being purified, the Patient will gradually return to his

his former Health and Soundness: Or if this cannot be effected, by reason of the Strength of the Disease, or the Greatness of the Obstruction in the small Vessels, the Person must unavoidably submit to Fate. But if such a Course be pursued more slowly, and by more moderate Degrees, and *Laziness*, or Want of Exercise is joined with it, so that the Acrimony of the Salts, and the Stock of the Humours, gradually encrease as the Solids are relax'd and weakened: then the flower, colder, more humourous and chronical Diseases are produced, with all the Pains, Miseries, and Torments arising in this low, sunk and dejected State of the Constitution. From all which it is evident, that these monstrous and extreme *Tortures*, are entirely the Growth of our own Madness and Folly, and the Product of our own wretched Inventions, from the Poison and Ordure, with which, for the sake of a little sensual Pleasure, we forcibly and tyrannically cram our poor passive Machins.

CHAP. V.

Of the surprizing and wonderful Effects of Salts, especially of the volatile, urinous, or animal Salts, upon human Bodies and Constitutions.

§. I. IT may perhaps seem incredible, nay, impossible, to those unacquainted with the surprizing and wonderful Effects of saline Concretions, especially of those call'd *volatile, urinous,* or *animal Salts,* upon human Bodies and Constitutions, to imagine how they should be sufficient to produce and account for those terrible Effects and Appearances, which I have describ'd in the former *Chapter.* But he who has considered and is acquainted with the surprizing *Energy*, Force, and Activity of Salts of all Kinds, together with the Tenderness and Delicacy

cacy of *animal Fibres* and Solids, if he at all ascribes them to natural and *second Causes*, and does not altogether run into Fatality, and resolve every thing immediately into *Miracle*, *Witchcraft*, *Enchantment*, or *Omnipotence*, must acknowledge that there is nothing else among all the minute Bodies, or their *Systems*, that surrounds us, or have any considerable Influence upon animal Constitutions, that can so readily and effectually produce the mention'd Appearances.

§. II. This will be more evident to those who have considered the wonderful Effects of *Nitre*, and its Composition *Gun-powder*; the surprizing Appearances of kindled *Camphire*, and the like congeal'd *chymical Oils*, the strange Energy of the *urinous*, and other Kinds of *Phosphorus*'s, the Effervescence, Firing, and detonation of several *chymical* Mixtures: In a Word, all the strange Appearances resulting from the Mixture of *pure Light* (or the same imprison'd in its more gross Vehicles, *viz.* the several Sorts of *Sulphurs*, *Oils*, *Balsams*, and *Bituminous* Concretions) with *Acids* and *vegetable*, or *mineral Salts*, producing in the Bowels of this our Globe, *Earthquakes*, Eruptions, and *Vulcanos*, overturning *Cities*, *Hills*, and *Mountains*, and raising new *Islands* in the Bosom of the *Ocean*, and in the *Air* generating *Thunder*, *Lightening*, *Meteors*, and all the Wonders of the *Atmosphere*. But that which makes more immediately for our Purpose, is the terrible, violent, and sudden Desolation and Destruction, Pain and Torture, produced by * *Plague*, *Pestilence*, *spotted and purple Fevers*, *Small-Pox*, *Venereal*, *Cancerous*, and *Leprous* Diseases, and all the other Epidemical and Infectious Distempers, with all their numerous Train of nauseous, loathsome, and painful Symptoms, their Scabs, Ulcers, Corrosions,

---

* Vide *Mead* on the Plague.

and Putrefactions, which by Reason or just Philosophy, can be ascrib'd to no other intelligible or natural Cause, but Corrosive and Caustick Animal Salts. If to these we add the quick and sensible Effects of *Cantharides*, Spirit and Salt of *Hartshorn*, and such *volatile* and *urinous* Salts, the Power of Spirits, *urinous* or *inflammatory*, of Aromaticks, *Emeticks*, the Preparations of *Mercury*, and *Antimony*, the sensible Effects of external Applications of the several Sorts of active *Cataplasms*, *Plaisters*, and *Sinapisms*, but especially of † *Poisons*, *Animal*, *Vegetable* or *Mineral*, upon human Bodies, (all which, as well as those beforementioned, plainly owe their Effects to Salts of one Kind or other, combin'd with Oils and Sulphurs) there will be found little Difficulty in this Matter.

§. III. It is plain there is a Mineral Source of Salts lodged in the Bowels of the Earth, (to which the Sea owes its Saltness) which transmits its Steams or smaller Particles to Minerals, Plants, and Vegetables, and seems to be the common *Mother* and Origin of all the several Kinds of form'd Salts or saline Concretions, according to its different Mixture with the other Elements, to wit, those of Earth, Water, Sulphur, (or perhaps imprison'd Light) and Air: There are likewise, possibly, two Kinds of most active Fluids, (Air, Water, and Mercury, being combin'd with the other passive Substances) one we know very little of, more than what I shall mention in a following *Chapter*. The other is that of *Light*, which actuates and enlivens the whole material *System* of Bodies here below, without which they would languish, deaden, chill, and be motionless, and this seems to be the active *energetick* Principle, (together with that other, which is suppos'd to be the Cause of their attractive Quality, as well

---

† Ibid on Poisons.

as that of all Matter, and of all the subtile Appearances of small Bodies on our Globe.) Salts of one Kind or another, seem to be its passive Instruments, which being driven and actuated by it, (and the other active Fluid mention'd) produce the Appearances we observe from them. Form'd *Salts* also are hard, and dissolvible only by Water, and from it, possibly, in a great measure, they originally spring †. They generally form themselves into regular, and sharp, or angular Figures, * whereby they become more piercing and penetrating: And this Regularity of their Figures makes it probable, that their Particles have plain Surfaces, which accounts for their extreme Degree of Union, or their running eagerly into one another's Embraces, as is evident from their Congelations and *Crystalizations*. The Volatility and Activity of Salts, seems to arise from several Sources: As first, from the smallness of their Parts, and the Sharpness of their Angles: Secondly, from their greater Degree of *Attraction*, than is common to other Bodies of the same Bulk: And thirdly, from their Union with *Light, Sulphur*, and other *sulphureous* Bodies, when they become *Urinous* or *Animal*. It is not my Affair to detail their Laws, or the *Mechanism* of all their Actions, my Design being only to give such a Sketch of the Matter, from the best Accounts of Philosophy, as may be sufficient to give my Reader a general Notion of the Force of this Argument.

§. IV. Mineral (or the Mother) Salt is, probably, simple, and of the plainest Figure (perhaps a *Tetrahedron* of an equilateral, triangular *Base*) which, with its Dissolubility in Water, and the Influence of the active Principle of Light, fits it to be readily introduc'd first into the Substance of Ve-

---

† Vide *Newton*'s Opticks.
* Vide Gulielmini de Salium Natura.

getables, where, by the Action and *Attraction* of their Tubes and Solids, and its Union with the Sulphurs and Earths of Plants, it is advanced one Degree farther in Activity and Volatility, its Angles are rendered more Acute, and it becomes, by Cryſtalization a Vegetable or fix'd Salt: But 2dly, it acquires a yet further Degree of Smallneſs and Agility, when introduc'd into animal Bodies as Food, being there again ground and ſubtiliz'd by the Force of animal Fibres and Solids, and blended with animal Oils and Sulphurs, and thereby becoming what we call properly *urinous* Salt: And 3dly, the laſt and higheſt Degree of Subtility and Volatility is produc'd, when this *Salt*, now in its *urinous* Form, becomes Food for Birds and Beaſts of Prey, or for human Creatures, being there mix'd with, and agitated by the lighteſt and moſt ſubtile of all Oils and Sulphurs: And when introduced into the Habit, in great Quantities, and urg'd or actuated by the higheſt Oils and Spirits, (as happen to the *European* Nations chiefly, and to thoſe of the *Eaſtern*, who follow their Methods, in Riots and Exceſſes of animal Food and ſpirituous Liquors) they become too ſtrong and powerful for the tender and delicate Fibres, and produce the diſmal * Appearance I have deſcrib'd.

§. V. The Reaſon why *mineral* and *vegetable* Salts, *Poiſons* and *Cauſticks*, have ſuch immediate and ſenſible Effects beyond animal Salts, ſeems chiefly to be owing to their Firmneſs and Solidity, whereby a greater Quantity of Salts is contain'd in the ſame Space or Volume, than can poſſibly be of animal Salts, becauſe the Cement of the firſt (even when ſubtiliz'd) being Earth or earthy Particles, a greater Quantity of them are combin'd in a ſmaller Space than can be of animal Salts, which are united with a great Quantity of a poroſe and light Sulphur only,

---

* *Vide Philoſoph. Tranſ.* No. 433. A Letter from *Micheli Pinelli.*

and so can neither become so compact, nor lodge so great a Quantity of Salts or attractive Particles in an equal Space. For these others, when admitted into animal Bodies, become true *Causticks*, and burn up the internal, as *Causticks* do the external Parts of Animals, as we see in *Arsenick*, *Vitriol*, *Alum*, &c. But after the several Degrees of *Alcoholization* and *Subtilization* formerly mention'd, the natural Salt being thus levigated and refin'd, and its Angles thereby render'd more acute, and its *attractive* Quality greater, (by the lessening of its Bulk) when Motion and Volatility is added to it, by its Mixture with the several Oils and Balsams, of Animals, Vegetables, and *Cannibals*, (pardon the Expression) it becomes so subtile and agile, as to be able easily to enter into the smallest Tubes, and there exert its Fury, which the grosser Salts, especially when mix'd with Earths, are either, by their Grossness, incapable of, or, by the Violence of their Action on the Parts they first touch, are thrown out, upon their first Approach, by the digestive Organs in convulsive Vomitings.

§. VI. The Sum of this present Argument is thus, *that* Salt, in its Origin, is but one; *that* by Division its Angles are made smaller and sharper, and its attractive Virtue greatly increased; *that* though it be the most penetrating and attractive among little Bodies, or their *Systems*, and becomes, as it were, like a *Lancet* or *Razor*, yet can neither hurt nor destroy, when sheath'd, or not put in Action by some *moving* Principle; *that* this Motion or Action is communicated to it by the most active and *energetick* of all Fluids, Light or Sulphur, Oils or Spirits; *that* when its Particles are cemented only by an earthy Matter, so that the greatest Number of them possible, may be crowded into the smallest Volume; it has its most deleterious or destructive Power on animal Bodies, but under that Form is incapable of being receiv'd or retain'd long in the Body for that Effect; *that* after two or three Divisions and Subtilizations, its Parts become so exceeding fine, that it is thereby render'd capable to be readily introduc'd into the inmost Recesses of animal Bodies, (when thus sheath'd with animal and vegetable Oils) and in small Quantities is not only safe, but absolutely necessary for exciting the innate Action of the Fibres and Solids, to wit, Contraction: But *that* when crowded in great or infinite Numbers and Quantities, and received into the smallest and finest Tubes, and there having Time and Leisure to drop its Oils, it unites and crystalizes in greater Volumes and Clusters, and it thereby acquires the Nature and Qualities of the first mention'd Salts or Poisons, that is, becomes hard, compact, and deleterious, and acts as *Poisons*, or a *Caustick*, upon animal Fibres and Constitutions. But I am weary of this Subject, and its tedious Detail; those who have Philosophy enough to understand or receive this Doctrine, will be convinced and satisfy'd by what has been said; or if they want any further Confirmation, may have it from what Sir *Isaac Newton* has said of the Actions of little Bodies, * as explain'd by Dr. *Keil*, and from the Explication of *chymical* Appearances of Dr. *Friend*, in his *Chymical Prelections*, or from the late ingenious and accurate Performance of Dr. *Bryan Robinson*, the Reverend and ingenious Mr. *Hales*, in his *Vegetable Staticks*, or even Mr. *Miller*'s Dictionary of *Gardening*, and the other Philosophical Gardeners, together with the Memoirs of the *Academy Royal*, and especially the *Philosophical Transactions*.

§. VII. I shall only now add, (to apply what has been said to the present Purpose) that it is past all Doubt from † Experiment, that rich Foods, high Sauces, Aromaticks, Delicacies, fine Flavours, and rich and generous Wines, owe all their

---

* Vide Sir *Isaac Newton*'s Opticks.
† *Vide Boyle*'s Chimical Works. *Lemery*, on Foods, and *Tournefort*'s Plants about *Paris*.

Surprizing Effects of Salts.

Poignancy, high Taste, and Gratefulness, to their abounding with such *Salts and Sulphurs*, in a much greater Proportion than those other Foods that have a lesser Degree of such Qualities: That* young and tender Plants and Vegetables have scarce any Salts, and few Oils or Spirits at all, at least, that can in any Quantity be extracted out of them; that Plants have them only when they come to Maturity, or rather in their Decline, and Animals most as they advance from Youth, thro' Maturity towards old Age, and so are more or less grateful to the Palate or Taste, as these Salts and Sulphurs abound in them; that *Aromaticks*, the Juices of vinous Fruits or Plants, owe their Virtue, Flavour, and Delicacy, to their abounding more eminently with such Salts and Oils, but especially to the *Spirits* extracted out of them, when the grosser Parts are thrown off by Fermentation and Distillations. Now if all these Considerations put together, are not sufficient to make out the true remote Cause, and give an Account of the Origin of these Diseases, even of the most excruciating Nature, (tho' a great deal more of the same Kind might be added) I despair of any Success with my Reader on this Subject. To conclude, *Salts*, of one Kind or another, seem absolutely necessary to carry on the Animal Life and Functions in the best Manner possible for our present Situation on this Globe; and it is not possible to have any Food without them, since even Water itself, with a Particle of Earth, if not the Origin and sole Matter of Salt, yet, at least, is never without it; but whether † Animal or Vegetable Salts are most proper, every one must judge from his own Feelings, his Constitution, and the Diseases he is most subject to, or from the Judgment of his Physician; to make

---

* *Vide Philosophical Transactions.*
† Vide Plutarch de Sanitate tuenda, & de Esu Carnium.

which Judgment I shall assist the Reader in the best Manner I can afterwards; I think there is no Doubt to be made, that Salts of any Kind, when too many in too large Clusters, and of the most pungent, provoking, and deleterious Nature, have the greatest Share in the Production of those Diseases to which Mankind are expos'd in this Life. And that therefore, in some Diseases it is extremely fit and convenient, to support Nature with those Foods which abound in them least, and where they are of the most benign Nature.

§. VIII. But lest any one should misunderstand what has been here said, by supposing that I consider *Salts*, according to the particular Qualities that distinguish one Kind of Salts from another, or their different Properties, whether *Acid*, *Alkalin*, or having this, or that particular Effect upon the Palate: or the Appearances arising upon the Actions of the several Kinds of Salts upon one another, and the other Appearances observ'd from *chymical* Managements (all which peculiar and distinguishing Properties and Appearances, probably arise only from the different Mixtures and Proportions of the other Elements in their particular Composition, or their different Degrees of *Attraction*.) For since that particular Formation or Union with the other Elements, and these different Qualities resulting thereupon, are mostly destroy'd as soon as they enter into an animal Body, and are mix'd and blended with the animal Juices; (at least, no such different Kinds of Salts are to be extracted out of these Juices) or *that* have such particular Appearances and Effects, as they had before they were received into the Habit: Therefore, I say, that there may be no Room to mistake my Meaning on this Head, I shall here add, that I consider Salts only in their general Nature, as Angular, Hard, and Attractive, and consequently active solid Particles of Matter,

and

Increase of Nervous Disorders.

and make use of those general Properties only, that are existent in all Kinds of Salts, whatever other peculiar and distinguishing Qualities any particular Kinds may have, since tho' these may remain in them while they are in the Stomach and Guts, where they are sometimes to be found, yet (as I have just now said) they are all confounded, soon after they have enter'd the Habit, and mix'd with the Juices; for which Reason I have rejected the Consideration of the violent and sudden Effects of some Kinds of Salts, and have only observ'd of *Salts* in general, that they are Hard, Solid, Sharp, and Angular Bodies, highly Attractive and Dissolvible by watery Fluids, and capable of being subtilized or divided into smaller Parts, and render'd sharper and more volatile by different Mixtures and Managements, which are equally applicable to all Kinds of Salts, and from thence deduce the Effects they have, or produce in the Fluids, or upon the Solids of Animals, when receiv'd into the Habit. The other Consideration of specifick Salts may have their specifick Effects on one another without the Animal. But they seem more proper and adapted for philosophical than medical Disquisition.

CHAP. VI.

Of the frequency of Nervous Disorders in later Years, beyond what they have been observed in former Times.

§. I. IF what I have advanced in the former *Chapter* have any Truth or *Verisimilitude*, it will be no hard Matter to account for the Frequency of Nervous Distempers observ'd of late Years, beyond what they have been in former Times. There is nothing more common, than to hear Men (even those,

those, who, on other Subjects, reason justly and solidly) ascribe their Distempers, *acute* or *chronical*, to a wet Room, damp Sheets, catching Cold, ill or under-dress'd Food, or eating too plentifully of this or the other Dish at a certain Time, and to such like trivial Circumstances, being unwilling to own the true Cause, to wit, their continu'd Luxury and Laziness, because they would gladly continue this Course, and yet be well, if possible. And there have not wanted learned Physicians, who have ascrib'd the Frequency of these Nervous Distempers of late, especially among the fair Sex, to *Coffee*, *Tea*, *Chocolate*, and *Snuff*: I would not affirm that there could be no Abuses of these, otherwise innocent Foods or Amusements, or that these mention'd Circumstances, and Accidents may have no Effects, but they are so Weak, Insensible, and Transitory, if they meet with Constitutions tolerably Clean and Healthy, that whoever would attribute any considerable Disorder to them, argues with as much Reason and true Philosophy, as he who ascribes his good Liquor intirely to the Yest or other Helps of its Fermentation, or the Death of a Man kill'd by a Gun-shot to the Paper or Tow that held down the Bullet: Health and Life, however Frail and Brittle, are too strong Forts to be taken or destroy'd by such puny and insufficient Pop-gun Artillery. The Matter, as I take it, stands thus:

§. II. Since our Wealth has increas'd, and our Navigation has been extended, we have ransack'd all the Parts of the *Globe* to bring together its whole Stock of Materials for *Riot*, *Luxury*, and to provoke *Excess*. The Tables of the Rich and Great (and indeed of all Ranks who can afford it) are furnish'd with Provisions of Delicacy, Number, and Plenty, sufficient to provoke, and even gorge, the most large and voluptuous Appetite. The whole *Controversy* among us, seems to lie in out-doing out-doing one another in such Kinds of Profusion. *Invention* is rack'd, to furnish the Materials of our Food the most Delicate and Savoury possible: Instead of the plain *Simplicity* of leaving the Animals to range and feed in their proper *Element*, with their natural Nourishment, they are physick'd almost out of their Lives, and made as great *Epicures*, as those that feed on them; and by *Stalling, Cramming, Bleeding, Laming, Sweating, Purging,* and *Thrusting* down such unnatural and high-seasoned Foods into them, these Nervous Diseases are produced in the *Animals* themselves, even before they are admitted as Food to those who complain of such Disorders. Add to all this, the *torturing* and *lingering* Way of taking away the Lives of some of them, to make them more delicious: and the Dressing of them, by culinary Torments while alive, for their Purchaser's Table: All which must necessarily sharpen, impoison, corrupt, and putrify their natural Juices and Substances. The *Liquors* also that are used for *Vehicles* to such Food, are the highest and most spirituous, the most scorched by the *Solar* Beams, or inflam'd by repeated Distillations, to carry off the present Load, and leave a Disposition and Craving for a new one in the shortest Time possible. Any one who has but a tolerable Knowledge in *Philosophy*, or is acquainted with the Animal *Œconomy*, can easily tell what the necessary Consequence of such a *Diet* must be in naturally weak Habits.

§. III. Not only the Materials of *Luxury*, are such as I have describ'd, but the Manner of Dressing or Cooking them, is carried on to an exalted Height. The ingenious mixing and compounding of *Sauces* with foreign *Spices* and Provocatives, are contriv'd, not only to rouze a sickly Appetite to receive the unnatural Load, but to render a natural good one incapable of knowing when it has enough. Since *French Cookery* has been in such Repute in *England*, and has been improv'd improv'd from *Spain*, *Italy*, *Turkey*, and every other Country that has any thing remarkably delicious, high, or savoury in Food; since *Eastern* Pickles and Sauces have been brought to embellish our continual Feasts. Dressing which was design'd to assist the Labour of Digestion, as it is now manag'd, not only counteracts that Design, but is become the most *difficult, curious, ingenious,* and at the same Time, one of the most profitable Trades*.

§. IV. Such a Course of Life must necessarily beget an Inaptitude for Exercise, and accordingly *Assemblies, Musick Meetings, Plays, Cards,* and *Dice*, are the only Amusements, or perhaps Business follow'd by such Persons as live in the Manner mention'd, and are most subject to such Complaints, on which all their Thoughts and Attention, nay, their Zeal and Spirits are spent. And to convey them with the least Pain and Uneasiness possible from Motion, or slavish Labour, to these still and bewitching Employments: *Coaches* are improv'd with Springs, *Horses* are taught to pace and amble, *Chairmen* to wriggle and swim along, to render the Obstructions more firm and fix'd in the small Vessels, and to prevent all the Secretions that would any ways lighten the Burthen. Is it any Wonder then, that the Diseases which proceed from *Idleness* and *Fulness* of Bread, should increase in Proportion, and keep equal Pace with those Improvements of the Matter and Cause of Diseases?

§. V. It is a common Observation, (and, I think, has great Probability on its Side) that *Fools, weak* or *stupid* Persons, *heavy* and *dull Souls,* are seldom much troubled with Vapours or Lowness of Spirits. The intellectual Faculty, without all manner of Doubt, has material and animal Organs, by

---

* Do you wonder that Diseases are innumerable? Number the Cooks.——— *Seneca* Epist. 95.

which it mediately works, as well as the animal Functions. What they are, and how they operate, as, I believe, very few know, so it is very little necessary to know them for my present Purpose. As a philosophical Musician may understand Proportions and Harmony, and yet never be in a Condition to gratify a Company with a fine Piece of Musick, without the Benefit of Sounds from proper Organs, so the intellectual Operations (as long as the present Union between the Soul and Body lasts) can never be perform'd in the best Manner without proper Instruments. The Works of *Imagination* and *Memory*, of *Study*, *Thinking*, and *Reflecting*, from whatever Source the Principle on which they depend springs, must necessarily require bodily Organs. Some have these Organs finer, quicker, more agile, and sensible, and perhaps more numerous than others; *Brute* Animals have few or none, at least none that belong to *Reflection*; Vegetables certainly none at all. There is no Account to be given how a *Disease*, a *Fall*, a *Blow*, a *Debauch*, *Poisons*, *violent Passions*, *astral* and *aerial* Influences, much Application, and the like, should possibly alter or destroy these intellectual Operations without this Supposition. It is evident, that in *nervous* Distempers, and a great many other bodily Diseases, these Faculties, and their Operations, are impair'd, nay totally ruin'd and extinguished to all Appearance; and yet, by proper Remedies, and after Recovery of Health, they are restor'd and brought to their former State. Now since this present Age has made Efforts to go beyond former Times, in all the Arts of *Ingenuity*, *Invention*, *Study*, *Learning*, and all the contemplative and sedentary Professions, (I speak only here of our own Nation, our own Times, and of the better Sort, whose chief Employments and Studies these are) the Organs of these Faculties being thereby worn and spoil'd, must affect and deaden the whole

System,

System, and lay a Foundation for the Diseases of Lowness and Weakness. Add to this, that those who are likeliest to excel and apply in this Manner, are most capable, and most in hazard of following that Way of Life which I have mention'd, as the likeliest to produce these Diseases. *Great Wits* are generally great *Epicures*, at least Men of *Taste*. And the Bodies and Constitutions of one Generation, are still more corrupt, infirm, and diseas'd, than those of the former, as they advance in Time, and the Use of the Causes assign'd.

§. VI. To all these Considerations, if we add the present Custom of Living, so much in great, populous, and over-grown Cities; *London* (where nervous Distempers are most frequent, outrageous, and unnatural) is, for ought I know, the greatest, most capacious, close, and populous City of the *Globe*, the infinite Number of Fires, Sulphureous and Bituminous, the vast Expence of Tallow and fœtid Oil in Candles in Lamps, under and above Ground, the Clouds of stinking Breaths, and Perspiration, not to mention the Ordure of so many diseas'd, both intelligent and unintelligent Animals, the crouded Churches, Church-yards and Burying Places, with putrifying Bodies, the *Sinks, Butcher-Houses, Stables, Dunghils,* &c. and the necessary Stagnation, Fermentation, and Mixture of such Variety of all Kinds of Atoms, are more than sufficient to putrify, poison and infect the Air for twenty Miles round it, and which, in Time, must alter, weaken, and destroy the healthiest Constitutions of Animals of all Kinds; and accordingly it is in such like Cities, that these Distempers are to be found in their highest and most astonishing Symptoms, and seldom any lasting or solid Cure is perform'd till the Diseased be *rusticated* and purified from the infectious Air and Damps, transubstantiated into their Habits, by a

great

great City, and till they have fuck'd in and incorporated the fweet, balmy, clear Air of the Country, and driven the other out of their Habit. For by innumerable Experiments it is certain, that the Nitre or Acid of frefh, new Air, is as neceffary towards Life and Health as frefh balmy Food.

§. VII. All thefe together will, I think, be fufficient to account for the Frequency of *Nervous Diftempers* of late. And, in fact, the fame Caufes pretty near, have been affign'd by all Obfervers, Phyficians, and Philofophers, in all Ages and Countries, to have produc'd fimilar Effects. The *Egyptians*, as they feem to have been the firft who cultivated the Arts of Ingenuity and Politenefs, fo they feem likewife to have been the firft who brought *Phyfick* to any tolerable Degree of Perfection. The ancient *Greeks*, while they lived in their Simplicity and Virtue, were healthy, ftrong, and valiant: But afterwards, in Proportion as they advanced in Learning, and the Knowledge of the Sciences, and diftinguifhed themfelves from other Nations by their Politenefs and Refinement, they funk into *Effeminacy*, *Luxury*, and *Difeafes*, and began to ftudy *Phyfick*, to remedy thofe Evils which their Luxury and Lazinefs had brought upon them. In like manner, the *Romans* fell from their former Bravery, Courage, and *heroick Virtue*, which had gain'd them the Empire of the World. As *Celfus* obferves, where he is giving fome Account of the Rife and Improvement of Phyfick, according to the Prevalency of thefe two general Caufes of Difeafes, *Idlenefs* and *Intemperance*; *That thefe two had firft fpoil'd the Conftitutions of the* Greeks, *and afterwards thofe of his own Countrymen the* Romans, *when become Mafters of the Luxury as well as the Country of thofe polite People.*

§. VIII. It were eafy to fhew, from the beft Philofophy, confirm'd by the moft folid Experience, that Diftempers of all Kinds owe their more remote

Origin, Cause, and Rise to the same Principles: And that the Pains and Trouble some have taken to search and discover from *History*, the Occasions and Times of the Appearance of such and such Distempers, ends only in gathering and collecting some new Names, which Mankind have arbitrarily bestow'd upon some particular Symptoms, Degrees, or Paroxysms of universally known Diseases; and that these Enquiries, tho' they may divert and amuse the Enquirer and the Reader, like any other Pieces of History; are of no further Use or Advantage to the World, than in so far as they at the same Time discover the Means and Medicines by which such Symptoms or Degrees of Distempers were remedied or overcome. For, I think, it is plain to a Demonstration, that all Diseases whatsoever, by whatever Names or Titles dignified or distinguish'd, so far as they are natural and internal Distempers, and not caus'd by Accident, must in the main proceed (if we suppose, as we must, that Mankind at first were healthy and sound) from Intemperance, or some Error in the Quantity or Quality of their Food, and Laziness or Neglect of due Exercise: by which as the Solids and Juices of the Parents have been spoil'd, so their Posterity by continuing the same Courses, have gradually suffer'd higher and more extreme Disorders or Symptoms, arising from the same general Causes: which upon their first Appearance receiving new Names by their Observers, as new and particular Distempers, have increas'd to such a Number, as to exhibit that numerous Train of Miseries with which our *Books of Physick* and *Bills of Mortality* are fill'd: And as the Age grew worse, and the same Causes have been continued, and consequently the Constitutions more deprav'd, not only more numerous, but higher and more terrible Symptoms have arisen, till they have come at last to such a Degree of Malignity, as to infect and contaminate by mere Touch or Contact;

nay,

nay, even by the Smoak or Steam emitted from such diseas'd Habits. Not that I would deny that *Seasons*, *Climates*, *astral* and *aerial* Influences, and many other Circumstances, had any Effect or Influence in begetting or propagating these Distempers, but that these are slight, partial, and occasional Causes only, in respect of those others mention'd. And he that will consult History, will find sufficient Arguments to draw the same Conclusions.

§. IX. All Diseases have in some Degree or other, or in Embryo, been extant at all Times, at least, might have been, if the efficient Causes, *Idleness* and *Luxury*, had been sufficiently set to *work*, which were chiefly in the Power of Men themselves. What we call Nervous Distempers, were certainly, in some small Degree, known and observ'd by the *Greek*, *Roman*, and *Arabian* Physicians, tho' not such a Number of them as now, nor with so high Symptoms, so as to be so particularly taken notice of, except those call'd *Hysterick*, which seem to have been known in *Greece*, from whence they have deriv'd their Name: But as they were probably a stronger People, and liv'd in a warmer Climate, the slow, cold, and nervous Diseases were less known and observ'd; the Distempers of all the *Eastern* and *Southern* Countries being mostly *acute*.

§. X. When these general Causes I have mention'd, came to exist in some more considerable Degree, and operate in the more *Northern* Climates, then these Nervous Diseases began to shew themselves more eminently, and appear with higher and more numerous, and atrocious Symptoms. *Sydenham*, our Countryman, was the Physician of Note who made the most particular and full Observations on them, and establish'd them into a particular Class and Tribe, with a proper, tho' different, Method of Cure from other chronical and humorous Distempers, tho' their true Nature, Cause, and Cure has been less universally laboured and known, than that

that of most other Diseases, so that those who could give no tolerable Account of them have call'd them *Vapours, Spleen, Flatus, Nervous, Hysterical,* and *Hypochondriacal* Distempers.

CHAP. VII.

Of the true Nature of the Fibres and Nerves.

§. I. THE Fibres are *small, transparent, solid,* and *elastick,* or springy Threads or Filaments.

By *Fibres,* I mean here the least and smallest Threads in the Composition, of which many unite to make one sensible *Fibre.* Our Hairs, which are a Kind of *Fibres,* may be divided and split into a great Number of small ones, evident to the naked Eye; but *Leewenhoeck,* by his Glasses, has discover'd five or six hundred of them in one visible *Fibre.* They are *transparent,* as is evident, when sufficiently wash'd and cleans'd from the Skins, Humours and Fluids that adhere to them. The *last* and ultimate *Fibres* must of Necessity be *Solid*; for a *Fibre* that has a Cavity must consist of several others that go to make up its Coat; but even the smallest compound *Fibres* may be likewise *solid,* and consist of the simple ones, as a Silk Thread is made up of the Filaments of the raw Silk; for the best Glasses discover no Cavity in them, at least, they are not fairly prov'd to be tubular or hollow by the Appearance they give of some Cavities, when view'd thro' a Microscope, since what appears to some to be so, may be no other than the Interstices between them; as seems highly probable from their lying oblique to the Length of the *Fibres,* to which they ought to run parallel, if these *Fibres* were tubular. But other Arguments to confirm this shall be assign'd in their proper Place. They are *elastick* or springy, as appears by

a *Fibre,*

a *Fibre*, or a Mufcle's contracting (when divided) towards both Extremities; and that Heat and Puncture ftimulate them into involuntary Spafms and Convulfions.

§. II. All the Solids of the Body, when duly prepar'd, refolve themfelves, or may be feparated into fuch *Fibres* at laft. They are probably platted and twifted together in the Manner I have defcrib'd, to make the larger fenfible *Fibres:* And thefe again are either united in Bundles to form the *Mufcles, Tendons, Ligaments,* &c. or woven into a fine *Web*, like Cloth, to make the *Membranes*, the Coats of the Veffels, &c. only in fome the longitudinal, in others the tranfverfe *Fibres* are larger and ftronger; or thefe laft are rolled *fpirally*, according to the particular Office or Function defign'd to be perform'd by them. The Structure of the Bones feems to be like that of a Piece of Linen roll'd upon a *Cylinder*, thro' which a vaft Number of Pins are ftuck perpendicular to the Surface, to keep it from unrolling. Thefe, and doubtlefs many other Methods of Texture are made ufe of by the Infinitely-wife Author of Nature, in the Fabrick of the Solids of the Animal Machin. We muft content our felves, in the Explication of the Works of Nature, with Allufions to thofe of Art, that come neareft the Cafe where philofophick Nicety is not intended.

§. III. The fenfible or compound *Fibres*, as they are found in the Structure of an Animal Machin, are of three Kinds. *Firft*, Some are of a loofer and fofter Texture, or of a weaker Spring and Elafticity, contracting eafily and readily, and requiring only a fmall Force to diftend them, being moiftened with a greater Quantity of Blood; (which makes them look red) and fuch are all the *Mufcular Fibres*, which are employed in the Compofition of the Inftruments of voluntary or animal Motion, whofe greater Action requires a greater Quantity of balmy, warm

warm Moisture, to preserve their due Degree of *Tension*, and repair their casual and ordinary Decays. *Secondly*, Others are of a closer and more compact Disposition, the smaller *Fibres* whereof they are compos'd, being more firmly and intimately united, and crowded or compress'd into a smaller Space, in consequence of which their *elastick* Force is greater, they contract with greater Strength and Quickness, and are with more Difficulty distended, being moisten'd with a thinner, more rare, milky and watery Fluid, because of their solid Texture, to keep them from growing rigid or hard, and such are the Fibres of the Membranes, Tendons and Nerves, whose Compactness and closer Union of Parts, seems to be the Reason of the greater Degree of Sensibility they are evidently endued with above those of the first Kind. The Motion or Impression communicated to them, being thereby less interrupted, broken or lost; and the last of these particularly, to wit, the *Nerves*, are made use of to communicate the Impression they receive from outward Objects, or the muscular Fibres to the *Sensorium* in the Brain, and by it to the sentient Principle or *Musician*, and from it to the Organs. *Thirdly*, There is yet another Sort of these compound Fibres of a hard and rigid Make, whose *Elasticity* is like that of Steel, and not of the so distractile Kind, like those before mention'd, and consequently, being neither fit for Sensation or Action, they are only employ'd as a Support or Security for the tender Solids, requiring only a little Oil to keep them from growing too dry or brittle; and of this Kind are the Fibres of the Bones. Every single Fibre has a particular Membran involving it, like the Bark on a Tree, and some particular Clusters have another Membran binding the Whole.

§. IV. From this Account of the *Fibres* in general, if just, it is plain, that in their original Constitutions they are much the same, and that their different Properties and Appearances arise only out

of

Nature of Fibres and Nerves. 45

of the various Methods of Texture employ'd in their Composition, according to the Uses they were intended for. It is likewise probable, that all the *Fibres* of the Body (except those of the hard and rigid Kind, whereof the Bones are compos'd) are sensible, more or less, according to their Density or Closeness of their Texture, or the Degrees of their *elastick* or *distractile* Force, consequent thereupon, and their Communication with the Brain; the *Nerves* being only some of these Fibres the most susceptible, by their Structure of communicating Action and Motion, made use of to convey such Impressions, as they receive from outward Objects, or the other Fibres (however this Intercourse is carried on between them, whether by Engrafting, like the Blood Vessels, or otherwise, I shall not determin) to the Seat of the intelligent or sensitive Principle, and to carry back from thence the first Tendency of Action to the *Muscular Fibres*, when they contract or relax, in order to the several Functions of the *Animal OEconomy*. To tell precisely in what Manner this is perform'd, is, perhaps, impossible, I am sure very difficult; nor do I think it any ways necessary to what I have to propose, concerning the Nature and Cure of *Nervous Distempers*, commonly so call'd. I am of Opinion, that these Disorders do not so properly depend upon one Kind of *Animal Fibres*, that particularly of the *Nerves*, as is commonly suppos'd, unless it be in small and Topical Disorders of the nervous Kind: but that when there are general internal Diseases, and that many of the *Fibres* and *Nerves* suffer, the whole *System*, or all the Solids of the Body (except those which are firm and hard) suffer together in some Degree or other.

§. V. That there is a certain *Tone, Consistence,* and Firmness, and a determin'd Degree of *Elasticity* and *Tension* of the Nerves or Fibres, how small soever that be, (for it must be in some Degree even in Fluids themselves) necessary to the perfect Performance

mance of the *Animal Functions*, is I think, without all Question, from an Excess *over* or Defect *under* which, in some eminent Degree, Diseases of one Kind or another certainly arise. Those I am chiefly concern'd for in the following Treatise, are what proceeds from the Defect, or that Degree which falls below the just Mediocrity necessary for perfect Health: That is, those Diseases that ensue upon a too lax, feeble, and *unelastick* State of the *Fibres* or *Nerves*: And that every one may, in some measure, judge whether this be their Case, I shall hereafter enumerate the Signs and Symptoms that determin it, after giving the Reader some Conjectures concerning the Use of the Fibres, and the Manner of their Functions.

CHAP. VIII.

Of the Use of the Fibres and Nerves; the Manner and Causes of Sensation, and of Muscular Motion.

§. 1. IT not being my Intent to run into *philosophical* or speculative Disquisitions in a practical Treatise, which I design chiefly for the Use and Benefit of my *fellow Sufferers* under *nervous* Distempers; I shall only, with all the Brevity and Perspicuity I am capable of, represent to the *curious Reader*, what I have found most probable among the *Physicians*, *Philosophers*, and *Mathematicians*, upon this intricate and perplex'd Subject, having, I think, consider'd Impartially, and with some Attention, all those who have offer'd any thing solid upon it; and on this Account chiefly, that the *curious Reader* may more readily relish some of the Reasons for Advices of less Moment, which I suggest for treating of these Distempers in the best manner my Observation and Experience have taught me. But I lay much

much greater Stress upon the Experience and Observations themselves, than upon any *philosophical* Reasons I, or any other, can suggest; tho', I think, they may not be without their Evidence, when drawn from the real Nature of Things, or from the best Accounts of the *Animal OEconomy* we have hitherto gain'd, and may sometimes approach near to a Demonstration in Subjects more simple, and more obvious to Sense and Experiment than those I now treat of.

§. II. In the *first* place, I take it for granted, that the *intelligent Principle* is of a very different, if not quite contrary Nature from this organical Machin which contains it; and has scarce any thing in common to them, but as they are Substances. It is well known to *Physicians* what wonderful Effects, the *Passions*, excited by lucky or unlucky Accidents, (which are justly reckon'd *Intellectual* or *Spiritual* Operations) have on the Pulse, Circulation, Perspiration, and Secretions, and the other Animal Functions, in *Nervous* Cases especially, even to the restoring from Death, and destroying Life, as innumerable Instances demonstrate. I have felt a Pulse languishing, interrupting, and just dying away, render'd strong, full, and free by a joyful Surprize, and on the contrary. * Dr. *Bryan Robinson*'s Reasoning is conclusive, and yet I shall give one Instance, of which I my self (with many others) was an Eye-witness, more coercive, where an *Effort* of the *Mind* restor'd to Life once and again (to all Appearances) extinct Animal Functions. Now if the Principle of both Parts of the Compound were one, or if the Whole had but a material or organical Principle, or if there were only an external Spring of Motion and Action, the Functions dying, expiring, and going down, the Whole would always

---

* Vide Dr. *Bryan Robinson*'s *Animal OEconomy*, Prop. xxi.

die and extinguish. But surely no different or independent internal Principle, could restore, invigorate and actuate the dead or just dying material and animal Functions, as in this last Case *. I have formerly suggested, that the best *Similitude* I can form of the Nature and Actions of this *Principle* upon the *Organs* of its Machin, is that of a skilful *Musician* playing on a well-tun'd Instrument. So long as the Instrument is in due Order, so long is the Musick perfect and compleat in its Kind. As it weakens or breaks, the *Harmony* is spoil'd or stop'd. Some of the Parts of this Instrument being more delicate than others, are sooner disorder'd or broken. The great and principal ones, which preside over and actuate the lesser, are Strong and Durable, and require a greater Force and Violence to disorder them; but when once they are worn out, spoil'd, and ruin'd, the lesser and dependent ones are involv'd in their Fate, and the *Musician* must necessarily shift his Place and Scene. It is the Nature of all material Organs to decay and be worn out by Time. The Divisibility of Matter, the Friction of the Parts upon one another, and the Action of the Bodies that surround them, make this inevitable; but Accidents, Violence, and Mismanagement will quicken and forward their Ruin.

§. III. Material Objects can act no otherwise upon material Instruments, than by communicating their Action and Motion to them, or, at least, to the *Medium*, Fluid, or subtil Matter that surrounds them; that is, material Objects can act no otherwise upon animal Organs, but either immediately by communicating their Action and Motion to these Organs, and putting their constituent Parts into particular Vibrations, intestine Action and Reaction upon one another: or mediately by the Interven-

---

* Vide Part 3d, the Case of Col. *Townshend*.

tion

tion of some *subtil Fluid* or Matter on which they impress their Actions and Motions, which are transmitted by the *Medium*, in the same Manner to the Organ. Small Bodies act upon one another in the same Manner, and by the same Laws and Mechanism, that the *Systems* of greater ones do: And he who would understand the Effects of little Bodies, Fluids, or material Spirits upon greater Bodies, and the Nature of the Action of their Particles upon one another, has nothing to do, (if he reasons justly) but to resemble small Bodies to great, under particular Laws and Conditions. To apply this general Doctrine to the Case in Hand: We may conclude, that *Smelling*, for Example, is nothing but the Action of an odorous Body, or the Steam or Vapour emitted from it, giving a determin'd Impulse to the Nerves or Fibres of the Nostrils, which, by their *Mechanism*, propagate this Vibration and Impulse, thro' their Length to the intelligent or *sentient Principle* in the Brain (which I resemble to the *Musician*). Again, *Feeling* is nothing but the Impulse, Motion, or Action of Bodies, gently or violently impressing the Extremities or Sides of the Nerves, of the Skin, or other Parts of the Body, which by their Structure and *Mechanism*, convey this Motion to the *sentient* Principle in the Brain, or the *Musician*. Lastly, *Seeing*, or the Perception of the Bulk, Distance, Situation, or Colour of Objects, is nothing but the Action of Light (a Fluid of its own Kind) reflected or refracted from the Surfaces of Bodies or outward Objects (some of which scatter the Rays from one another, in an infinite Variety of *Angles*, and so by *Experience* determine their *Distance* and *Bulk*: And transmit one Kind of Rays more copiously than another, to determine their *Colour*) which being variously refracted in the Humours of the *Eyes*, are at last united on the *Retina*, so as there to form an *Image* analogous to that of the outward Object, which by striking the Nerves of the *Retina*,

tina, (in the same manner that the Object it self would have done) is by them transmitted to the *sentient Principle*. It is much after the same Manner in all the other Instruments of the Sensations.

§. IV. What is the true Cause of *Elasticity* in general, or that of the *animal Fibres* and *Nerves* in particular, is, I think, an unexplicable *Problem*, unless we admit of a centrifugal or repelling Fluid. Even the true Nature and Cause of *Cohesion* and *Continuity* it self was uncertain till of late, and as yet is too general, as far as this Kind of Fluid or subtile Spirit explains it. The Principle of *Attraction* both in great and little Bodies, is evident from innumerable Experiments; but what the Laws of this general Principle may be, in all *Systems* of Bodies; or what Limitations or Restrictions it may undergo, to solve the particular Appearances, is, I fear, as yet imperfect. Perhaps Generals, in natural Philosophy, (as well as some other Sciences) are all that we can attain to in our present State (for it seems Precision is a Contradiction to Finitude). We see indeed that Bodies of plain, smooth Surfaces, or in which many Points come into Contact, cohere most strongly, which must necessarily follow from the Principle of *Attraction*. Sir *Isaac Newton* has shewn the *Analogy* of Bodies flying from one another; or their having a Principle of *Repulsion*, to *negative Quantities*, in *Algebra* and *Geometry*, and to some other Appearances in Nature: whereby he hints a probable Account of the Elasticity and the Compression of the Air: And the same Manner of Philosophising, duly applied and suited to Circumstances, will equally account for the *Elasticity* of all Fluids whatsoever, and perhaps of Solids too. There are some Experiments upon Bodies, that seem to prove the real Existence of such a Principle in Nature as *Repulsion:* for Example, (not to mention others, of which there are a great Number, that enforce the same Conclusion) *That* whereby a smooth
Prism,

Prism, rubb'd strongly, drives Leaf-Gold from it, and suspends it till its Influence is withdrawn, *Hawsbee*'s Experiments on an exhausted Glass *Sphere* or *Cylinder*, violently turn'd on an *Axis:* Water rising in a *hyperbolick* Line above the Surface, and *Mercury* subsiding below it in the same Curve, and a great many other such Experiments. We see also, that a Body under a circular Rotation, has a constant Tendency to fly off in the Tangent, which a certain *late Author* has made Use of to explain *Elasticity* by (tho', I think, with indifferent Success). Now tho' all these Appearances may possibly be accounted for from other Principles, different from that of *Elasticity*, yet, I think, they may be sufficient to illustrate this Principle of *Repulsion*. *Animal* and *Vegetable* Substances, such as *Ivory*, *Whale-Bone*, the *Tendons* and *muscular* Substances of Animals, *Cork*, *Sponge*, &c. are the most perfectly *elastick* of any Bodies known, which makes it highly probable, that the Actions, Sensations, and Functions of Animals and Vegetables, are owing, in some measure, to this *Elasticity* in the Solids: And *Metalick* and *Mineral* Bodies (as is well known) have their elastick Properties increas'd and augmented by *Animal* and *Vegetable Salts* united with them while they are in *Fusion* by Fire.

§. V. The most difficult Problem in all the Animal OEconomy, is, to give any tolerable Account of *Muscular Action* or *Animal Motion*. The Similitude of a Machin put into Action and Motion by the Force of Water convey'd in Pipes, was the readiest Resemblance the *Lazy* could find to explain *Muscular Motion* by. It was easy, from this Resemblance, to forge a thin, imperceptible Fluid, passing and re-passing through the Nerves, to blow up the Muscles, and thereby to lengthen one of their Dimensions, in order to shorten the other. On such a slender and imaginary Similitude, the precarious *Hypothesis* of *Animal Spirits* seems to be built.

But as their Existence is, I fear, precarious, so, were it real, they are not sufficient to solve the Appearances, as shall be more particularly consider'd hereafter. All I shall further say here, is, that this and the other abstruse Appearances in the Animal and Vegetable Kingdoms, particularly *Vegetation, Elasticity, Cohesion,* the Emissions, Reflexions and Refractions of *Light, Attraction* in the greater and lesser Bodies, and all the other secret and internal Actions of the Parts of Matter upon one another, are with some Shew of Possibility suspected, and by some Observations (not otherwise to be accounted for) made not improbable by the late *sagacious and learned* Sir Isaac Newton[*], to be owing to an infinitely subtil, elastick Fluid, or Spirit, (as he strongly expresses that subtil Matter) distended through this whole *System*, penetrating all Bodies with the greatest Facility, infinitely active and volatile, but more condens'd in *Vacuo*, or Spaces void of grosser Matter, than towards the Surfaces of Bodies, or in them: And by this *Æther, Spirit,* or most subtil Fluid, the Parts of Bodies are driven forcibly together, and their mutual attractive Virtue arises, and the other beforemention'd Appearances are produced. The Existence of this *subtil Fluid* or *Spirit*, is made probable by what he has observ'd of Liquors, *heating* and *cooling,* Mercury rising and continuing rais'd, and smooth Bodies clinging together, and requiring an equal Force to separate them in *Vacuo,* or in an exhausted Receiver, as in Air: And a great many other Experiments have been suggested not otherwise to be so readily accounted for. And it is probable, that those other mention'd Appearances may be owing to the same Cause, since we find always *similar* Effects have *similar* Causes, and that Nature is frugal in *Causes,* but various and manifold in *Ef-*

---

[*] Opticks, Book III.

fects:

Existence of Animal Spirits.

fects: But Sir *Isaac* not having been able to make a sufficient Number of Experiments to determin all the Laws of this Fluid, nor indeed sufficient absolutely to prove its Existence, he leaves it to the Sagacity of future Ages to determin them, and to apply them to the Appearances; and finding nothing in the Writings of other *Philosophers, Mathematicians,* or *Physicians,* of equal Probability with this, tho' imperfect Account of these Difficulties, I will offer the Reader no other.

CHAP IX.

Of the Existence of animal Spirits, and of their Use to account for animal Motion, and the other animal Functions.

§. I. THE Doctrine of Spirits, to explain the animal Functions and their Diseases, has been so readily and universally receiv'd from the Days of the *Arabian* Physicians (and higher) down to our present Times, that scarce one (except here and there a *Heretick* of late) has call'd this *Catholick* Doctrine in Question. And those who perhaps had Courage or Curiosity enough to doubt of, or examine the Matter, either out of Laziness, or to avoid a tedious Way of expressing themselves, have implicitly gone into the common Dialect which is now very convenient. The *System* at first was but rude and imperfect, but having been adopted by *Philosophers* and *Mathematicians,* as well as *Physicians,* they have brought it to a more consistent and less absurd *Theory.* *Borelli* gave it a great Countenance, by receiving it to explain *muscular* Motion, in his Book *De Motu Animalium. Willis* gave it all the Advantages of Eloquence and Metaphor. *John Bernoulli* has added to it a Kind of Geometry and Calculation. And last of all Monf. *des Molieres,* in the *Memoirs*

moirs de l' Academie Royal for 1724, has added Plainness, and some Conformity to the Natural Appearances, and taken off most of the common Objections. I shall not tire myself, nor the Reader, by detailing the *System* at length, nor the several Steps by which it has been reformed and amended. *Goelike*, Professor at *Frankfort*, in a small Treatise, has solidly expos'd and ridicul'd it as far as *Borelli* went, or the precedent or co-temporary Physicians: And that admirable Geometer Dr. *Pemberton*, has, I believe, *geometrically* shewn the Insufficiency of what *Bernoulli* has advanced to mend the Matter, in his Preface to Mr. *Cowper*'s Book on the *Muscles*. I shall therefore only suggest some general Reflections, which perhaps equally distress this *System*, however improv'd or amended.

§. II. I will not urge, that the best Eyes or Senses, however assisted, have not hitherto been able to discover any Cavity in the Substance of the *Nerves*, or in the small Filaments into which they are divided. That, on the contrary, as far as *Leewenhoeck* (the best Observer doubtless) or others who have examin'd the Matter with great Accuracy, could perceive: they appear solid, transparent, and with broken Reflexions, even when dry, like crack'd *Glass-Wire*, *Horn*, or any other solid Substance, without any apparent Cavity. Nor that by compressing them by *Ligatures*, stopping the Influx, or by stroaking and milching their Lengths, are any Appearances to be observ'd like those in other Vessels, which we know do carry Fluids in them, more than must necessarily happen from compressing the small Arteries that go along by them. It is true, that by stopping and tying the Trunks of the greater Nerves, the Muscle it self will turn *Paralytick* and motionless, but it will equally do so upon intercepting the Motion or Influx of the Blood, which concludes nothing but this, that these *Nerves* are necessary towards the Action of the Muscles, whether from their

car-

Existence of Animal Spirits.

carrying a Fluid, or from their own *Tonick* Nature, their internal Configuration, or any other Manner they may act, is not thereby determin'd. And if Probabilities could any way influence a Fact, they must lie on the other Side of the Question, since that thin and soft Liquor, which seems only fit to keep them moist and lax, rather derogates from the Existence of any spirituous Fluid in them proper for the intended End. Nor, thirdly, will I urge against it Dr. *Glisson*'s Experiment of putting the Arm of a strong, brawny Porter into a large Tube full of Water, and fixing it close to his Shoulder, that the Water might not get out, but ascend into a small *conical* Tube, passing out of the Side of the larger one: whereby he found, that upon the strongest Action of the Muscles, the Water subsided and fell in the small Tube, and rose again upon their ceasing to act; from whence he concludes, that *Muscular Motion* is not performed by the Inflation or Swelling of the Muscles, but that, on the contrary, when they are mov'd, they are contracted into a lesser Figure, and more compact Substance, or are hardened: which would scarcely happen, if any Matter, how subtil soever, flow'd in the Nerves, and thereby was added to the Substance of the Muscles: For since the *Impenetrability* of Matter is demonstrable, the least such an Addition could effect, was, that tho' the Fluid, by its Subtilty, would not sensibly increase the Bulk, yet surely it could not lessen it. I say, I shall not urge these obvious Objections against this Doctrine; because, tho' I think they cannot be solidly answer'd, yet they may be evaded; but shall proceed to offer a few Considerations, which I think equally distress it, in all the Improvements that have been made on it.

§. III. Some have imagin'd the Nature of this Fluid of *animal Spirits*, to have some Resemblance with that of Light, (the most subtil, active and penetrating Fluid apparent in this our *System*) which would

would make them quickly penetrate, fly through, tear, break, and consume their rare and tender Prisons, which would be of no more Use to them to determin them to regular and uniform Motions, than Glass Tubes are to Light. And were they like *urinous* or *inflammable Spirits*; yet neither would such slender Prisons contain them any Time, or convey them uniformly for regular Purposes. And *lastly*, if they were like Water or aqueous Fluids, they could neither have Activity nor Subtilty sufficient to solve the Appearances, nor could they move with Velocity enough to answer the Purposes of Volition, Sensation, and voluntary or involuntary Motions, under that more gross and sluggish Form, and would even then ouze thro' their containing Tubes.

§. IV. In a Word, give them what Nature you will, they will never answer the *animal Functions* and Appearances. For suppose them to have any Resemblance to the other Fluids in our *System*; if extremely volatile and active, they would fly away, and tear in a very short Time their containing Tubes and Canals the *Nerves*, and could not receive regular Determinations from them; and yet such they must be, to answer the Ends of Volition and Sensation: And if they were grosser, denser and less refin'd, they would not answer quick and sudden Motion, and its Cessation. And they can never be suppos'd to be extremely active and volatile, and gross and thick at the same Time We find in *Dropsies*, that a grosser Fluid, than they can be suppos'd to be, will ouze in great Quantities thro' Vessels of as close a Texture as theirs; not to mention the sudden Effects of all Kinds of Spirits (taken inwardly) upon the *Nerves*, which from this Appearance must even be suppos'd to penetrate the Substance of these *Nerves*, and yet the nervous Fluid must be, at least, as subtil and penetrating as they.

§. V. Quick and instantaneous, strong, and violent Motions (increas'd by adding great Weights, as we we know by Experience) seem absolutely to have determin'd the Nature of animal Spirits, to that of the most active and volatile Kind of Fluids imaginable, because none else is capable of so quick and strong Actions, in order to determin the instantaneous Obedience of the Muscles to the Orders of the Will: And such strong, violent, and quick Motions must necessarily make a great Waste and Expence of these animal Spirits, so as to require a constant Supply of such fine and subtil Parts from the Food: And yet we find that aqueous, vegetable, and earthy Substances only, make up most of the Nourishment of those who have the best and strongest Spirits, and live in a constant Course of such Action; and the animal Heat, employ'd to generate them, rises no higher than that of Vegetation or Incubation only, which is not sufficient for any other Kinds of Spirits, inflammatory or urinous. *But* how any Fluid at all, of what Kind soever, can be suppos'd or imagin'd to go backwards and forwards in the same indivisible Instant almost, (to convey Pain, for Example, to the sentient Principle, and muscular Action at the same Instant, to shut the Eyes upon Appearances of Danger, or to actuate all the Muscles necessary for running away under a *Panick*, and a thousand other Instances that may be given) seems very hard to explain from the Nature of Fluids known here below.

§. VI. The Existence of animal Spirits, has been chiefly contriv'd to solve the Appearances of *nervous Distempers*, viz. Obstructions of the Nerves, or their Incapacity to act under some Circumstances. Now if these Appearances can be accounted for, more conformably to the *Analogy* of Nature without this Supposition than by it, then the Dispute will be at an End, and they useless. Of this last the Reader will be a better Judge, when he has consider'd the whole of this Treatise. As to the Obstructions of the *Nerves*, since they are plainly

cylin-

cylindrical, (or nearly such) it does not seem agreeable to *Mechanism*, that any Fluid should readily be obstructed in them. For whatever Fluid, of whatever Nature, can enter the one Extremity in the *Brain*, will move on by the same Impulse to the other. For *Example*, a Ball of the same or less *Diameter* than the Cavity of a *cylindrical* Tube will move (by the Force first impress'd) from one End to the other, without Stop or Hindrance from the Tube; unless it be from external Accidents or Bruises altering the Figure of the Tube; and the same may be concluded of any Fluid: which makes *Obstructions* pretty unaccountable in *cylindrical* Tubes: Besides, it is no small Prejudice against any Fluids moving in the nervous Fibres, even that their Figure is *cylindrical*; for we see in all Tubes that contain Fluids, (as the *Veins*, *Arteries*, and *Lympheducts*) to accelerate the Motion of the Fluid, their internal Figure is *conical*, or tapering, or nearly so, which readily accounts for the Obstructions in these last mention'd Vessels; and it is not improbable, that Nature, which is always similar, or consistent with it self, had the Nerves been design'd to carry a Fluid, would have hollowed them in this Form. And, on the contrary, the frequent Obstructions that happen in those Vessels, which are of this mention'd *conical* Figure, and the Hardness of such Obstructions, may be sufficient to account for the Obstructions of the *Nerves* themselves. From all which we may, I think, pretty firmly conclude, that the Notion of *animal Spirits* is of the same Leaven with the *substantial Forms* of *Aristotle*, and the *cœlestial System* of *Ptolemy*.

§. VII. Perhaps there may be in Nature material Systems of Fluids of several Degrees of Rarity and Subtilty, even indefinitely many and different. What makes it not impossible, that there may be more such *Systems* of subtil, elastick Fluids, than that mention'd *Æther* describ'd by Sir *Isaac Newton*,

Newton, is, that the *Elasticity, Attraction,* and other Qualities of this *Newtonian Æther,* must necessarily be caus'd by some other more *ætherial* and subtil Fluid, else we must admit *Elasticity, Attraction,* and *Activity* in the Particles constituting this *Newtonian Æther* without a Cause; or we must suppose these Qualities innate to them, and to have been impress'd on them immediately by the *first* and *supreme Cause*. And thus we are necessarily thrown into one or other of the two *Horns* of this *Dilemma,* either to admit of Fluids descending *in infinitum,* in Tenuity and Subtilty, to produce *Elasticity* and *Attraction,* or allow Particles of Matter impress'd with these Qualities in their Creation immediately by the *supreme Being*. It is true, this *Newtonian Æther* advances us one Step further into the Nature of Things; but here we must necessarily stop, the Works of *God* appearing literally inscrutable to Perfection. A few of the first Steps we may go in this *infinite Progression,* but in all the Works of *God*, there is a *ne plus ultra;* perhaps it may be in the inanimate material *System* of Things, as it is most certainly in the *Animal* Kingdom, that Nature and its Author, to distinguish itself from finite *Mechanism*, always operates by *Systems* and *Organs* in Number even infinite, if not *infinite* in the highest Sense, yet certainly indefinite or *infinite* in a *relative* Sense, and in Regard to a finite *Capacity;* and thus he leaves *Images* and *Signatures* of himself on all his Works, as is manifest in *Quantity, Time,* and *Motion,* and their Signs or Characters, *infinite Divisibility, infinite Progressions, Eternity, Series's,* and *Fluxion,* &c. *Mercury* is grosser or denser than *Water, Water* than *Air, Air* than *Light, Light* than *Æther,* and how far further Nature may go in descending in Tenuity, Subtilty, and Refining of other *Systems* of Fluids, none alive can certainly tell. This as a Conjecture the *Analogy* of Things, the infinite Divisibility or Encreaſe of Matter, from finite, till it becomes infinitely great or ſmall, at leaſt, as to our Conceptions; Nature's never paſſing from *Poſitive* to *Negative* Quantities, till it goes thro' the Medium of *Nothing*, or infinitely ſmall of the ſame Denomination; its never paſſing from Motion to Reſt, but thro' infinitely ſmall Motion: In a Word, its never acting in Generals, by *Starts, Jumps*, or unequal Steps; I ſay all theſe Hints ſeem to point out ſomething like this. From all which, and a great deal more might be urg'd, it may not be improbable, that as in Quantity there is one or more *Means* between the *leaſt* and the *greateſt*: ſo in *Subſtances* of all Kinds, there may be Intermediates between *pure, immaterial Spirit*, and *groſs Matter*, and that this intermediate, material Subſtance, may make the Cement between the human Soul and Body, and may be the Inſtrument or *Medium* of all its Actions and Functions, where material Organs are not manifeſt: And may poſſibly be the Cauſe of the other ſecret and inſcrutable *Myſteries* of Nature, and the ſame (for ought I know) with Sir *Iſaac Newton*'s infinitely *fine and elaſtick Fluid*, or *Spirit*, mention'd in a former Chapter; for ſince he has not, I believe none elſe will take upon him to determine its *ſpecifick* Nature, or, indeed, whether it actually be or not: The innumerable Appearances ſeem to imply ſome ſuch Thing.

§. VIII. To conclude this dark Subject of *animal Spirits*, if they muſt be ſuppos'd, we may affirm they cannot be of the Nature of any Fluid we have a Notion of, from what we ſee or know. Indeed, the large Size, the wonderful Texture, and the great Care and Security Nature has employ'd about the *Brain*, makes it probable it has been deſign'd for the *nobleſt* Uſes, *viz.* to be the Temple or *Senſorium* of the *ſentient and intelligent Principle*. And its Reſemblances, in many Circumſtances,

Existence of Animal Spirits. 61

cumstances, to the other *Glands*, which certainly separate Liquors, makes it not impossible that it may have Uses *analogous* to those. But how to assign them, explain, or accord them with what has been suggested above, I know not. May not the *sentient Principle* have its Seat in some Place in the Brain, where the Nerves terminate, like the *Musician* shut up in his Organ-Room? May not the infinite Windings, Convulsions, and Complications of the Beginning of the Nerves which constitute the Brain, serve to determine their particular *Tone*, *Tension*, and consequently the Intestine Vibrations of their Parts? May they not have interwoven Blood Vessels and Glands to separate a milky Liquor, to soften, moisten, and continue their *Elasticity*, and innate Mechanick Powers through the whole *nervous System*? And also to keep them in a proper Condition to play off the *Vibrations*, *Tremors*, and *Undulations* made on them by Bodies, or their *Effluvia*? May not these *Vibrations* be propagated through their Lengths by a subtile, spirituous, and infinitely elastick Fluid, which is the *Medium* of the Intelligent Principle? As Sound is convey'd thro' Air to the *Tympanum*, and by it to this *Medium* or *Æther*, and from the *Medium* to the *Intelligent Principle*, and as *Sight* is perform'd through or by Light. And is not the *Analogy* of Nature and Things thus, in some measure, preserv'd? I own it is much easier to confute than establish, and I should not be very *Sanguin* about the Non-existence of animal Spirits, but that I have observ'd the dwelling so much upon them, has led Physicians too much to neglect the mending the Juices, the opening Obstructions, and the strengthening the Solids, wherein only the proper and solid Cure of nervous Distempers consists; and apply to *Volatiles*, *Fœtids*, and *Stimulants*: which, at best, are but a Reprieve, and is not unlike blowing up the Fire, but at the same Time forcing it to spend faster, and go out sooner;

sooner; for *Volatiles*, *Aromaticks*, and *Cordials*, are much of one and the same Nature, and all but Whips, Spurs, and pointed Instruments to drive on the *resty and unwilling Jade*.

CHAP. X.

Of the Generation, Animation, Nutrition, and Growth of the Solids and Fluids of Animals, and some other Functions of the Animal Oeconomy.

§. I. I Think it next to a *Demonstration*, that there is a *self-active* and *self-motive* Principle in all Animals whatsoever, both in the *perfect* and *imperfect*. Mere *Mechanism* (that is, Foreign impress'd Motions, according to certain Laws, and in Proportion to the Surfaces of Bodies only) may possibly account for the Appearances of *Vegetation*; but it can never account for *Animation*, or the *animal Life* even of the lowest *Insect*; and this, I think, is the universal Opinion of all the ablest and wisest Geometers, who are most knowing in the Laws of Mechanism. How far a *perpetual Motion* is possible, in the present State of Things, and under the present established Laws of Nature, I will not take upon me absolutely to determine. I should think the *Friction* of Bodies, the perpetual Loss of *communicated* Motion on our *Globe*, and the Impossibility of any *Curves* being describ'd by one and the same Impulse, should make it as impossible, as the *squaring* the *Circle*, or expressing *Surds* by Integers or finite Fractions, under the present State of our *Arithmetic*. But that every Animal is a *perpetuum Mobile*, from a *Self-Motive* Principle *within*, and from its own *innate* Powers, I think, is past all manner of Doubt; and to explain *Mechanically*, from Matter and Motion alone, and all the Powers of our Numbers and Geometry joined

Generation, &c. of Solids & Fluids. 63

join'd to them, the Functions of any living Animal, is mere *Jargon* and *Ignorance*, as I conceive.

§. II. May not *Life* and *Animation* have some Resemblance to Light, in its Activity, and acting from a central Point of *Self-Motion* and *Self-Activity* Radiat in a limited *Sphere*, and where it finds proper *Organs*, concurs and *analogises* in these Organs, with the established Laws of Bodies? For it is as utterly impossible to account for *Animation* from mere *Mechanism*, as to account for *Thinking* or *Willing* from that Principle. Might not the *Self-Motive* and *Self-Active*, the Intelligent and Free-willing Principle (that is, the several Degrees and Extensions of this animating and actuating *Spirit*) have been at the same Time and Instant created with the *organical infinitesimal* Body, in the first Originals of each different Species of Animals, and have been forming and extending the organiz'd Body under certain Laws and Restrictions, till it was fit to bear *Light* and *Day*, and had its Organs compleatly finished, to play off the *Musick* and *Harmony* it was originally design'd for? Is not every Animal a *Machin* of an *infinite* Number of *organical* Parts, fitted with a proper *Musician* or *Self-Motive* and *Self-Active* Principle, of an Order, Rank, and Extension proper for the intended Ends and Purposes of the Compound?

§. III. By an *Organ*, I understand a Part of a Machin, compleat in itself, necessary towards the Perfection and intended Use of the Whole: Thus a Wheel, with its *Axis* and *Pivots*, is an *Organ* in a Watch or Clock: On this Definition, are not the *Organs* of every Animal in Number actually *infinite*, which nothing less than a *Geometer* of infinite Capacity and Power, could adjust and fit to each other, and to their intended Purposes and Uses? If we consider the Number of *Veins*, *Arteries*, *Lymphaticks*, *Nerves*, *Fibres*, *Tendons*, *Ligaments*, *Membrans*, *Cartilages*, *Bones*, *Muscles*, and *Glands* discovered in every Animal, and this infinite Number still encreased

and

and made further conspicuous by *Injections* and *Microscopes*: Add to these, the Sensibility of each the smallest Point and Particle of Animal, where the Circulation reaches, we shall be easily persuaded that they surpass all finite Skill and *Mechanism*, to form and frame; and that they are without Number, and without End. That the whole Fabrick is but an *Assemblage* of an infinite Number of such *Organs*. Every minute Point, and Atom of which, is fitted and contriv'd for a particular End and Purpose, and for the Benefit of the Whole *. The *Structure, Contrivance*, the *Use, Beauty*, and *Perfection* of the human *Hand* alone, made *Galen* a firm Believer in a first Cause infinitely Wise, Good and Powerful.

§. IV. But that the whole *System* of these *Conjectures* may be brought into one View, I shall draw them out into a few *Propositions*, without offering at any thing, that may be suggested to make them more probable, and leave the Reader to correct, or reject them at his Pleasure, being in no manner necessary to the main of my Design, and calculated only to amuse and divert.

Prop. 1. Matter is capable of infinite *Division* and *Addition*.

2. There may be *Systems* of Bodies of all Sizes, from indefinitely *small*, to indefinitely *great*. The Stars may be consider'd as a *System* of Bodies indefinitely *great*, and *Light* a System of Bodies indefinitely *small*, and how many other such *Systems* there may be, none can tell.

3. There may be *Animalcula* or Organised living Bodies of all Sizes, from those of a *Pepper Corn* and lower, up to a *Whale* and higher, and these may be for many Ages growing and encreasing to their appointed *Magnitudes*, under certain Laws and Restrictions.

---

* Vide *Galen* de Usu *partium*.

4. *LIFE* and *Animation* seem impossible, and a Contradiction to mere *Mechanism*, that is, to Matter, acted by determin'd Laws of Motion, and in Proportion to the Surfaces of Bodies only.

5. *LIFE* and *Animation* admit of all the Degrees of Quantity.

6. *MECHANISM* takes Place and operates by it self only, on dead *Matter*; but is actuated and govern'd in its Operations, by animated living Bodies or *spiritual* Substances.

7. The *Self-Motive, Self-active*, and *living* Principle concurs with, and *homologises* to *Mechanism* in the animal Functions and Operations. The second is subordinate to the first in all its Effects, which take Place according to its own Laws.

8. Organised Bodies fit for *Animation*, and living Functions, consisting of Organs, in Number *infinite*, can only be the Work of infinite Wisdom and Power.

9. The *Self-motive, Self-active* Principle cannot act *harmoniously*, or according to its intended Uses and Purposes, on an unfit, unfinished, unorganised Body, any more than a skilful *Musician* can produce fine Musick or *Harmony* on an unfinished, imperfect Instrument.

10. Might not the *organised* Bodies of all the Species of Animals have been included in the first original Pairs, decreasing continually in a *geometrical* Progression, or as *second, third*, and subsequent *Fluxions* are contain'd in their first Fluxions, and all in their Fluent?

11. Might it not be, that the *organis'd* Bodies of all Animals might be included in the *Male* of each original Pair? and that the *Female* might only supply a more convenient Habitation for them during a determin'd Time, while by their quicker Encrease they were fitted to bear *Air, Sun,* and *Day*?

12. The

12. The original *Stamina*, the whole *System* of the Solids, the Firmness, Force, and Strength of the Muscles, of the Viscera, and great Organs, are they not owing to the *Male*? And does the *Female* contribute any more but a convenient Habitation, proper Nourishment, and an *Incubation* to the seminal Animalcul for a Time, to enable the *organised* living Creatures to bear the *Air*, *Sun*, and *Day* the sooner?

13. If the *Brain*, *Heart*, *Lungs*, *Liver*, or *Kidneys* of the *Male* be spoil'd and corrupted, the same Juices in him that spoil'd these *Viscera*, may they not spoil and corrupt the same *Organs* in the *Animalcul* while lodged in him, and in some kind fed and encreas'd by his Juices?

14. Since then the *Female*'s Juices are what, for a certain Time, also feed the *Animalcul*, as they are Good or Bad, proper or improper, may they not alter, spoil, or mend the Juices of the *Fœtus*?

15. The *Solids* therefore seem neither eminently (or in such a Degree as the Juices) capable of being repair'd, renew'd, nor mended when broken, wounded, or taken away, no more than a *Tinker* can mend a Hole in a Brass Pot or Pan, *viz.* not by new forming or joining and uniting the *Metal*, but by a *Soder* or *Patch*; and so Nature seems only to have provided proper Juices to fill up the *Discontinuity*, and supply the Breaches: As in Animals, we see by the *Cicatrices* of Wounds and Sores of all Kinds, *viz.* their continuing for almost ever after, a Botch. For this Cement never makes them the same continued *Organ*, scarce any thing but a botch'd or clouted one.

16. The Solids seem scarce subject to any eminent Alterations in their innate Tension, Force, and Elasticity naturally, till they are almost quite spoil'd and putrified, but merely as they are made thicker or grosser, harder or softer, by this adhering

Glew

Glew or Soder, or from these Juices within, and their agglutinating Patch-work.

17. *NUTRITION* seems only to be the supplying the several solid Parts with a suitable *Glew* or *Soder*, to augment and encrease the Bulk, and but little to alter the innate Force and *Elasticity* of the original and primitive Solids.

18. The *Solids* seem to be capable of being contracted, as it were, into an indivisible Point, *viz.* in seminal Animalculs: By *Plicatures*, *Foldings*, *Twistings*, and *Swaiths* or *Membranes*, and yet to preserve a proportional Degree of Elasticity and Spring: As we see in the *Nymphæ* of Silk-worms, and the other Insects of the *papilious* Kind. Or they may be shut up, one Part within another, as a Fishing-rod: and the different Shapes of these seminal Animalculs, from their Figure when full grown, seem to imply this. And these *Swaiths* and *Membranes* burst and break naturally, by Accretion and Encrease of Bulk, as we see in seminal Plants, and in the Formation of Animals.

19. The *Solids* therefore seem to be the great, the proper, the only Instrument of *Life* and *Animation*, and the true *musical Organ* of the living *Musician*. And the *Fluids* to be only intended to preserve them in due *Plight*, *Glibness*, *Warmth*, and *tonical Virtue*, and to soder and repair their Wounds, Wastes and Decays. But it is on these Fluids that *Medicines* and *Medical Operations* have place chiefly.

20. This general Sketch, tho' imperfect, and, perhaps, not real, yet is the most consistent I could frame on a Consideration and View of the whole of *Animal Nature*, in all its Kinds and Species; by it the *Analogy* between *Vegetables* and *Animals* is preserv'd, and many Appearances in *Generation*, *Nutrition*, and *Animation* may be solv'd, which otherwise appear unaccountable: The *philosophical Gardeners*, the *philosophical Breeders* of Cattle and other Animals, and those best acquainted with *Na-*

tural History, will be the fittest Judges of its Truth and Justness. I thought it might amuse the ingenious Valetudinarian; and therefore let it pass as it is, without the Arguments and Instances that make it probable, tho' I could produce innumerable.

CHAP. XI.

Of the Signs and Symptoms of a too relaxed, loose and tender State of Nerves.

§. I. THOSE who have weak, loose, and feeble or relax'd Nerves, have generally a small, weak, languid, and sometimes an intermittent Pulse. Exercise, strong Liquors, high Food, or that which is hard to digest, or too great a Quantity of these last, taken down, quicken and accelerate the Pulse, and discover a Labour and Struggle in the Circulation. The Strokes of such a Pulse are seldom clean and free, and sometimes quite stopt and interrupted for some small time; especially in great Lowness, Fainting or Fits; and, at best, are like a Force not apply'd at once, but by straining, and struggling, and slow Degrees.

§. II. * Those that have by Nature soft, thin, and short Hair, which, with great Difficulty, receives or retains a Buckle, and those who readily run into Baldness or shedding of the Hair towards the Spring, are certainly of a loose, flabby, and and relaxed State of Nerves: For the Hair seems to be only some of the fleshy Fibres lengthened outwards and hardned, at least they seem to be of the same Kind and Nature, with the other Fibres,

---

* Vide Essay on Health and long Life, Chap. vii. §. 4.

consist of a great many lesser Filaments, contain'd in a common Membrane, and are solid transparent, and elastick: And as the Hairs are in Strength, Bulk, and Elasticity, so generally the Fibres of the Body are; and those whose Hair sheds, turns thin, lank, or refuses Buckle, if it does not happen to them after recovering from an acute Distemper, ought to take care they fall not into nervous Disorders, which anointing their Hair with sweet Oils, or washing their Heads with Honey-Water will scarce prevent.

§. III. Other Things being equal, those of the fairest, clearest, and brightest colour'd Hair, are of the loosest and weakest State of Fibres and Nerves, not only because the fairest and lightest is the most rare, transparent, and fungous, but because Bodies of the lightest Parts, consist of Parts of a weaker Union, which adhere with less Force, and consequently are less elastick, firm, and springy than those of the darker and more opake Colours. We generally observe, that People of very fine and white Hair, especially if so after they are come to Maturity, are of weak, tender, and delicate Constitutions: And those who deal in making artificial Covers for the Heads of Men or Women, find that such Hair will never, with any Credit to them, serve these Purposes, and seldom honestly employ it for that End.

§. IV. Those of large, full, and (as they are call'd) mastiff Muscles, and of big and strong Bones, are generally of a firmer State of Fibres, than those of little Muscles and small Bones, because the Muscles and Bones being similar to the Fibres, and made of them, these being bigger and stronger, so must those be; and, on the contrary.

§. V. Soft and yielding, loose and flabby Flesh and Muscles, are sure Symptoms of weak and relaxed Nerves or Fibres, as hard, firm, prominent and brawny

brawny Muscles and Flesh are constant Signs of firm Fibres.

§. VI. A White, fair, blanch'd, wax or ashen-colour'd Complexion, constantly indicates a weaker State of Fibres, than a ruddy brown or dark Hue.

§. VII. A Fat, corpulent, and phlegmatick Constitution is always attended with loose, flabby, and relax'd Fibres, by their being dissolv'd and over-soak'd in Moisture and Oil, especially if it belong to young Persons, or happen long before the *Meridian* of Life; for in the Decline, when the Fibres have acquir'd their utmost Degree of Tension, Hardness, and Firmness, it then serves to preserve them in that State, from the Dryness that old Age always introduces. But those of a dry, firm, clean, and brawny Make have generally the strongest and most tense Fibres.

§. VIII. Those who are subject to Evacuations of any Kind, in any Degree greater than what is natural and common to sound Constitutions; or those, who by any Accident, a Fever, or any acute Distemper whatsoever, have suffer'd long under any preternatural Evacuation, are already, or soon will, become subject to a loose, relax'd, or weak State of Fibres and Nerves: Those who frequently run into Purging and Costiveness alternately, or into Floods of pale Water, or into profuse Sweatings, upon little or no Exercise, into a constant Spitting or Salivation at the Mouth, or too plentiful Discharges from the Nose and Eyes: Those who have lost much Blood, or frequently fall into *Hæmorrhages:* Those who have labour'd long under an obstinate *Diarrhœa,* or Looseness: Or those of the Sex who have purified long in greater Quantities, or oftener than is usual or natural: All these originally are, or commonly become of weak and relax'd Nerves, and suffer under them.

§. IX.

Signs of relaxed Nerves.

§. IX. Those who are naturally of a cold Constitution, are apt to fall into Chilling and Coldness on their Extremities, or feel frequently like the trickling of cold Water over some Parts of the Body, are ready to catch Cold, upon the slightest Occasions, are apt to run into Rigours and Shiverings upon a sharp North-East Wind; are too sensibly and violently affected, and feel too much Pain and Uneasiness from cold or frosty Weather; who want too much Covering, Cloaths, or Heat; or, on the contrary, are too much sunk and dis-spirited, spent and wasted with excessive hot Weather, are all of loose and weak Fibres. For all these are Signs of a too slow Circulation and Perspiration, which manifest a weak Spring in the Fibres of the Coats of the Vessels, and of the other Solids, and shew too great a Degree of Sensibility or Easiness of being acted upon by external Objects, which argues a Weakness or Slenderness in them, either natural or acquir'd.

§. X. Those who are subject to acute or chronical Distempers of the cold and viscid Kind, though they have not commonly their Denomination from nervous Distempers, such as an *Atrophy*, *Dropsy*, *Diabetes*, *Diarrhœa*, white and *leucophlegmatick* Swellings upon the Joints or other Parts of the Body; glandulous and *schirrous* Tumours, the *Scrophula*, viscid Quinseys or Swellings in the Glands of the Eyes, such (besides all those who are subject to Diseases denominated Nervous in their Kind) are all of weak Nerves and Fibres.

§. XI. Those who stutter, stammer, have a great Difficulty of Utterance, speak very low, lose their Voice without catching Cold, grow dumb, deaf, or blind, without an Accident or an acute Distemper; are quick, prompt, and passionate; are all of weak Nerves; have a great Degree of

Senſibility; are quick Thinkers, feel Pleaſure or Pain the moſt readily, and are of moſt lively Imagination.

§. XII. Theſe are, at leaſt, the moſt material of the Signs and Symptoms of a relax'd State of Solids or Fibres; ſo that whoever labours under them for any Time, or in any eminent Degree, may certainly conclude, whatever other Diſorders he may labour under, that theſe are certainly attended with a State of looſe and relax'd Fibres, and conſequently, that in preſcribing Medicines for ſuch, whatever their Diſeaſe otherwiſe may be, or may be call'd, great Care is always to be had, both in doſing the proper Medicines for ſuch particular Diſorders, and joining with them ſuch Medicines as may keep up the due Tenſion of the Solids, as much as poſſible, while they are under the Cure, and alſo ordering ſuch Remedies as may corroborate and ſtrengthen them, when the Cure is effected. For in all ſuch Caſes, where the Solids are greatly relax'd, the Conſtitution of the Patient differs as much from the ſame Caſe in ſtrong and robuſt Perſons, as the Conſtitution of a Child, from that of a grown Perſon.

§. XIII. But the fundamental Propoſition, on which the Manner of treating ſuch Diſtempers is, and ought in Reaſon to be grounded, and which Experience always juſtifies, is, that a Laxity, Weakneſs and Want of due Tone and Elaſticity in the Solids, produce viſcid, ſharp, and ill-condition'd Juices. And, on the contrary, that ill-condition'd, ſharp, and viſcid Juices, neceſſarily produce weak and unelaſtick Solids, ſo that they mutually exaſperate each other, and differ only as Cauſe and Effect, though the Fault of the Fluids always precedes that of the Solids. Put the Caſe, that the Blood and Juices are viſcid, ſharp, and ill-condition'd, the Fibres ſubſiſting nearly in their proper Tenſion and

due

due Degree of *Tone* and Elasticity, that they ought to be in perfectly found and robust Persons, the necessary Effect of such a State of Juices, would be a Retardment of their Circulation by a greater Pressure upon the Sides of the Vessels, and the forming of Obstructions in the small and capillary Tubes, which by rendring these impervious, forces a greater Quantity upon the pervious ones, than they are accustom'd or able to drive about, and so by Degrees break and loosen the Texture, and relax the Tone of all these Solids. For when once the Ballance between the Force and Strength of an Instrument, and the Body to be moved by it, comes to be destroy'd, and the Advantage thrown upon the Side of the Body to be moved, the Instrument must be soon shatter'd and broken. On the other hand, supposing the Juices sound and good, and of a due Consistence and Balsam, but that the Solids are of a laxer, weaker and less elastick Make than they should be, it must necessarily follow, that the Circulations, Perspiration, the Digestions and Secretions must be weaker and more languishingly perform'd than they ought to be, by which neither will the Food be sufficiently broken and digested in the alimentary Tubes, nor the Size of the Particles of the Blood sufficiently small, nor divided by the Force of the Circulation, nor its Recrements thrown off with due Force and in sufficient Quantity, that the Juices may be duly purified, insomuch, that they must necessarily become viscid and sharp; and their Parts necessarily increase in Bulk and Hardness, especially under a *mal-Regimen*. From all which it is evident, that a weak State of Nerves or Fibres must necessarily imply a bad State of Juices, and so on the other hand, and that they mutually attend or produce one another, unless a proper Regimen of Dyet come in to their Relief.

THE

THE
Engliſh Malady:
OR, A
TREATISE
OF
Nervous Diſeaſes of all Kinds,
AS
Spleen, Vapours, Lowneſs of Spirits, Hypochondriacal and Hyſterical Diſtempers, &c.

PART II.

Of the Cure of Nervous Diſtempers.

By *GEORGE CHEYNE*, M.D.
Fellow of the *College of Phyſicians* at *Edinburg*, and F.R.S.

———— *Nunc retrorſum,*
Vela dare atque iterare curſus
Cogor relictos. ————   Horat.

DUBLIN:
Printed in the Year, MDCCXXXIII.

THE
English Malady.

PART II.

CHAP I.

Of the general Method of Cure of Nervous Distempers.

§. I. THERE are some Persons, who, being far advanced in Age, have not sufficient Time remaining for a perfect Cure; and others, in whom the Disease is so deeply rooted, by a bad Constitution, derived to them from their Parents, that they are not capable of a total Cure; and both these must be contented to submit to the *Orders of Providence*, and make the best of their Misfortunes, resting satisfied with a *Partial* or *Palliative* Cure, and relieving the Symptoms as they arise. But those who are

are in better Circumstances, will have better Success, by following with Patience and Perseverance, the Directions here to be laid down.

§. II. From what has been said in the former Part of this Treatise, concerning the Sources and Causes of Chronical Distempers, and the general Causes of the Disorders of the *Nerves* or *Solids*, there will arise three *Indications* in the Cure of *Nervous* Distempers, from the three principal *Causes* concurring towards their Production.

1*st*, The first *Intention*, and that which has the greatest Influence on all the rest, and will often, in smaller Degrees of this Distemper, or when the Solids are not much weaken'd or spoil'd, render the other two unnecessary (at least, in a great measure). The first *Intention*, I say, will be to thin, dilute, and sweeten the whole Mass of the Fluids, to destroy their Viscidity and Glewiness, to open the Obstructions thereby generated, make the Circulation full and free, the Perspiration current, and the Secretions flow in their due Proportion and Tenor. This, if fully obtained, lays the Foundation of all the rest of the Cure, and will even, during that Time, take off the Violence of the *Symptoms*, and make their Intervals greater.

2*dly*, The *second Intention* will be to divide, break and dissolve the saline, acrid and hard *Concretions*, generated in the small Vessels, and to destroy all *Sharpness* and *Acrimony* lodged in the Habit, and to make the Juices soft, sweet, and balsamick. This will be more readily effected, if the first *Intention* has been sufficiently and successfully pursued; and, indeed, will, in a great measure, be fulfilled by it; for as it is the Sizyness and Sharpness of the Juices, that retards the Circulation, obstructs the small Vessels, and thereby leaves the stagnated Juices to corrupt and putrify, by giving Time and Occasion for the smaller *saline* Particles to approach nearer one another, exert their innate Quality of *Attraction* and
Chrystal-

Chryſtallization, and unite in greater Cluſters and larger *Concretions*, (which, tho' never ſenſible, yet, from the Neceſſity of Nature and its Laws, is never the leſs real) ſo when the Blood is made ſufficiently thin and fluid, theſe ſaline Concretions will be either diſſolv'd or broken, by the Thinneſs of the Juices, and the Force of the Circulation, and ſo fitted to be thrown out of the Habit, by the proper Diſcharges, or will be kept at a due Diſtance from one another, or more eaſily reach'd, and then remedied by ſuch Medicines as will produce this Effect.

3*dly*, The *third* and laſt *Intention* in order, is to reſtore the *Tone* and *elaſtick* Force, to criſp, wind up, and contract the *Fibres* of the whole *Syſtem*, which is the laſt, and indeed the moſt imperfect Part of the Cure, and the leaſt, I am afraid, in the Power of *Art*. It is much like the Caſe of *Hair* that has loſt its Buckle, by Length of Time and much Uſe; tho' by *Art* it may be harden'd, ſtiffen'd, and reduced in ſome Degree to a greater Firmneſs and proper Figure, yet will not retain it long, nor bear the Injuries of the Weather ſo readily, without returning to its former Laxity: If this could be always and totally effected, the Cure would be a true *Rejuveneſcence*, and no body needed grow old or die. But the Laws of Mortality will ſuffer this Intention to riſe only to a certain Height, and no further; for this, if ſolidly and fully effected, would be the true *Cyclus Metaſyncriticus* of the Ancients, ſo little underſtood. However, there are not wanting Means to effect this Purpoſe in ſome Degree, if duly and judiciouſly choſen, eſpecially if the Perſon is under the *Meridian* of Life, while Nature has Warmth and Vigour to aſſiſt *Art*. After that *Date* the Difficulty is greater, there remaining little more than the Aſſiſtances of *Art*, upon the Signs of Laxity, to criſp, wind up, corrogat, and contract the Fibres of the feeble and relax'd Solids from Time to Time as they drop.

drop. There is certainly an innate *Firmness* and *Force* in the Solids, which, tho' Age hardens and stiffens, yet the *Tone* and *Elasticity* is not augmented thereby in Proportion: But this *Tone* is scarce ever so much broken and lost, but that it is sufficient to circulate well-thin'd and sweeten'd Juices, and to perform all the animal and intellectual *Functions:* and if Care be taken to keep up the Juices in this middling State of Fluidity and Sweetness, the Party will be free from all great Pain or violent Disorder, and will be subject only to some transient Lowness or Weakness, which may be presently remedied, or to the unavoidable Infirmities of *Age* and *Mortality*.

§. III. These are the general *Intentions*, to be pursued towards a *total* and perfect Cure of *Nervous Disorders* of whatever Sort or Kind; nor are they ever to be confounded or blended, at least, not in the first Attempts towards such a Cure: For as in diluting the Juices, unless the Solids are left to their innate Force only, the Medicines employed for that Purpose, being *active* or *ponderous*, and those which are employed to restore the *Tone* of the Solids being astringent, must in some measure again thicken the Juices, and so if mixed and blended together, must unavoidably interfere with, counter-act, and destroy the Effects of each other. And therefore these three *Intentions* I have mention'd must religiously follow one another, in the order I have propos'd them, in deep *Cachexy's* especially, to effect this Purpose of a *total* Cure: Not that I mean, that they should never be interrupted nor combined with each other, for some small Time at least, and as it were, for the Patient to take Breath and recover Spirits a little, in order to the further prosecuting the several Intentions. Nor that they may not be gone on with entirely, in a mix'd and blended Manner, both in Method and Medicines, in slight Cases, and the low Degrees of *Nervous* Disorders, with good Success; but that in obstinate, deep, and dangerous Cases of this

this Kind, from an universally spoilt Constitution, every *Intention* is to be pursued by it self for a due Time, without Confusion or interfering with one another, more than the Prosecution of the then *Intention* requires, till the Effect is obtained.

§. IV. What the Time necessary for each *Intention* must be, it is impossible absolutely to determine; that must be proportion'd to the Violence of the *Symptoms*, and the Obstinacy of the Distemper. But to give some general Idea or Notion of the Time: That which is necessary for the first *Intention*, may be conjectur'd from the State of the Blood. If the Size on the Top is much gone, if the Colour and its easily yielding to any dividing Instrument, and the Proportion of the *Serum* to the globular Part, upon bleeding (a few Ounces only for the Trial) be such as they are found commonly in sound Persons, and if the *Serum* be clear, or not too tawny, then may it be concluded, that the first *Intention* has been pursued sufficiently. The *second* may also be guess'd from the healing up and cicatrizing of any Ulcers, Sores, or the Cure of any *cutaneous* Foulnesses, and the Removal of any acute Pains and *Paroxysms*, principally caus'd by the Sharpness, and *Acrimony*, and *Saline* Quality of the Juices. The *last* is obvious, after these two are ascertain'd by the *Strength, Vigour, Vivacity*, and *Freedom of Spirits*, the natural and easy Performance of all the *Animal Functions*, necessarily following upon the *last* Intention's being prosecuted for a due Time, and in a proper Manner. But that every one may more certainly judge of the State and Condition of the Blood and Juices, and the Necessity of prosecuting the *Intentions* I have propos'd, I shall here give some general Account of the different Changes that happen in them under Diseases of all Kinds; but particularly those I am here principally concern'd about.

§. V. The *Blood* as it flows in the greater or larger Vessels by the ordinary Course of the *Circulation*,
G seems

seems to be a pretty uniform Mass, much like Cow-Milk; but when drawn out of these Vessels, and left without Heat or Motion to settle in the Air, it separates into two Parts, one of a more glutinous and solid Texture, call'd the *Globular*, and the other of a more thin and fluid Nature, called the *Serous* Part; and both these are found in different Proportions, and of different Natures, Consistence, and Colours, according to the Diseases of the Persons in whom they are found. I shall only here mention *three* of these different States, wherein the distinguishing Marks are most evident, tho' there are many intermediate Degrees between these, which it were endless to enumerate; but these will include them all, and are the most general, remarkable, and useful: 1*st*, The *first* is, when the *globular* Part is of a moderate Cohesion and Firmness of Parts, in a pretty equal Proportion to its *Serum*, and of a red and Scarlet Colour, when expos'd a due Time to the Air; and the *Serum* is about the Consistence of common Water, pretty clear, and almost insipid, or, at least, not biting saltish. This I take to be pretty near the State of the soundest and best Blood. 2*dly*, The *second* State I would mention, is, when the *globular* and grumous Part is in a far greater Proportion than the *Serum*, more thick and viscid, having a Glue or Size on its Top (of a blueish at first, and afterwards of a whitish or tallow Colour, increasing sometimes to half or more the Thickness of the Whole) the *Serum* being in a smaller Quantity, and of a yellowish or tawny Cast, sharp, acrid, and saltish to the Taste. This seems to be of a middling Nature, (I speak not here of that accidental Size, generated by the Nitre of the Air in catching Cold, which evanishes in a few Days by proper Management) between the best and the worst, and is common to *Pleurisies, Rheumatisms*, &c. 3*dly*, The last State of the Blood, I shall speak of, is where the *fibrous* or *globular* Part is scarce any at all, and the *Serum*

above

above ten or a dozen times the Quantity of it, where the globular Part swims like an *Island* amidst the Ocean, the *Serum* being sharp, saltish and urinous, to the highest Degree in its Taste. This I take to be the worst State, when the Sharpness and *Acrimony* have arriv'd at their utmost Height, like that of those in a confirm'd *Consumption* or *Dropsy*, and some other mortal Distempers. But in all these three *States* of the Blood, the *Sharpness*, *Heat*, and *Acrimony* may rise almost to an equal Degree, even to that of the worst State, of which we have no Means of judging, but by the Taste, which is but gross and inaccurate, and therefore we must be contented with Probability. The *first* of these is commonly call'd *good Blood*, the *second rich Blood*, and the *third poor Blood*. The *Blood Globules* (consisting probably of Parts of an equal Degree of *Attraction*, and equal Density) seem to be form'd of the more solid Parts of the Food, by the Action of the digestive Powers in the *alimentary Tubes*, the Force of the Circulation, and the Grinding of the Blood Vessels, and to receive their *globular* Figure from the equal Pressure, on all Sides of the watery Fluid wherein they swim, and the equal Degree of Attraction in their Parts. When the Quality and Quantity of such Food is duly proportion'd, the *red Globules* and *Serum* are pretty near of an equal Quantity, the *first* being perfectly red in the Air, and the *second* mostly limpid, like that of the first State. But when the solid Food is in too great a Proportion in the whole Mass, either in Quantity or Quality, a greater Proportion of *Blood Globules* will necessarily be generated: And if the Solids be strong, so as to comminute them sufficiently, and drive them about with a due Force, they will produce an inflammatory State of Blood, from whence *acute Fevers*, *Inflammations*, *Pleurisies*, and the other hot and inflammatory Obstructions and Diseases will arise. But if the same Proportion of Food, both in Quantity and Quality, is thrown in, where the Solids are lax and feeble,

feeble, and consequently, the *digestive Organs* weak, and the *Circulation* languid, the Blood thence arising will be viscid and sizy in Proportion, and exhibit the Appearances describ'd in the *second* State, from whence Obstructions and Diseases of the cold, *chronical*, or *nervous* Kind will arise. On the other hand, when the *Drink* is in too great a Proportion to the solid Food, when great Quantities of strong and spirituous Liquors are thrown into the Habit, and the small Quantity of Food that is taken is also strong, and full of *Salts* and *Spirits*, the *fibrous* Part of the Blood will be produc'd in a smaller Proportion to the *serous*, or will be consum'd and burnt up by the greater Quantity of *Salts* and *Oils* in the *Serum* proceeding from such Nourishment, and so the *last* State of the Blood I have taken notice of will be produc'd: whereby the Solids being stimulated and corroded, and the Circulation carried about with too great Hurry and Violence, or some great noble *Bowel* attack'd, destroy'd and spoil'd, various Diseases of the inflammatory-chronical Kind will ensue, as *Hectick-Fevers*, *Consumptions*, &c. the Blood-Vessels being burst or corroded will occasion *Hæmorrhages*, or the Solids being weaken'd, relax'd and broken, will suffer this thin and acrid Serum *to ouze* thro' their Substances, and thus beget a partial *Dropsy*, or a true *Ascites*. Something like the same State of Blood may be occasion'd by a *Hæmorrhage*, or any great Loss of Blood, tho' tolerably good, in what manner soever it happens, either by a Wound or otherwise; the remaining Part being robb'd of its *red Globules*, or of too great a Quantity of the Compound to be soon repair'd, it will be unable to resist the Force of the Solids, but will be reduc'd to a poor, thin, watery State, so as, if not presently or speedily restor'd to its former *Balsam* and Texture, to end in a *Dropsy*, in the Manner I have just now describ'd, especially if a *Mal-Regimen* has proceeded or succeeds it.

§. VI.

§. VI. But to apply this more particularly to the Diseases I am now treating of: In all *Nervous* Disorders produc'd by Excesses, especially after the *Meridian* of Life, the Blood is generally viscid and sizy, like that of the *second* State, which I have describ'd. I have not for these many Years let Blood of any one (if it were but an Ounce or two to make Observation on, of which I have had innumerable Instances) who being subject to *Nervous Distempers*, *Lowness*, *Vapours*, or *Melancholy*, have not had it *Sizy*, *Rheumatick* and *Viscid*, with a sharp yellow *Serum* in some Degree or other. I have always observ'd the Blood of the younger and those under the *Meridian* of Life, in these who were violently subject to Nervous Disorders, to be hot, fiery, inflam'd, acrid and sharp, tho' the Colour and Consistence might be tolerably good, and then found it occasion'd by dealing too much in hot Liquors, in Proportion to the original Weakness of their Solids. But if the Viscidity of the Juices was produc'd, as I have said, by an Overproportion of Food receiv'd into the Habit, the Weakness of the Solids, and Slowness of the Circulation being consequent thereupon, Obstructions must necessarily be form'd in the small Vessels and *Glands*, especially of the Liver, the Mesentery, *&c.* and then the stagnant Juices putrify, corrupt, turn acrid and corrosive (like what we see in some other Cases of Obstructions that lie more immediately under our Observation, particularly that produc'd by a Blow on the Breast, which terminates in a *Cancer*); and the urinous or *animal Salts* being let loose, tear, corrode, and destroy the Solids, from whence the highest Degrees of *Nervous* Disorders spring: Indeed, in the last Stages of *Nervous* Distempers, the Blood sometimes approaches to that which I have describ'd as the last and worst State; but then the Case is gone, I think, beyond the Reach of human Means or Art to remedy, since it generally attends the entire Corruption of some of the great
Viscera;

Viscera; or the highest Degrees of such Obstructions, whereby the whole Mass of Blood is infected with the Poison, and the Juices dissolv'd and fus'd into a putrid Thinness, like what is found in the last Stages of the *Black Jaundice*, or some other mortal Distempers.

CHAP. II.

Of the Method and Medicines proper for the first Intention.

§. I. IN order to attenuate the Juices, to break the Cohesion of their Parts, to destroy their *Viscidity* and *Glewiness*, and to make them sufficiently thin, and fit to flow in the small Vessels with Ease, those Medicines are chiefly to be chosen, which either by their own Nature are the most *active*, by the *Figure* of their Particles are the most sharp and dividing, by their *Weight* are endu'd with the greatest Force and *Momentum*; or lastly, which by Experience are found (without knowing a Reason why) to be the most effectual for producing these Ends.

§. II. I need not mention here the Necessity, before any Course be enter'd upon for this Purpose, of premising the common and proper universal Evacuations, as *Bleeding*, *Purging*, *Vomiting*, &c. some one or more of which will always be found necessary to be first of all perform'd, not only to lessen the Quantity of the corrupt Fluids in general, but to cleanse the alimentary Tubes, that the proper Medicines may be more easily and readily convey'd into the Blood. But as these Evacuations are never to be undertaken without the Advice and Assistance of some skilful and honest *Physician*, so it is by his Direction that the *Repetition Dose* and Materials are to be adjusted: For these Evacuations are so essential in this Case in its first Stage, that by going about them indiscreetly, or neglecting to do them as the Symptoms require, the Patient may be ruin'd, by trusting

Medicines for the first Intention.

ing to his own Judgment, or relying upon general Rules, which in all severe, but particularly in *Nervous* Cases, are both precarious and uncertain.

§. III. Among the chief and principal of such Medicines, are *Mercury* and its Preparations, *Calomel, Mercury alcalisated, precipitat per se, Quicksilver, Silver-Water, Æthiops Mineral, Cinnabar of Antimony, Antimony Diaphoretick, Bezoar Mineral, Crude Antimony, Bezoardicum Joviale, Salt of Tin, Ens Veneris,* and the like, whose chief Efficacy seems to lie in their Weight, after they have dropt their Salts in the alimentary Tube. *Next* to these are the Woods *Guajacum, Sassafras, Sarsaparilla, Lignum Nephriticum,* the several Sorts of *Saunders,* Wood of *Aloes,* &c. In the *third* Order are the *fix'd Salts,* such as *Salt of Tartar, Salt of Wormwood, Broom, Fern,* &c. The *last* Class contains such Vegetables as are of an acrid and austere Taste, such as are all the *Antiscorbutick* Plants, of which there is Choice and Variety in all the modern Writers and Collectors of the *Materia Medica*; so that it is needless here to detail them. These may be compounded or combined in the best Manner possible, to make them easy and agreeable to the Stomach, by the Skill of the *Physician* in ordinary: and if given in a proper Dose, and for a Time sufficient, will scarce fail of their Effect.

§. IV. In the Administration of *Calomel,* for such a Purpose, it may be necessary to observe, that however it may be manag'd in Cases of another Nature, yet where it is intended for the Cure of *Nervous* Diseases, which suppose weak Solids, and consequently tender Bowels, it will always be necessary to give it in the smallest Dose, as an *Alterative* only, and not an Evacuant; for *Example,* in two, three, or four Grains, once, twice, or three times a day, because thus it may be given with Safety for a much longer Time,

Time, and will not be thrown off by the greater Conduits of Evacuation, nor meerly circulate thro' the greater Blood-Vessels, but gently and gradually insinuate it self into the smallest *Capillary* ones, where its Virtue and Efficacy is most wanted, and where it can do the most Service. For this Reason it is chiefly, that in many deep *Venereal* Cases, *Salivation* by the internal Exhibition of Mercurials only, seldom succeeds: whereas by *Inunction* it seldom fails, *viz.* that when it happens to be perform'd on People of weak Nerves, and tender Constitutions, and patent Glands, it is generally thrown off by the greater Out-lets, with great Danger to the Patient; so that a few Grains commonly raise a scorbutick *Ptyalism,* which few can distinguish from a Mercurial Salivation, and so they are scarce able to go on: or at best, it circulates only thro' the Trunk of the greater Arteries and Veins, to be thrown off by the more patent and larger *Glands,* and seldom or never gets Admittance into the Capillary Vessels: whereas by *Inunction,* or in small and often repeated Doses, it is receiv'd into these last immediately or gradually, and there does its Work. In *Nervous* Cases the same Effect is obtain'd by the longer Time, and lesser Doses, these Constitutions neither admitting nor requiring so violent and quick a Deobstruent. But even this Method, in its gentlest Degree, will fit none but the *Nervous* Disorders, of the stronger and robuster Constitutions, which having been originally sound, have contracted these Disorders by a *Mal-Regimen.*

§. V. The Medicines next to this the most effectual for the first Intention, are *Æthiops Mineral,* the *Æthiops Antimoniatum, Cinnabar,* but especially *Mercurius Alcalisatus,* or the other Preparations of Quicksilver, with the various Preparations of *Antimony,* of which there is great Variety

Medicines for the first Intention. 89

riety (and might be more). And this *Æthiops Mineral* is indeed an excellent Remedy both from the Weight of the *Mercury,* and the cleansing Nature of the *Sulphur* entring its Composition, and would do the whole in Time necessary for this Intention, were it not that even few, but those of the stronger Sort, can bear the Slipperiness, and violent Cholicks and Gripes, which it brings on their Bowels: which not only sinks them more, but occasions the Medicine to be carry'd off before it enters the Habit; and therefore when it is us'd in such a Case, I should always advise an Astringent, or warm Medicine, such as *Diascordium, Mithridate, Venice Treacle,* and the like, to be join'd with it: perhaps a less Quantity of *Sulphur* in the Preparation would mend it, and make it go further than the alimentary Tube. But those who are strong, and whose Bowels are firm, bear it easily; and in some I join *Gum Guajac* to it, with *Salt of Wormwood,* to make it more cleansing, attenuating and deobstruent, with great Success. *Belloft*'s Quicksilver Pills are of the same Nature and Vertue for this first *Intention,* as well as for *Asthmatick* Cases, and, I think, the best way of taking *Quicksilver* inwardly.

§. VI. That which I generally prefer in viscid Juices, in Persons subject to Nervous Disorders, in very low Cases, is *Cinnabar* of *Antimony,* both because it creates fewer Tumults in the Stomach and Bowels, passes more readily into the Blood, and seldom keeps the Bowels slippery, unless it be in exceeding low Cases. Those who are robust, or still in a great measure strong, may bear the *Æthiops;* but both the very Young and very Weak, if their Juices be either too viscid or too sharp, will find the greatest Relief from this Medicine duly fitted to their Constitution, and continued for a long Time, if any of the whole Tribe of the *Materia Medica* (in my Judgment) can possibly do it. Its Efficacy in Childrens *Epileptick* and *Convulsive* Fits, and indeed

in

in all their *Chronical* Diftempers, is fufficiently known and acknowledg'd. And I have found the fame Effects in many Cafes both *Nervous* and *Chronical*, even in adult Perfons, both to my Surprize and Admiration. If it has fail'd, it is becaufe it has not been long enough continu'd. A *Patient* of mine, now alive, has us'd it thefe twenty years. It firft (by my Advice) cured him of his *Nervous* Complaints; and whenever he ails, he has recourfe to it on occafions to this Day. It ought to be given frefh, or the leaft ftale poffible, otherwife it may become turbulent in the Bowels; and it ought to be as finely levigated as Art can make it, to enter more readily into the fmall Veffels. And indeed, when I confider that moft other *Mercurial* Medicines, tho' they are the moft powerful Attenuants of the Juices, yet (as all ponderous and very active Medicines muft neceffarily do) they, with the Salts united, fcrape thin, and relax the Solids. I think this the fafeft and moft effectual of all the Attenuants, in very low Cafes, efpecially if a little of the *Refin* or *Extract* of the Jefuits Bark be added to it, to keep up the Force of the Solids, at the fame time that it is diffolving the Vifcidity of the Juices, and opening the Obftructions in the fmall Veffels: for it is impoffible to get any *Mercurial* Medicine that has not fome Tendency to weaken them.

§. VII. There is nothing I could more earneftly wifh were brought into the common Practice of *Phyfick*, than the more free and general (but cautious) Ufe of the Preparations of *Mercury* and *Antimony* in Chronical and Obftinate Cafes: efpecially when join'd to a thin, cool, foft and mild Diet, to anfwer this *firft* Intention of a total Cure. Dr. *Charlton*, who had the licenfing of the *Quacks* in King *Charles* II. Time, told on his Death-Bed (as I am well inform'd) that all the ufeful or fuccefsful Cures perform'd by the *Mountebanks* of his Time, were owing to the Preparations of *Mercury* and *Antimony* only;

only; and it is a great Pity, that such glorious Remedies should be in the Possession chiefly (I mean the Preparations of *Mercury*) of such unskilful, unprincipled Wretches. For a regular reputable Physician may endanger his Reputation among the weak and prejudiced, who deals freely in it, tho' it be a Remedy only fit to bear the Name. *Mercury* is the only Fluid in Nature (except Water) fit to circulate thro' hollow Animal Tubes; (Two of the others, Light and Æther, can scarce be retain'd in them) its greater Weight than any other Kinds of Matter (except *Gold*) makes it the most capable to force its way: but then *Gold* and all other Minerals having no innate *Fluidity*, nor Natural Rotundity of Particles, must be always carry'd on Water to be introduc'd into an Animal Habit, with which they never kindly mix. *Mercury* in all its Divisions, Mixtures and Unions with other Bodies, is still reducible to liquid *Quicksilver*: which makes it not improbable, that when it has drop'd its Mixtures in Animal Vessels, in the *Alimentary Duct* especially, it returns to its primitive *Fluidity*, and acts with the united Force of the whole then collected Mass of Particles; and we know what Efficacy Shot and small Bullets of Lead have in cleaning foul Bottles or small Tubes. * The Rotundity of its Particles (in all its visible and sensible Divisions, and even in its Ascent in the *Retort*, and in all its other Preparations, apparent by fine Glasses) with its *Fluidity*, makes them probably smooth, and so without any Injury to the *Capillaries*, except from their Weight only. The infinite Smallness of its Particles, evident by its ready Ascent in a Retort from the least even a Sand-Heat only, and its almost infinite Force of *Attraction* (from these general Principles of its Weight and Quantity of Matter, and from many Experiments) makes it always run

---

* Vide *Boerhaave*'s Chymistry.

into a fluid Mass, when its *spherical* Particles are brought near enough: whereby its Force is greatly increas'd. From all which Consrderations (obvious even to common Sense, without *finessing*) it is evident what a *Noble Medicine* it might be made in *Chronical* Cases of all Kinds, viscid Juices and Obstructions of the Organs, if duly prepar'd, dosed and fitted to the Patient and the Distemper. The *Mercurius Alcalisatus* (of *Quicksilver* and *Crabs-Eyes prepar'd*, and rubb'd together till the first disappear) is an admirable *Medicine*, and in a small Dose gives no Trouble or Uneasiness, and is specifick in *Cutaneous Foulnesses*, and almost all other Chronical Cases, especially *Nervous*, to this First Intention, as well as is the *Precipitate per se:* I have often us'd them both with great Success, even in *Nervous* Cases, since they have been so universally known. Liquid *Quicksilver* will do great Service in beginning *Plicatures* of the Intestines, Obstructions of their Glands and Valves, and in Foulnesses and hard Concretions or Obstructions, bred in the Mouths of the *Lacteals* which are often Cases where the Symptoms common to other Diseases, will not admit a certain Distinction) but eminently so in *Asthmatic* Cases, above all other Medicines. By its Weight only, forcing open the obstructive Mouths of the *Lacteals*, and it Steams thereby entring the Habit, attenuate the viscid Juices of the *Lungs*, and render them pervious, and so promotes *Expectoration*; and, I think, other more appropriated and specifick Medicines not succeeding, this ought to be try'd in all Cases of the *Alimentary Tube*, since it is as innocent and safe as Asses Milk. And even the *Aq. Mercurialis* or Silver Water, as it succeeds beyond any thing in Childrens Worm Cases: so I am satisfy'd, were it try'd in other Cases, might do Wonders: especially in *Decoctions of the Woods*, *Antiscorbutick* Waters, or other appropriated Liquors; for as it neither alters Taste, Smell, nor any other sensible Quality

Quality of the Liquid, it may be safely us'd as long, and in as great Quantities as one pleases, without any Trouble, Pain or Danger. I am therefore of the Opinion, that the most effectual Remedies in Nature in Chronical Cases and their first Stages, is the Preparations of *Mercury*, of one Kind or other, together with *Diet*. Where it has not succeeded, it is chiefly because proper *Diet* has not been join'd; and, I believe, there are few Cases and Constitutions, where some of these mention'd Preparations may not agree in proper Doses; and, if duly continu'd, are not of wonderful Benefit, where the *Viscera* are not quite spoil'd. But the Management must be in the Hands of a sober, careful and experienc'd *Physician*, who well understands and considers what Nature will bear, and what not; for it is not an indifferent or trifling Medicine, but a *Divine Antidote*, or a certain Poison, according to the *Case* in which, and the *Person* by whom, it is prescrib'd; and I scarce willingly ever advise it at a Distance in any Preparation, for it ought always to be watch'd. Where the Vessels are very lax, putrify'd, or thin: or the Obstruction very hard or *schirrous*, the more active Preparations must be cautiously avoided, and nothing but the gentlest Preparations try'd, *viz.* the *Æthiops*, the *Cinnabars*, the *Mercurius Alcalisatus*, the *Precipitat per se*, *Aq. Argentea*, and the like. For as to the Opinion of some, *viz.* that these mention'd Preparations get no further than the Alimentary *Duct*, I think it without all Foundation, either from Philosophy or Experience: when we see the *Æthiops* and the *Cinnabars*, liquid *Quicksilver* and the *Silver Water*, cure Cutaneous Distempers, Inflammations of the Eyes, *St. Anthony's Fire*, the *Itch*, the *Piles*, and the like; and when they will soil the Silver and Gold about the Patient. Nay, as I am satisfy'd all the Kinds of them will at last raise a kind of a *Ptyalism*. But even tho' then its principal Action were only on the *Glands* of the Stomach and Intestines, yet the opening these, and enabling them to perform their *Functions* may be sufficient, by *Derivation* to propagate a proportional Benefit over the whole Habit. *Lastly,* when we see Mercury boil'd in Water only, without losing the least estimable Weight, have such sensible Effects, as in Time to do all that any other Preparation can, as I am convinced it will: we can easily conceive how any Preparation of it, impregnating the Chyle with its infinite small Particles, may enter the *Lacteals* and pervade the whole Habit, and when long continu'd, may have wonderful Efficacy on the most distant Parts of the Body; for the even actually almost infinite Smallness of its Parts, the *Sphericity* of its Particles, and its exceeding great *Weight,* will make it in any *Shape* pass readily thro' any Animal Substance in Time. The Preparations of Antimony may possibly be of great Vertue, if sufficiently try'd and examin'd; but I having us'd none but the common Shop ones, finding the Preparations of *Mercury* sufficient, can say nothing of them. The Preparations of *Mercury,* some one or other, seem much more proper for this Intention.

§. VIII. I shall say nothing of the other *Attenuants,* especially those of the Vegetable Kind, whose Virtues may be easily learn'd from the Books of the *Materia Medica* *. As for those of the Mineral Kind, of which I have said nothing in particular, I leave them to the Judgment of those Physicians, who have had more Experience of them; my Practice and Observation having confin'd me pretty much to those I have remark'd on, finding them the most ready, sufficient, and, by their Nature, fittest. I shall only add a Word or two concerning the *Wild Valerian* (so much commended by *Fabius Co-*

---

* Vide *Phytobasanos* of *Sir* John Floyer.

lumna)

lumna) in all *Nervous* Cases, but especially the worst and highest Degrees of them. It is certainly one of the most *active* and *volatile* of the Vegetable Kingdom, and seems to act chiefly by promoting the Perspiration, and a gentle *Diaphoresis*. The Root powder'd and given with *Cinnabar of Antimony* and Powder of *Black Hellebor*, has frequently good Success; and a Tea made of its Leaves, is an admirable Diluter, and may be long continu'd with Advantage in these Cases. I will say nothing here of the *Misletoe*, it belonging (in my Opinion) to another Class of Medicines (to wit, *Astringents*) to be mention'd afterwards.

CHAP. III.

Of the Medicines proper for the Second Intention.

§. I. WHEN the former *Intention* has been sufficiently and successfully pursu'd, so that the Blood has return'd to its due Degree of Thinness, Fuidity and *Balsam*; when the Acuteness of the Pains, and the Violence of the Symptoms are lessen'd by the ponderous Remedies, and the *Fits* or *Paroxysms* are less severe or frequent: then the Medicines of *this* Class may be united and compounded with those of the *former*, to sheath and blunt the *Acrimony* of the Salts, and the Sharpness of the Juices, discharg'd from the small Vessels: to scour and cleanse the internal Sides of these Vessels yet further: and drive the ponderous Medicines into the most remote *Capillaries*, where the Disorder first begins, and is most rooted: there to open a Passage for the Circulation and Perspiration, and remove any Obstructions, putrid or stagnant Juices, and so to bring all the Secretions to a regular Order, and the whole Mass of the Fluids to a due Degree of Sweetness and *Balsam*. This Method and
Order

Order must necessarily be follow'd, where a total and absolute Cure is intended or expected: But where a *Palliative* Cure only is design'd, these may be blended with the former, even from the beginning of the Cure. And where the Blood is in that Condition, which I have mention'd as the last and worst State: they may even take the Place of the former and go before them, if there be any reasonable Hopes of Success; because the great Degree of Acrimony diffus'd thro' the whole Mass of Blood, requires a more immediate Attention and Application, than the removing of Obstructions; (which is often the Case in many *Scorbutick, Hectick, Icterical, Scrophulous* and *Cancerous* Habits:) at least the Medicines for the Second Intention are the absolutely necessary, and the only Means that can effectuate a *Palliative* Cure, and relieve the Symptoms then.

§. II. Water is acknowledg'd to be the most universal *Dissolver* of Salts of all Kinds, and would certainly dissolve these mention'd *Concretions* in the greater Vessels, and help to carry them out of the Habit; but it not having Activity or Agility enough to get into the small Vessels, where the Danger is greatest, and the Want most, it cannot alone be sufficient here. Those Medicines therefore that are of the most *active* and *volatile* Kind, which have, as it were, a *penetrating* Steam or Vapour flowing out of them, like that of Fire or Light: which can most readily pervade the Solids, and get into the inmost Recesses of the Habit, seem to be the most effectual for this Purpose; especially if a soft Balsam be added to these Qualities, which may both sheath the Salts in the great Vessels, as it goes along to the small ones, or so guard against their Irritation and Acrimony, as to hinder their otherwise destructive Effects. Of this Kind all the *fœtid* and *volatile* Substances seem to be the chief: or those which emit the strongest *Effluvia*, or in the greatest Quantity, such are particularly the *volatile Gums* and Juices,

Juices, the volatile *Salts* and *Spirits*, which are nothing but solid or liquid Natural *Phosphori*, or Fire Substances. To these may be join'd the Soaps, and *Saponaceous* Substances.

§. III. The principal Medicines of this *Tribe* are, *Gum Ammoniacum, Galbanum, Assa fœtida, Sagapenum, Myrrh, Guajacum, Camphire, Castor, Amber, Salt of Hartshorn, Salt of Amber, Salt* and *Spirit* of *Human Skulls,* and of *Raw Silk, Castile Soap, Saffron, Garlick, Horse-Radish,* and the like, of which there is sufficient Variety; but these seem to be the most powerful.

§. IV. Among these I should prefer the *Ammoniacum, Galbanum, Sagapenum,* but especially the *Assa fœtida,* since we are at the last come to judge of and easily find out the true, from, and in the Adulterated, by its cutting white, and turning afterwards of a Pink-Blossom Colour, according to the Description of it by the *Antients* [*], by whom its Virtues are celebrated with Praises, even above the Merit of any natural Remedy. It certainly deserves (as a present Relief in extreme Cases) as much as any one Thing in the *Materia Medica* in such Cases, it having all the kindly Effects of quieting *Anxiety* and *Oppression,* procuring Rest, and all the other Benefits of *Opium*, without leaving that Lowness and Depression behind it, which this last, when its Force is wrought off, does in most Persons, like Brandy or Inflammatory Spirits: insomuch that in a great many Cases and Constitutions it is a great Question, whether the present Relief be sufficient to ballance the subsequent *Oppression* and *Anxiety*: for which there is no other Remedy, but repeating one Dose as another wears off, as the *Turks* do, or as Drunkards do with their Drams, till both come to be without Measure or End, and have made the Dis-

---

[*] Vide *Plinii Hist.* Nat. Lib. XIX. Cap. 3.

ease perhaps irremediable by any Means, but the Death which it certainly brings on. But this natural *Phosphorus* having Light and Activity without Fire or Heat, easily pervades the whole Habit, and penetrates the smallest Vessels, and makes the Perspiration flow readily, as * *Sanctorius* observes, and thus gives a Relief for some considerable Time; and and when other proper Methods are join'd with it, will help forward a lasting Cure. The *Soots* of some or any Woods are or seem to me to be of the same Nature and Efficacy, and are, I think, *Phosphorus*'s, (where the remaining Fire is actually, but lies hid under the Ashes) which by their Activity and *Volatility* getting into the small Vessels, the Joints and Muscular Substances, dissolves and melts the Jelly and Size, (as actual Fire does Hartshorn Jelly and Glew) and thereby enables them to circulate for some Time, and so become at best but Reliefs and Reprieves, but no Cures; for accordingly, if not constantly repeated, the Complaints return, as a Man of a chilly Constitution, must be always hovering over the Fire.

§. V. I should say something of *Ammoniacum* but that its Virtues are sufficiently known in *Asthmatick* and *Pulmonick* Cases, (where it is the sovereign Remedy, and most effectually attenuates viscid Phlegm) to make its Efficacy believ'd in the Cases of viscid Juices I am speaking of. *Sagapenum* likewise and *Galbanum* are very effectual for the same Purpose. Nor ought the Product of our own Country, *Garlick* and *Horse-Radish*, to be neglected, the first of which is as effectual in *Lung* Cases, as the mention'd *Ammoniacum*. The only Inconvenience of these *fœtid* Medicines is the disagreeable Taste and Scent they leave, which is so offensive to delicate Persons; but that may be in a great measure overcome by

---

* *Medicina Statica*, Sect. 3. Aph. 82.

Medicines for the Third Intention. 99

proper Mixtures, or muſt be born with in extreme Caſes. Under this *Claſs*, and chiefly to anſwer this *Intention*, the *Acidulæ* or *Mineral Waters* ought to be rank'd, but moſt eminently the *Bath* Waters, becauſe of their *Sulphur* as well as *Steel*; and it is becauſe the ponderous and active Remedies have not been ſufficiently ply'd before, in habitual and obſtinate *Nervous* Caſes, that *Bath Waters* have not always theſe ſenſible and laſting Effects, as they moſt infallibly would have, if duly claſs'd and manag'd; and in all ſuch *Cahectical* and *Nervous* Caſes, *Mineral* Waters, *theſe*, eſpecially, are the beſt and ſafeſt Vehicle for *ponderous* Medicines: and in want of theſe *Barley Water*, with Syrup of *Marſhmallows*, Decoction of *Comfrey Roots*, with *Syrup of Mulberries*, or ſweet *Cow-Whey* drank plentifully, are beſt to ſeparate, diſſolve and ſheath theſe burning and deſtructive Salts, of which the *Element* Water in itſelf is the ſureſt and moſt effectual *Antidote*, the *Mineral* giving it Activity and Penetration chiefly.

CHAP IV.

Of the Medicines proper for the Third Intention.

§. I. WHEN the two former *Intentions* have been follow'd for a due Time with ſuitable Succeſs, ſo that the *Symptoms* are abated, and tolerable Eaſe is obtain'd, it will be then convenient to enter upon the Method and Medicines of the *Third* Intention: which will make the Caſe both more comfortable, and bring Spirits and Courage to go thro' with it, being the laſt Stage towards a compleat Cure. For the Medicines here are more grateful to Nature, ſtrengthening the digeſtive Powers, and making all the *Functions* more full and ſtrong, so that Vigour and Chearfulness flow in daily. And surely there is not a more agreeable Entertainment, both to *Physician* and *Patient*, than to observe the growing Steps of such a flattering Prospect, advancing gradually without Fear or Danger of Relapse, unless the Patient return to those Indiscretions that first begot these Disorders. This Pleasure I have enjoy'd myself once and again in both Capacities.

§. II. The Medicines which answer this Intention, will be those of the Strengthening and Astringent Kind, which *contract, corrugate*, wind up, and give Firmness and Force to the weak and relaxed Solids, Fibres and Nerves. Of this *Tribe* are all the *Bitters, Aromaticks* and *Chalybeats*: such as the *Jesuit's Bark, Steel, Gentian, Zedoary, Cassamunair, Calamus aromaticus, Snakeweed, Contrayerva, Cinamon, Winter's Bark, Chamomile Flowers, Wormwood* and *Centaury-Tops, Terra Japanica*, &c. Here likewise the *Oak Bark*, and its Offspring the *Misletoe* and *Acorns*, seem to have their proper Place, and every thing that is subacid, whether Mineral or Vegetable.

§. III. I think there is not a more wonderful Strengthener of the Solids in all the Compass of Medicine, than the *Jesuit's Bark*. The first time I us'd it myself as a Strengthener and bitter *Astringent* (after having diluted and thinn'd my Juices sufficiently by Medicine and Diet) I can say it with Truth, never any thing in Nature (Medicinal) affected me in so sensible and surprizing a Manner, or gave me so quick an Appetite, such Activity, and so serene clear Spirits, as the *Bark* did, after taking it for some Time. It is true, these Effects did not last in their greatest Heighth always, but they were still considerable for a long Time: and I went on gaining Ground by it in that *Period* (for I continued it

near

Medicines for the third Intention.

near a Year) till I had a perfect Recovery. I have seen pretty near the same Effects from it in others, and in the like *Nervous* Cases: tho' it had not the same Degree of good Success in my next Relapse, as was not to be expected in a further advanc'd Age; but still it had better than any other, and I take it universally to be the best and only cool bitter Astringent known to Men. I have known People labouring under an internal *Goutish* Humour (even those belonging to the *Profession of Physick*) who have affirm'd to me, that they were never vapour'd or low-spirited to any Degree, while they continu'd the Use of the *Bark* under the *Gout*, which they had interrupted only, because they had been assur'd that it confin'd and ty'd up the *Gouty* Humour from being thrown outward: than which there is nothing more false and absurd; for nothing so much promotes the *Gouty* Humour towards the Extremities, because it strengthens the Solids: And I have frequently given a Fit of the *Gout* with it and *Steel*, when nothing else would effect it; and I always found it the most effectual of all Medicines, to recover Appetite, Strength and Spirits, after a severe Fit was over, as is now universally experienc'd and acknowledg'd.

§. IV. Next to the *Bark* (or even beyond it) is *Steel*, or *Chalybeat* Medicines and *Mineral Chalybeat* Waters, which act principally by constricting, crisping, and winding up the relax'd Solids. Weak and young Persons, and slight Cases, do well with liquid Steel, such as the *Vinum Chalybeatum*, *Tinctura Martis*, the Solution of *Sal Martis* in common Water, *Elixir Vitrioli*, and the like. But those who are stronger and older, require *Steel Rust*, join'd with Aromaticks and Bitters, and the *Bark*; for they are all of one *Tribe* and *Class* of Medicines, and differ only in Degree: in which the Preparations of *Iron* is the strongest, as is evident

dent from its *Energy* in Externally ſtopping Hæmorrhages, and corrogating tender Fibres, and its partaking the Nature of Vitriol and Acids. Where theſe do not relieve at leaſt, the Caſe muſt be very bad, or the Medicines apply'd much out of Time, while the Juices were too viſcid, or not ſufficiently thin and ſweet. *Sydenham* ſeem'd to doubt, whether Purgatives ought to be join'd with *Chalybeats* in the ſame Courſe; but that can be no Difficulty to thoſe who have underſtood what has been before ſaid, or are well acquainted with true Philoſophy and the Animal *Oeconomy*. For the Purgatives are either ſimply deſign'd (in ſuch a Caſe) to cleanſe the *Prima Viæ*, or to *fuſe* and thin the Blood: in the firſt Caſe they are abſolutely neceſſary, and in the ſecond more ſo, if the *firſt Intention* has not been fully purſu'd before: As we find by *Lower*'s bitter Tincture, eſpecially when a Purgative and Chalybeat with the *Bark* is combin'd, which ſucceeds wonderfully in ſuch Caſes, where the Habit is pretty full, and the Solids not much relax'd. But a long Courſe of *Chalybeat* Mineral Waters is ſtill the moſt effectual for the Purpoſe: *Spaw*, *Pyrmont*, or *Tunbridge*, in the hot Weather; and *Bath* in the temperate and cold Weather. Some fearful and apprehenſive People have been diſſuaded, by intereſted Perſons, from the Uſe of the *Bath* Waters in *Lowneſs*, *Oppreſſion*, and *Vapours*; and ſome unexperienced People have even imagin'd they have had more Vapours than ordinary under the Uſe of them. But theſe may as well affirm, that *Opium* purges, and *Jullap* binds. For if they mend the Faults and Weakneſſes of the Stomach and Bowels, (as all the World acknowledges they do, and muſt do by their Nature and Compoſition) they muſt then infallibly be moſt beneficial in theſe Diſorders, as from my own, and the Experience of many thouſand others, can be teſtified, who will affirm them to be the moſt certain Relief of any in ſuch Caſes.

Cases. And indeed, as by their *Sulphur* thus dissolv'd in hot Water, they are the most cleansing and diluting of all Medicines, so their *Steel* (as I have already said) is the most effectual for bracing the Solids: And with such a Composition it would be pretty strange they should not (if any Means could) be successful in such Cases. They may raise some Mist and Dimness before the Eyes in foul Stomachs, nay even occasion some Head-Achs and Flatulence, which may properly enough be call'd *Vapourish* or *Nervous*; but the same every active Remedy will produce; and these may be easily remedied, by joining some *Volatiles*, *Aromaticks* or *Bitters* along with them. If they have not the greatest Benefit is expected, it is because the *ponderous* Medicines mention'd, and those for the *first Intention*, have not before, upon first drinking them, been sufficiently and long enough persisted in; for certainly they are the most agreeable and beneficial *Vehicle* for such Medicines, and the most sure Remedy, after such a Course, to be found on the *Globe*, as I have long experienced. The greatest Misfortune is, that their Relief does not last for a very long Time, at least not at an equal Heighth. But that is the Misfortune of all Remedies in bad Cases and Constitutions, and their beneficial Effects will last longer than that of any other Remedy, under the Management I have mention'd.

CHAP. V.

Of the Regimen of Diet proper for Nervous Distempers.

§. I. HAVING deliver'd, in the best Manner I am able, the general Method of Cure of *Nervous* Distempers, the several *Intentions* to be follow'd in the Prosecution of it, and the best Medicines

dicines I can suggest from Experience, Observation, or the Nature of Things, for fulfilling each of these *Intentions*; I come now to the *Diætetick* Management, *that Part* which has the greatest Influence in the Cure of *Chronical Distempers*, without which the best and surest Remedies fail of their Effect, and yet in these later Ages the least *cultivated* and most neglected of all the curative Parts of Physick in *England*, (till of late, that *my worthy, learned* and *ingenious Friend*, Dr. *Arbuthnott*, thought fit to treat it according to its *Use and Dignity*, in the masterly Manner he executes every thing he undertakes) insomuch that he hazards the Charge of introducing new and whimsical Opinions, who would pretend to stand up in its Defence, or bring it into his Practice. And yet, if we will make but a slender Enquiry into the Practice of the early and purest Ages of *Physick*, or the great and universally approv'd *Writers* in the healing *Art*, we shall find *Diet* no such contemptible Help towards the Prevention or Cure of Diseases, as it is now held or imagin'd. On the contrary, we shall find the Works of all the most judicious and celebrated Practitioners full of particular Directions and Advices on this *Topick* in every Disease they treat of; and demonstrating that their *Authors*, as they did not find, so they did not imagine, that any (at least habitual and rooted) Distemper, could be remov'd without such Assistance. We are certainly provided with a greater Choice of more perfect Materials, as well as more elegant Forms of Medicines, than the *Antients*, and this probably will still increase, by length of Time, with *Arts*, the Knowledge of Nature, and even of our Diseases; but what is, and will be ever admired among the *Antients*, is their *Method of Cure*, the Truth and Justness of their *Rules* and *Maxims*, and the Solidity of their *Intentions* in following the Directions of Nature in the

Way

Diet for Nervous Distempers. 105

Way she intends or points out. *Hippocrates*, the Father of the *Physicians*, thought a *Regimen of Diet* of such Consequence, both to the *Healthy* and the *Sick*, that of about *ninety Books* of his which remain, or that pass under his Name, there are eight of them which treat of that Matter only or principally; and thro' all the rest of his Works, he mentions much more of his *Diætetick* Management, than any Assistance he took from the *Materia Medica*. He complains, that * those who went before him, had written nothing concerning the *Diet* of sick Persons, which was nevertheless one of the most essential Parts of *Physick*, even in his Time, which we may justly suppose wanted it less than later Ages. *Galen*, tho' more abounding in Medicines, yet is far from depriving Diet of its due Place. On the contrary he declares, † " *That Physick has no Remedy so effectual as to be able to bring its wanted Relief where the Regimen of Diet either counter-acts or does not assist it.* And in another Place he says, § " *That by means of that part of Physick which prescribes a proper Diet, those who have deriv'd too tender and weakly a Constitution from their Parents, have brought themselves on to extreme old Age, without any Weakness of their Senses, free from all Pain and Diseases.*" He adds afterwards concerning himself, " *Even I, tho' I had not a healthy Constitution from my Birth, nor led a Life of much Freedom and Ease of Mind, yet by the Precepts of this most useful part of Physick, which I practised after the 28th Year of my Age, I never fell into any Distemper, except a slight Fever of 24 Hours through Weariness or Excess of Labour.*" The *Methodists*, a celebrated *Sect* among the Antient Physicians,

---

* Epidem. lib. 6.
† De usu Theriaces ad Pamphylianum.
§. Lib. 5. De Sanitate tuenda.

laid

laid the main Stress of the Cure upon *Diet* and *Evacuations*; and some of them carry'd this to an extravagant Heighth. But *Celsus*, who seems to have judiciously distinguish'd and kept in a proper *Medium* between the Extreams, that the different *Sects* of *Physick* in his Time, had carry'd each their particular and favourite Doctrines to, was yet sufficiently sensible and convinc'd of the Necessity of a proper *Diet* in the Cure of Diseases; for he is not only large and full in his Directions and Regulations about it, in every particular Disease he treats of: but where he distinguishes between internal and external Disorders, he calls the *first* those in which the Regulation of *Diet* is the principal Part of the Cure, and the *latter* those where *Medicines* make the chief Part of it. Even in the same Place, where he takes some Pains to refute the Doctrine of *Asclepiades*, who maintain'd that all Diseases were to be cured by *Diet* alone, and to restore Medicines to their proper Place. He goes further, to enjoin *absolute Fasting* in the first Attacks of a Disorder, and a strict Moderation in the Quantity as well as Quality of the Food, during all the Time that the Disease continues; for nothing, *he says*, is more beneficial to a sick Person, than *timely Abstinence*. Then he proceeds to shew the Reasonableness of such a Conduct, and to blame and reprove those luxurious Persons, who will allow their *Physicians* to determine the Kind and Quantity of their Food, but reserve to themselves the Times of taking it; or who think they act very generously if they submit to his Regulations in every thing besides the Kinds or Qualities of it: and ends with assuring them of the extream Hurtfulness of any Error, either in the Quality, the Quantity, or the Times of taking their Nourishment. It were endless to produce Authorities for a Thing that makes a great Part of the Works of all the standard Writers in Physick, I mention these only, because they are acknowledg'd

the

the great Masters in this *Science*, and whose Evidences must of Consequence include the Suffrages of all their Approvers and Admirers; and as they will be sufficient to give the Reader, who is not conversant in these Matters, a just Notion of the Consequence of *Diet* in the Cure of Diseases. For I do not pretend to add (by what I have here said) any thing to the Knowledge of those whose Study or Profession has led them to search into these Affairs, since they will not want Conviction. But here one will naturally inquire how so necessary and essential a Part of *Physick* comes to be in such Disgrace, and so little regarded, as it is at present, since it was so much recommended, and made up so great a Part of the Practice of the most admired *Physicians*. The Original of this Evil seems to be owing to some over-zealous Abettors of *Chymistry*. The *Alchimists*, or more conceited and whimsical sort of *Chymists*, were the great Men, that, depending solely upon Medicines, endeavour'd to discredit *Diet* in the Cure of Diseases, bragging and ranting in Honour of their *Panacæa's*, *Elixirs of Life*, and other wonderful *Secrets*, which, if you will believe the Inventors and Admirers of them, were sufficient, without any other Means, even a *Regimen of Diet*, or whatever all Physicians before had thought most indispensible, to work infallible Cures in the most desperate Diseases. It was this, and nothing else, they pretended to. When once such an ill Practice is set on foot, the Patients themselves, as *Celsus* observ'd in his Time, are so averse to being confin'd by disagreeable Restraints, that they are prepar'd to believe every Impostor, that will take upon him to dispense with the most necessary Condition of Cure, and entertain a Prejudice against those who will honestly insist upon the Necessity of what they dislike, being more willing to believe such Physicians are not sufficiently acquainted with the *Virtues* and *Powers* of Medicines, than that Medicines have no such Virtues as they

they would so fain find them possess'd of: And they are generally so fond of being prescrib'd to rather in the most agreeable than in the most effectual Manner, that not only few of them will submit to any Restraints in Diet, but by their Squeamishness and intemperate Delicacy, bring some of the most powerful Medicines into Disgrace, and less and less common Use; so that we may fear, not only the *Bark* (the Aversion of every nice Palate) but *Mercury, Steel,* and several other of the best Medicines, which on the first Discovery were look'd upon as great *Gifts of God* for the Relief of human Miseries, will in time be quite disus'd, and perhaps forgot. However, since we who are *Physicians* are bound *by a most solemn Oath* * (contriv'd by *Hippocrates,* for ought we know, at least it is handed down to us amongst his other Works, and is the Substance, I believe, of the Obligation and Vow that *Candidates* take in all the *Universities* in *Europe,* when they receive their Degrees of *Physick*) to order a *Regimen of Diet* proper and peculiar to each Distemper we undertake the Cure of, as well as proper Medicines. I shall proceed to inform the Reader of what I have found most beneficial or successful on this Head towards the Cure of the Disorders I am now treating of.

§. II. It is highly probable, that the infinitely wise Author of our Nature has provided proper *Remedies* and *Reliefs* in every *Climate,* for all the Distempers and Diseases incident to their respective Inhabitants, if in his Providence he has necessarily placed them there: And certainly the *Food* and *Physick* proper and peculiar to the middling Sort of each *Country* and *Climate,* is the best of any possible for the Support of the Creatures he has unavoidably placed

---

* Vide Hippocrat. p. 42. Vol. I. Edit. Vander Lind. or Edit. Fæsii, Sect. 1, 23.

Diet for Nervous Distempers. 109

there, provided only that they follow the Simplicity of Nature, the Dictates of Reason and Experience, and do not lust after *foreign Delicacies:* as we see by the Health and Chearfulness of the *middling Sort* of almost all Nations. And whoever is acquainted with the *History* of the *Origin of Nations,* and the Manner in which they liv'd, preserv'd themselves in Health, and got rid of their Diseases, while they liv'd in their Simplicity, and had not yet grown luxurious, rich and wanton, or had frequent Commerce with other Nations, and communicated with them in their *Luxury* and *Arts*, will be pretty well satisfy'd of this Truth. But where the *Luxury* and *Diseases* of all the Nations on the *Globe* are brought together, mingled and blended, and perhaps heighten'd by the Difference of *Climates*, there is an absolute Necessity that the *Materials of Physick*, and the Methods of Cure, should be various and extended in an equal Proportion: which is the Cause of the Multiplicity of our Medicines, and the Necessity that *Physicians* are under to know almost every thing that is knowable in Nature, for the Use of *Physick:* and to bring from each *Country* and *Climate* the proper *Antidote* for the Distemper brought from thence.

§. III. There is also another *infinitely wise* Contrivance in Nature, that *Loathing* and *Inappetency*, or at least a Difficulty in Digestion, always attends, in some Degree or other, all Disorders whatsoever. Were every one that is a little ill, capable of the same *Riot* and *Excess* during their Distemper, that they were when in perfect Health, when they laid in the Materials of their Disorders, they would infallibly and quickly ruin themselves, and perish without Resource: Whereas by this wise Necessity, they are not only hinder'd from adding *Oil* to the *Flame*, but find a new Increase of their Pains and Punishments, upon the smallest Excess, which puts them under the Necessity of forbearing: if the Pleasure of gratifying their Sensuality is not greater than the Sense of the Pain. And in some Cases, where there has been a great Disposition towards *Luxury* in the Patient, and where the Cure depended only or chiefly upon *Abstinence*, I have with Pleasure admired the Art and Ingenuity of a *Physician*, who, to keep up his Patient's Spirits during the tedious Cure, and gain the Advantages of Temperance and Abstinence as much as he was able, has prescrib'd a Course of innocent, tho' neither palatable nor appetizing Medicines, for a long time, without teazing his Patient with the dispiriting and mortifying Doctrine of *Self-denial*, which either he had despised, or not receiv'd in its proper Degree and Manner, and thus effected the Cure, which otherwise had been impossible.

§. IV. There is no surer or more general *Maxim* in *Physick*, than that Diseases are cured by the contrary or opposite Methods to that which produc'd them. If *Nervous* Disorders are the Diseases of the Wealthy, the Voluptuous, and the Lazy, (as I have already shewn) and are mostly produc'd, and always aggravated and increased, by *Luxury* and *Intemperance* (tho' perhaps not always an absolute and outragious Intemperance, yet certainly by one relative to the particular Constitution and Strength of the Patient) there needs no great Depth of Penetration to find out that *Temperance* and *Abstinence* is necessary towards their *Cure*. But as there are different Stages or Degrees of these Disorders, and even seemingly different *Kinds* of them, according to the Prevalency of this or that particular Quality in the Materials of the general Cause: whereby different Effects, Appearances, and Symptoms are produc'd with greater or lesser Violence, and longer or shorter Duration; so different Regulations in the Quantity and Quality of the Food, is necessary towards their Removal: I shall therefore first give some *general* Directions in these two last Particulars, and afterwards

wards subjoin some Considerations, to be made in the Application to particular Cases.

§. V. As to the Qualities of the solid Food, it is necessary, 1*st*. That it be soft and tender, light and easy of Digestion, and affording a mild or *Balsamick Chyle*; that its Materials be sound and good in their Kind, and fitted for Use, without the artful Composures of *Cookery*, or the Means us'd commonly in making it more *luscious and palatable*; and likewise, that it be the most simple and uncompounded, and that fewest different Materials possible be receiv'd into the same Meal; for as they will only serve to provoke Excess, so, as *Celsus* * observes, "*Variety of Foods, tho' they may go down with greater Ease and Pleasure, yet they are not so easily digested.*" 2*dly*, That it be endu'd, as much as possible, with Qualities contrary to the *Nature* of the *Distemper*, and the *Vices* of the Fluids: † That it be *thin* and *diluting*, where there are viscid or sizy Juices, great Obstructions, or gross Habits: That cooling and liquid Things be preferr'd to heating and drying Foods, where there are acute Pains, and violent or inflammatory Symptoms: That Seeds be preferr'd before Roots, Greens, or Fruits, in Cases of Flatulence; and that soft, mild, sweet, or at least insipid Things, be chosen, rather than those that are sharp, salt, or sour, in *Scorbutick*, *Hectick*, *Scrophulous*, or *Cancerous* Cases and Constitutions; or when there are any Ulcers, Foulness of the Skin, or other Signs of sharp and acrid Juices: And so in other Cases. §

§. VI. The Quantity of the Food must be proportion'd to the Strength of the Digestion, and the

---

* Lib. III. Cap. 6. Vide etiam Sanct. Med. Static. Sect. 3. Aph. 51.
† Vide Sanctorii Aphorismata de Cibo & Potu.
§ Vide *Arbuthnott* of *Aliments*.

Waste

Waste or Decay of the Fluids, from Exercise or bodily Action, or to the present Fulness of the Habit, and Obstruction of the natural *Secretions*. But as it is impossible to give *general Rules* in these Cases, wherein almost every individual Person differs from another, or even from himself at different Times, so the precise Regulation of this must be left to the Patient's own Feelings, and the Honesty and Experience of his *Physician*. A few Observations upon the Quantity that agrees best, sits easiest and lightest upon the Stomach, gives no Oppression, Heaviness, Heat or Feverishness, while it is digesting, and passes off without any ill Effects, will most readily determine it for the Patient; and it is of so great Consequence to the Welfare of the Patient, that no Pains ought to be spar'd for attaining the Knowledge of this precise and precious *Mediocrity*, which ought, as seldom as possible, to be transgres'd either way.

§. VII. Those who have only a few transient Symptoms of these Disorders: whose Constitution is yet sound, and their Juices good and sweet: if they live with a due Degree of Temperance suited to their Constitutions, and take care not to increase their Disorders by Excesses, will need no other Restriction, than to abate of their Quantity while they are more immediately under these *Symptoms:* will gradually get rid of their Distemper, and avoid violent Shocks, or great Sufferings: and be restor'd to their former Health and Freedom of Spirits, by the other Assistances of Medicine and Exercise. Those who have deeper, more habitual and violent *Symptoms*, will need a greater Degree of Care and Caution; and their Stomach being weaker, and their Digestion going on slower, will be necessitated to choose the lightest and most easily digested Foods, and the smallest Quantity of *spirituous Liquors:* and will suffer in Proportion as they exceed the Quantity that is determin'd by the mention'd Observations.

tions. For such the lightest, young, and *white* Animal Foods only, are necessary, and these also only at Dinner. And if they are subject to violent and acute *Paroxysms*, they must be more than ordinary careful about these Times, and then even use a cooler, softer, and more liquid Diet. In general, they must govern themselves by their Feelings, and take no more at a Time than their Stomach will easily bear, but rather repeat it oftner; and they ought always to wait till their Appetite returns in its usual Degree, and they will even find, however moderate or abstemious they may seem, that upon any Lowness, Heaviness, or Want of Spirits, still lighter Meals will restore their Chearfulness.

§. VIII. But as for all those whose Constitutions are spoil'd, who have bad or corrupted Juices, violent and dangerous *Symptoms*, great *Obstructions*, are subject to the great and eminent Degrees of these Disorders, are threaten'd with *Hectic* or *Consumption* (or a Destruction of some of the great *Viscera*, and who have tried all the other Methods and Medicines that could be suggested without Success) for these I have found no other Relief than a *total Abstinence* from Animal Foods of all Kinds, and all Sorts of strong and fermented Liquors, keeping only to Milk, with Seeds or Grains, and the different Kinds of Vegetable Food, according to the Nature of the Distemper: from which they have never fail'd to find a present Relief, and a considerable Abatement of the Violence of their Symptoms. Many have been led into this Method without any Advice or Direction, but merely from their own Feelings, and observing what they were easiest under. And many more have been absolutely cur'd and free'd from all their Disorders by it: some even from a very short time after they enter'd upon it, and others in a longer or shorter Time, according to the Obstinacy of their Distemper, if the Disease has not been so far gone, as to be past all possible Relief from natural Means.

In these last Cases it has done all that was in the Power of *Art*, has lessen'd their Miseries, and protracted their Fate, and has given more Ease and Quiet than they could receive from any other Method they could turn to, except *Opiates* and *Anodyn*'s: to which one is never to give himself, till he has given up all Hopes of a total Cure. Where the *Nerves* or Solids are naturally weak, or the Person subject to *nervous Disorders* from their Infancy, there is no Method will absolutely free them from some slight Returns of their former Symptoms; but this *Diet* I have found to do more than any other Method whatever: however, no one ought to undertake this Regimen, without the Advice of some honest, able, and experienced *Physician*, who has consider'd his Case and Constitution, and can direct him aright in the proper Management of it, and the Methods of keeping up the due *Tension* of his Solids, which such a *Diet* may probably somewhat relax, while it is purifying the Juices, and cleansing the Habit: and can likewise judge of his Constancy, Firmness, and Resolution to go through with it, since in some deep rooted and confirm'd Distempers of this Kind, tho' the Patient may find a considerable Relief for many Months, yet possibly when the gross Impurities, the *Choler*, *Phlegm*, and *Salts* stor'd up in the Habit, come to be thrown off on the *alimentary Tube*, as into the common Shore, and all the *Emunctory* Glands become loaded with the *Despumation* of the whole Habit: raising Sickness, Lowness of Spirits, and a Return of all, or many, of the former Disorders: this may blast all his Hopes, and mightily discourage him, and make him condemn the Method, and blame the Physician who advis'd him. But if he stands this Shock with Firmness and Patience (which will be readily relieved by proper *Evacuations*, *Volatiles* and *Astringents*) he may be assured of Success, and his perfect Recovery is at hand. But as there are incurable Disorders, which no Method or Medicine will

will reach, so it frequently happens in this: And even after the Patient is recover'd by this Method, he must resolve to continue in it ever after, at least, not to indulge himself in a much higher Degree of Food, without suffering presently, or hazarding a Return of all his Disorders; for as *Celsus* observes, in all Disorders of the Stomach, *by whatever Methods the Patient is recover'd, he must continue in the same when he is well, for the Disease will return, unless Health be protected by the same Means that restor'd it.*

§. IX. I would not be understood here (as some have maliciously and artfully misrepresented me, contrary to my most deliberate Intention) to recommend a *total Milk* or a *Vegetable Diet*, or indeed any particular one, to every one that is sick, or out of Order: I never once had such a Dream. I have given the Preference in my *Essay on the Gout*, to the common Diet of well-chosen Flesh Meat, and good middling ripe Wine, even in that obstinate and painful Distemper, commonly treated by a Milk Diet. And in my *Essay on Health and Long Life*, I have endeavour'd, as far as I could, to enable the Patient to make the proper Choice of Animal Foods fit for his Constitution, and the Disorders he labours under; and have, from considering the Nature of the Distemper, actually order'd some who were in a *Vegetable Diet*, to change it for an *Animal* one. A total *Milk and Vegetable* Diet, besides its being *particular* and inconvenient in a Country where Animal Food is the common Diet, and affording no sufficient Store of Animal or Mechanical Strength (to Persons naturally weak, or who have not been habituated to it from their Cradles) may bring the Patient into such a State, that, without the utmost Risque or Danger, he can never leave it off again. And even while he is under it, by relaxing and softening the Solids, (in some Degree) when it is a sweetening the Juices, it brings him under a Necessity of keeping up their Tenfion with proper aftringent, warm, and cordial Medicines, (which are of the fame Nature with a more generous Diet) and inceffant Labour and Exercife: And in grofs foul Bodies, or thofe fubject to *goutifh, fcorbutick,* or other *inflammatory Diforders* and *Paroxyfms:* requires the utmoft Care and Caution that the Difeafe be not thereby at firft, thrown inwards, and fo the extream Degrees of Vapours, Lownefs, and other *Nervous* Diforders enfue, which this *Diet* is defign'd to prevent. Indeed there are fome Cafes wherein a *Vegetable* and *Milk Diet* feems abfolutely neceffary, as in *fevere* and *habitual Gouts, Rheumatifms, Cancerous, Leprous* and *Scrophulous* Diforders, extream *Nervous Cholicks, Epilepfies,* violent *Hyfterick Fits, Melancholy, Confumptions,* and the like Difeafes mention'd in the Preface, and towards the laft Stages of all chronical Diftempers; in fuch Diftempers I have feldom feen fuch a *Diet* fail of a good Effect at laft. But in moft other *Chronical Diftempers, Nervous* or *Humorous,* and in all their tolerable Degrees, and firft or fecond Stages, a common middling, plain and moderate Diet is certainly the beft and fafeft; a little *Animal* Food of the youngeft, lighteft, tendereft, thinneft, and fweeteft Kind, and a fmall Proportion of generous Liquors, to keep up the due *Tenfion* of the Solids, under the Regulations I have mention'd; weak Broths and Soops made of tender young Animal Subftances, without Fat or Butter, and thicken'd with a due Proportion of Vegetable Seeds or Grains, fuch as thofe of Wheat, Barley, Rice, Sage, Oats, Millet, and the like: Such a *Diet,* I fay, will, in my Opinion, anfwer all the Ends of pure *Milk* and *Vegetables*; and as I have often found fuch an one lefs dangerous, fo it is a more eafy Regulation, as things now ftand: and wants only a few Months in the fame Courfe, of that Cure that might be gain'd perhaps by going into fuch a particular Method of Diet. I am never for entring upon *extream* or uncommon

common Means of *Diet* or *Medicines*, but in extream and mortal Cases; for I always think that *common Sense* is the best Indication of a sound Mind, and *common Life* the best Means of temporal Happiness, else they had never been common.

§. X. One great *Advantage* that a *Milk* and *Vegetable Diet* has over a Flesh or *Animal* one, lies principally in this, that one may thereby avoid the loading the Juices with too many *Salts* of any Kind, or thickening them with more gross and hard earthy Particles, or such as cannot be broken and comminuted by the natural Force of the weak Solids: and by it Patients will not be so readily led into Errors in the Quantity; Nature not being tempted to receive or retain such unprovoking and impoignant Viands, whereby they avoid the *Snare* and *Temptation* that Liquorishness and high Relish throws many into. *Another* Advantage is, that it effectually dilutes and cools too thick or hot Juices, and that a sufficient Quantity of it may be taken to keep the Bowels and Blood Vessels full, and sufficiently turgid, whereby the *Circulation* and natural Evacuations and Secretions will be more uniformly carried on in such weak Habits, than can possibly be under an *Animal Diet* of so small a Quantity as must be necessary in such Cases, unless it be extreamly diluted with Water, and the farinaceous Vegetables, which brings it to the same State: And therefore, in greatly deprav'd Habits, and such deep and dangerous Diseases as I have mention'd, it is the most proper and absolutely necessary Regimen to carry on the natural Functions without Pain and Uneasiness, and to preserve the Sides of the Capillary Vessels from *coalescing* and growing together, and so preventing irremediable Obstructions; though in other more slight Cases, it may be not only not necessary, but even sometimes inconvenient and hurtful: For though it will always produce at length Freedom from Pain, and Freedom of Spirits, and a greater

Capacity for intellectual Functions, yet it will never beget *mechanical* Force and Strength, or a hardy, strong Constitution, which in some Circumstances, Employments, Trades, and Professions, is indispensably necessary; so that such a Course and *Regimen* is only proper for those who follow *Intellectual* Occupations, and expect chiefly mental Pleasures, Freedom from Pain, Chearfulness and Length of Days, or, in short, for the Studious and Sedentary.

§. XI. The Sum of the Whole, in my Opinion, is this: Our Distempers generally arise from *Oils, Salts,* and *Spirits,* carried into the Habit by our Food; nothing else but these, in the Nature of Things, having *Force* enough to produce them. Some certain Proportion of these is absolutely necessary to excite, rouze, and carry on the *Circulation, Perspiration,* and all the *Secretions* with their proper Force and Vigour: When the Juices are too viscid or acrimonious, or the Obstructions many and great, *Diet* offers us one of the surest Means to cure these ill Qualities. All *Salts,* in their general Nature, are of the same kind, hard, and highly attractive, and differ only as they are smaller or greater in their Parts, and according to the Earths, Oils, and other Mixtures that unite them, or mix with them. *Milk* and *Vegetables* have but little saline Matter in Proportion to their Bulk, and therefore a *total Milk* and *Vegetable Diet,* may, in some Cases, defraud the Constitution of that due Proportion of *Salts* necessary for the mention'd Purposes, and for want of which the Solids may become too lax and feeble. But, on the other hand, too great a Quantity of Flesh Meat, and hot fermented Liquors, or that which is of too *saline* and *spirituous* a Nature, will load the *Habit* with too many of these Salts and Oils, and so beget the mention'd Distempers. The great *Art of Life* then, in *chronical* Distempers, is to ascertain the *Mediocrity* of such a *Diet* as neither makes the Salts and Oils

Oils too many to increase the Distemper, nor too few, to let the Solids become too much relax'd. Animal Food then, and spirituous Liquors become more tolerable in *Northern Climates*, where the Want of sufficient *Sun*, and the Moisture of the *Air*, makes the Solids of somewhat too loose and flabby a Nature, and so require a greater Proportion of Salts and Oils, needful to rouze and twitch them, than in more *Southern Climates*. Suppose, for Example, a Dram of Salts, and Oils or Spirits in twenty-four Hours was necessary; then certainly that *Diet* which conveys this Dram of Salts and Oils in the whole Substance of the Food, according to the Bulk, Age, and Expences of the Life of the Patient, into the Habit, will be the best, of whatever Kind it may be. But if, by an Over-charge of Salts and Oils, Diseases are brought on, and are to be remedied by a *Diet* wherein one half of this Quantity is found; then such Food is to be chosen, or such a Quantity of it taken, as will convey into the Habit only half a Dram of such: and if that End can be obtain'd by following the common and ordinary *Diet* of the Country and Climate, and of the healthiest People in it, then that is, beyond Dispute, the best Regimen in general to preserve Health. Under Diseases the Case is different. So that there can be no Room for mistaking the proper Kind of *Diet*, nor the Validity of the Reasons on which it is founded. The only Difficulty that remains, will be in chusing such Kinds, and that Quantity of *Animal Food* which best suits the Age, Bulk, and Constitution of the Patient, and conveys only the necessary Quantity of *Salts* and Oils. To determine which was the chief Design of my *Essay on Health and Long Life*, and of Dr. *Arbuthnott's Book of Aliments*, and which is evidently of the greatest Consequence to all who would secure these two in the most effectual Manner Mortality will permit.

CHAP. VI.

Of the Exercise proper for Nervous Distempers.

§. I. THERE is not any one Thing, more approv'd and recommended by all *Physicians*, and the Experience of all those who have suffer'd under *Nervous* Distempers, (since the Distinction has been made) than *Exercise*, of one Kind or another; and this without the least Exception or Limitation, but so far as the Strength can admit; if it is without Weakening, Fatigue, or Hurry of Spirits. In the *Southern* Climates, as there is scarce any, at least few, *Nervous* Distempers of the lingering and *chronical* Kind, so there is very little Room for *Exercise* meerly for Health: The Warmth and Action of the *Sun*, keeping the Blood and Juices sufficiently fluid, the *Circulation* free, and all the *Secretions* in their due Degree and Plenty, so as to prevent Obstructions, to which the Thinness, Coolness, and Lightness of their almost *Vegetable Diet* contributes not a little. But in the more *Northern* and colder Climates, where the Food is more gross, higher and harder of Digestion, being mostly Animal; where the *Perspiration* is small, or scarce any at all, especially in *Nervous* or *chronical* Distempers, there is an absolute Necessity of due *Exercise* and Labour to supply the Want of *Sun* and thin Air, and remedy these Defects: The Neglect of which, in our *cold* Climates, ought to be, in Reason, reckon'd as absurd, ridiculous, and unnatural, as our using it appears *fantastical* to *Orientals*. The few Instances brought from *Spain*, *Italy*, *Portugal*, and even more *Northern* Countries, of People that live there to a great Age, and without Distempers, meerly sitting still, are little to the Purpose, consider'd as a *Rule* for our Conduct (since, setting aside the above-mention'd Advantages, which they enjoy in common with other

Exercise for Nervous Distempers.

other *Southern* Countries, whereby *Exercise* becomes less necessary for them than for us they are in a great measure excluded from the Benefit they might possibly reap from it, if it was necessary, by its being impracticable in any high Degree: For it would be absurd to propose to them to take long continu'd Journies in their scorching *Climate* for the Cure of Distempers.

§. II. When Mankind was simple, plain, honest, and frugal, there were few or no Diseases. *Temperance*, *Exercise*, *Hunting*, *Labour*, and *Industry* kept the Juices sweet, and the Solids brac'd. The *Spiritual* Passions, however, raged and boiled high; those, to wit, of *Ambition*, *Malice*, *Revenge*, and *Pride*, which beget *Usurpation*, *Conquests*, *Murder*, and *Wars:* *Labour* and *Exercise* were observ'd to beget Firmness, Strength, and Activity for these Purposes. It was afterwards introduc'd into the *Religious Worship*. *Rewards* and *Honours* were appointed for the *Victors* in these *sacred* Contests. But Luxury and Intemperance having gain'd Ground, through Peace, Security, Ease, and Plenty, Diseases sprang up and multiplied, *Exercise* and *Labour* were introduc'd into their Cure by *Physicians*, who had observ'd the Health and Vigour of the Laborious and Active. * *Hippocrates*, *Diocles*, *Paraxagoras*, and *Erasistratus* first introduc'd it into *Rules*, *Laws*, and *Order;* appointing the Times and Kinds of it, appropriated to each particular Distemper. The *Grecians* in general, the *Athenians* and *Lacedemonians* in particular, erected *Academies*, *Gymnasia*, or publick Places, for the common Conveniency of all Kinds of Exercise, with all proper Accommodations and Services for that End, both to train up the People for *War*, and to preserve them from and cure their Diseases. These *Gymnasia* were dedicated to

---

* Galen. Cap. 58. lib. ad Thrasybulum.

Apollo, as *God* of *Physick*, and thither *Physicians* sent all those who labour'd under chronical Distempers, of which *Exercise* and *Diet*, limited and managed according to the Nature of the Case, made up all the Cure. By Degrees it spread over all the *Eastern* and *Southern* Countries, and at last had so general an Approbation, as to be universally received all the World over, where Health was regarded, or the Cure of Distempers studied. Such has been the original Rise, Reception, and Approbation of *Exercise*, as is evident from ancient History and universal Tradition. Whoever will consult *Le Clerc*, will be abundantly satisfied in this Matter.

§. III. The *Romans* (as wise and brave a People as ever was formed upon the Foot of mere Nature) received it with all their other *Arts* from the *Greeks*, and thought it so necessary, tho' in a much warmer Climate than ours of *England*, that they founded a great Part of the Cure of Distempers, as well as the preservative Means of Health, upon it, in its various Degrees and Kinds. Those who are curious may find all the Learning of the Antients, collected to entertain them on this Subject, with the best Reasons and Philosophy of the Times; and the Account of the Origin of new Diseases among the *Romans*, by *H. Mercurialis*, in his Treatise *de Arte Gymnastica*, in which every thing useful, ingenious, or that has been invented for this Purpose, is brought together. *Sydenham*, our Countryman, has enlarged in its Praises, as one of the most sovereign Remedies hitherto known; and mentions several Instances of its wonderful Success, and of its conquering the several Effects of *Nervous* Distempers by long and constant Journies on Horseback. *Fuller de Arte Gymnastica*, has done what he could to encourage and explain it. Many others of the best of the Moderns, have given its due Commendation: But it is not my Business to collect Authorities, for a thing so

uni-

universally * acknowledged, and so little disputed. As to my own Experience, I never saw any thing done to the Purpose in Nervous Cases, or with a Success complete, and subsisting for any long Time without the Assistance of these two, *Diet* and *Exercise*. I have even found the necessity of adding to these, in some Cases to make the Recovery durable and solid, Change of a thicker Air and of a colder Climate, to that of a *warmer Sun* and *purer* Air; which have seldom ever failed, when any Thing would succeed. But that not being in every one's Power, they must be contented with using the Means they can find within their Reach. The Benefit and absolute Necessity of a pure fragrant, fresh Air, and the Balm, Nitre, or Acid of it, both to Health and Life, are demonstrably proved from the Experiments of Sir *Isaac Newton*, Mr. *Hales*, and Dr. *Bryan Robinson*, both in the Vegetable and Animal Kingdom.

§. IV. Tho' Experience, which extremely confirms the Benefit of this Remedy, is the only solid Foundation to go upon, in the Cure of Distempers, yet the Reason of the thing speaks so loudly, that it cannot but be hearken'd to by every reasonable Person. As *Diet* and *proper Medicines*, in due Time, will certainly rectify the *Juices*, so Labour and Exercise will most infallibly strengthen the Solids, by promoting and continuing their constant Action and Motions. It is much like the constant Buckling of Hair, (I mean as to its Vertue and Efficacy, however different the *Mechanicks* of these Effects may be) or keeping it for some time fixed in a certain Position, to give the internal Parts new *Contacts* and *Cohesions*, and to confirm and settle them in these, which makes them retain the Form and Figure we design. 'Tis true, it is very hard, if not impossible to give a strong and lasting Union and Cohesion to

---

* We must sometimes force the Timorous from their Beds, and rouse the Lazy and Sluggish. *Hippoc. Epidem.* lib. 6.

the weak, disjoined, and discontinued *Fibres* of People of weak and relaxed Solids; but *Exercise* constantly continued does this (and will do it always) as much as the Nature of Things will admit of. There is an *innate* Power of *Contraction*, a *Spring* and *Elasticity* in all Animal Solids, as being contrived and designed as Instruments of Action and Motion; by Action and Motion only, this innate Power is nourished, preserved, increased, and recovered. And on the contrary, without them, it grows languid, feeble, and weak. Not only is the Circulation promoted, the Perspiration and all the other Secretions forwarded by *Exercise*; but by the *Muscular* Actions, the Blood and Juices are kept in a due State of Fluidity, their Viscidity broken and dissolved, and all Obstructions hindered or removed. There seems likewise, as it were, new Particles to be forced by this Action, into the Interstices and Ruptures of the Solids, to knit and solder them, and recover their lost Union, Cohesion, and Spring: So that *Exercise* seems the only, at least, the sovereign Remedy, in relaxed and weakened Solids. And as a low, light, and temperate Diet is necessary, and the best means of diluting and sweetening the Juices: and as at the same Time, it sometimes weakens and relaxes the Solids, so *Exercise* is more eminently useful in that Case, to keep up the due Force and Strength of the *Fibres*, else the Patient can never receive the full Benefit of such a *Diet*. All those in a *low Diet*, who have long preserved themselves in any Degree of Force and Spirits, have been constantly great Followers of Exercise, without which, even their *low Diet* would not have been so beneficial, especially after the *Meridian* of Life, when there is little Hopes of an *adventitious Force*. And one Reason why *Hypochondriacal* and *Hysterical* Persons relapse so frequently, after having been so wonderfully recovered by the Force of *Diet*, *Exercise*, and Change of Air, is, because they either intermit their *Regimen*

men of Diet, their *Exercise,* or perhaps both: and therefore he who, under *Nervous* Disorders and Complaints, will continue tolerably well after he is got better, must continue both his *Regimen of Diet,* and his *Exercise,* in some certain Degree ever after. It is true, *Diet* will do infinitely more than Exercise, and have more lasting Effects, but both should be joined.

§. V. It is of no great Consequence of what Sort or Kind the *Exercise* be, provided it be but *Bodily Exercise* and Action; certainly *riding* on Horseback is the best of all, because of the almost erect Posture, the lesser Weariness, and the more universal and natural Motion of all the Organs, with the constant Change of Air: and that the lower Regions of the Body, and the alimentary Instruments and *Hypochondres* are thereby most shaken and exercised. Next to that, is riding in a *Chaise* or *Chariot*. *Walking,* tho' it will answer the same End and Purpose as well as any, and may be more readily and easily used, because it may be equally followed within Doors and without, in Winter as well as Summer, yet it is more laborious and tiresome. Next to these are the active Games and Sports, such as *Hunting, Shooting, Bowls, Billiards, Shuttle cock,* and the like. I have known those who have exercised themselves by strongly working their Arms backward and forward; and some have used Weights for that Purpose, swinging and shaking them in their Hands. And some have done it with a *Cane,* rubbing it strongly over the whole Muscles of the Body and Limbs. The *Flesh-Brush* has supplied those who could not afford, or were not able to use any other Kind of *Exercise*. But certainly the best of all is, where *Amusement* or *Entertainment* of the Mind is joined with Bodily Labour, and constant Change of Air, as in *Hunting, Bowls, Billiards,* and the like, and riding Journies about Business: For the Entertainment of the Mind, and keeping it agreeably diverted from reflecting on its

Mis-

Misfortunes or Misery, makes Exercise infinitely more beneficial, as *Thoughtfulness*, *Anxiety*, and *Concern* render it quite useless.

§. VI. It is upon this Account that I would earnestly recommend to all those afflicted with *Nervous* Distempers, always to have some innocent entertaining *Amusement* to employ themselves in, for the Rest of the Day, after they have employed a sufficient time upon *Exercise*, towards the Evening, to prepare them for their Night's quiet Rest. It seems to me absolutely impossible, without such a Help, to keep the Mind easy, and prevent its wearing out the Body, as the Sword does the Scabbard; it is no matter what it is, provided it be but a *Hobby-Horse*, and an Amusement, and stop the Current of Reflexion and intense Thinking, which Persons of weak Nerves are aptest to run into. The common Division of Mankind, into *Quick Thinkers*, *Slow Thinkers*, and *No Thinkers*, is not without Foundation in Nature and true Philosophy. Persons of slender and weak Nerves are generally of the first Class: the Activity, Mobility, and Delicacy of their intellectual Organs make them so, and thereby weakens and relaxes the *Material Organs* of the intellectual Faculties; and therefore ingenious flattering, easy and agreeable Amusements, and Intervals of No-thinking and *Swiss-Meditation*, (as it is maliciously called) is as necessary for such, as Sleep to the Weary, or Meat to the Hungry, else the Spring will break, and the Sword wear out the Scabbard. *Study* of difficult and intricate Matters will infallibly do Hurt. *Reading* must be light entertaining and diverting, as well as Food. *Conversation* must be easy and agreeable, without Disputes or Contradiction. The *Diversion* innocent and inexpensive, else the Remorse and Reflexion afterwards will do infinitely more Prejudice than the present *Amusement* can recompense; and it must end at seasonable Hours;

Hours, without leaving a *Hurry* and *Fatigue* upon the Spirits of the Patient. To determine absolutely the Kinds and Quantities of the *Exercise*, *Amusement*, or even *Diet*, or the Times most proper for such, is impossible to any but the *Patient* himself. In the general, I shall only say, that as *Nervous Distempers* and *Old Age* reduce Men to the Weakness, the Tenderness, and Delicacy of Children, or very young Persons, they must be treated, and treat themselves as such, 'till Strength and a perfect Recovery come, if ever they are so lucky as to arrive at it, much in the same way, as a Child must be treated in his *Non-age*, till he arrives at Manhood.

CHAP. VII.

Of some of the more Immediate and Eminent Causes of Nervous Distempers.

§. I. I NEVER saw any Person labour under severe, obstinate, and strong *Nervous* Complaints, but I always found at last, the *Stomach, Guts, Liver, Spleen, Mesentery*, or some of the great and necessary Organs or *Glands* of the lower Belly were obstructed, knotted, schirrous or spoil'd, and perhaps all these together; and it may be very justly affirmed, that no habitual and grievous, or great *Nervous* Disorders, ever happened to any one who laboured not under some real *Glandular* Distemper, either *scrophulous* or *scorbutical*, original or acquired. So that in general, great Nervous Disorders may justly and properly be termed *Glandular*. The Stomach is often the first and principal Organ (or at least by Consent and Consequence) in the Fault: Either it is too thin and weak by Nature, or the inner *villous* Membrane is worn off by Luxury, so that it cannot contract close

close enough to embrace the Food; or it is become too soft, flabby, and relaxed, so that it cannot, with sufficient Spring, squeeze its Contents; or its *Glands* are growing *schirrous*, *hard*, and *knotted*, so that its Action is weak and languid, and interrupted, or *lastly*, there may actually be a discoverable *Imposthume*, *Schirrosity*, or *Cancer* already extant in it. And hence the Necessity of frequent, but gentle Vomits (at least in all these Cases but the last) to empty these weak *Glands*, when full of indigested *Flegm*, *Wind*, or *Choler*, in such *Nervous* Cases, and a thin, light, cool, and balmy *Diet*, proportioned to the Weakness and Infirmities of the Stomach and Solids (to give it the least Labour, and most Rest possible, as we cure broken Bones, by using them little) as well as to cut off the Sources of more Infection in them all, without Exception.

§. II. A vitious *Liver* seems to be one of the primary and immediate Causes of *Nervous Distempers*. I never once in my Life saw an *Hysteric* or *Hypochondriac* Case, of a deep Nature, or extreme Degree, in strong Persons especially, where the *Liver*, and it's Appendages were not eminently faulty, either by a præternatural *Size*, *Tumefaction*, *Obstruction*, or *Schirrosity*; and when by *ponderous*, alterative, active Medicines, join'd with a cool thin Diet, the Obstructions have been opened, the *Gall Bladder* and *Porus Biliarius* pervious, then, either *green*, *yellow*, or *black Choler* has poured out abundantly into the Stomach. The *Liver* is the *Organ* designed by Nature (or, at least, Nature makes Use of it) to suck out, draw off, and convey into the common *Shore* of the Body (the *Guts*) all the Poison, Malignity, and destructive Part of high rank Foods, and too great a Quantity of rich Liquors, taken into the Habit. This wise and bountiful Contrivance of Nature becomes an *Antidote*, or is a Receptacle (for some time) for the

destructive

destructive Effects of *Luxury* and *Intemperance*. And hence it comes to pass that gluttonous and voluptuous Animals, whether *Brutal* or *Rational*, have always overgrown *Livers*, and accordingly among the *Romans*, those Animals whose *Livers* were delicious, had their whole Entrails almost turned into *Liver*, by unnaturally cramming them with high and generous Foods; and no plentiful and *full Feeder* was ever opened, but he was found with some gross Fault in his *Liver*. It has indeed a noble and indispensible Use in all Animals (the human more especially) who live on Animal Foods and fermented Liquors, even beyond any Organ of the Body, next to the *Heart*, *Brain*, and *Lungs*: for it not only sucks out all the Venom, as it were, of the whole Mass of Blood, and carries it into the Guts (*the common Shore*, to be thence carried out of the Habit in Part) but there also the *Bile*, by its natural Acrimony and Stimulation, is the great Spring and Cause of the *Peristaltic* Motion: (that Function so necessary to Digestion and throwing off the Redundancy and Feculence); besides that it unites, by its *soapy* Nature, the various Particles of which the *Chyle* is compounded, and renders it a *similar* and *uniform* Fluid: and by its Bitterness, and this *Saponaceous* Quality, it cleanses and scowers the Mouths of the small and delicate *Lacteal Tubes*, from their Obstructions and Filth. But as all good Things, perverted and abused, have Pains and Punishments annexed to them, in Proportion to their Advantages and Benefits, so the *Liver*, when præternaturally large, tumified, obstructed, or *schirrous*, becomes the Cause of the most terrible and frightful Miseries incident to human Nature; from hence generally and chiefly spring all our horrible and dire *Hysterics* and *Hypochondriacs*, our *Epilepsies*, *Apoplexies*, and our *Manais*, our *Cholicks*, *Scurvies*, *Gouts*, *Jaundices*, *Hot Ulcers*, &c. and were there any Art or Medicine to turn or make *Choler* (*Adust*, Black,

Black, *Yellow*, or *Green*) an innocent, acid, active Liquor only (as it is in the Animals that live only on Vegetables) it would infallibly cure these Disorders; but I believe there is none, nor can be any such Art or Medicine, considering the established Laws of Nature, and those of the *Animal Oeconomy* : But the ponderous Remedies which open Obstructions (such as Preparations of *Antimony* and *Mercury*) gentle *E-meticks*, which pump up the peccant Humour as it flows (for *Catharticks* do little or nothing in such Cases, it being impossible to carry forcibly vitiated *Choler* so great a Length without Violence to Nature, besides that all Kinds of Purges pass through this gross Fluid, when vitiated, and leave it much as they found it) and a thin, mild Diet, that cuts off the Sources of the Evil. What is here said of the *Liver*, may be readily applied to the *Spleen*, in a certain Degree, and therefore 'tis needless to add any more of either.

§. III. The *Glands* of the *Mesentery*, or of the *Guts*, being knotted or obstructed, are less obvious by any other Symptoms, than these of a general *Weakness*, *Thinness* of Habit, a Tendence to *Hectical* Heats after Meals, and especially an Inappetence and Weakness of Digestion, Faintings, cold Sweats, Lowness of Spirits, and Oppressions, and the other *Nervous* Complaints to be described, those particularly of thin and *valetudinary* Persons. And those who continue weak, thin, and valetudinary, after Youthhood is over, are much to be suspected of *knotted Glands* in the *Mesentery*, which obstruct and hinder the free and easy Passage of the *Chyle* thro' the *Lacteals*, whose common *Bason* is in, and most general Course is thro' that *Membrane*; or of *knotted Guts*, and their obstructed Valves, which hinder the free Play of the *Peristaltick* Motion, so necessary towards the Progress of the Digestion, and the Expulsion of the Feculence; and all these more immediate Causes of *Nervous* Distempers shew the Necessity,

cessity, Expedience, and Benefit of ponderous Remedies, in the Beginning of a Cure: gentle Evacuations upwards or downwards, in the Process; and mild Astringents and Strengtheners to finish it; and an universal thin and low Diet in the whole Progress, and for future Preservation.

§. IV. It is very possible, neither the *ponderous* Remedies, nor the Evacuations may dissolve, or even much soften knotted, *schirrous*, or obstructed *Glands* in any Part of the Habit; but a cool, thin, soft, *balsamick Diet* will always make the Juices circulate easy, and without Rubs and Resistance; as a clear, thin, equable Stream of running Water will glide gently and calmly by the Sides of *implanted Islands:* and these *Knots* and *Tubercles* may thereby lie as easily and quietly in the Body, as the Nails on our Fingers and Toes, or as Bones surrounded with Muscles; and we know sweet thin Blood will make its way into the Circulation, through the lateral Branches, when the Trunk of the Artery is cut through: and that is all *Art* can do, or the Laws of the Animal *Oeconomy* will admit. And it is highly probable, when any one of these more immediate Causes of *Nervous* Disorders happen, they are all together in greater or lesser Degrees. Cutaneous Disorders also, such as the *Leprosie*, *Elephantiasis*, *Impetigo*, *Itch*, *Scurvy*, and *Erisipelas*, have a most powerful Influence in producing those violent, inveterate, and high, *Nervous* Disorders. But the Reason of the violent *Fits* under them is, that the *Glands* and great *Viscera* are loaded more than ordinary by *Debauches*, *high Diet*, and too great Fulness: so that the Circulation is thereby hindered and stop'd, and this makes these cutaneous Foulnesses recoil inwards, for Want of due Force and Freedom in the Circulation, to press them out, where they are safest; and none will be perfectly and safely cured under them, but by a long Course of the *ponderous* Medicines, and a thin, cool, soft Diet.

§. V. It is also possible, that none of all these mentioned immediate Causes may be the true one, and yet *Lowness of Spirits*, Sickness, and even *Fits*, *Fainting*, and *Convulsions* may happen: and when there may be none of these mentioned great Causes, by particular and special Symptoms to be suspected or justly supposed, a *Polypus* in the Heart, or *Great Artery*, or some præternatural Formation, *Excrescence*, or *Mal-Formation*, in some necessary Organ, may be the Cause of them; or *lastly*, the Juices may be so thick, *viscid*, and *glewy*, as may interrupt the Circulation, and the easy Performance of the Animal Functions. But as such Cases are more *rare*, they do not so immediately come under such general Directions as my Design must necessarily confine me to, and can therefore receive here no particular Consideration. It is, in my Opinion, that it is here as in the great *Venereal* Cases, where, if the *Grand Remedy* be sufficiently and duly pursued, there will be little or no need of Application to particular and *Topical* Complaints, which will drop off, and evanish, of themselves, as striking at, and cutting the Root of a Tree, will render the lopping of the Branches useless. In all *Chronical*, *Cachectical*, and obstinate Cases, I can allow of, and could never learn or discover, but *two* universal, certain, and natural *Antidotes*, *Remedies*, or *Methods of Cure*, viz. the ponderous and Mineral Medicines (the chief of which are *Mercury*, *Antimony*, and *Steel*, with Evacuations) and *Diet* and *Regimen* (the secondary Assistants of which are *Air* and *Exercise*) and both skilfully joined together, and duly persisted in, is the highest Pitch *Art* can, in my Judgment, arise to, under the present Laws of Nature, and of the *Animal Oeconomy*: the Application, tho' to particular Cases and Constitutions, will require the Skill, Address, and Attention of the most knowing and experienced Physician.

CHAP.

CHAP. VIII.

Of the Spleen, Vapours, Lowness of Spirits, Hysterical, or Hypochondriacal Disorders.

§. I. THE Title of this Chapter is so large a Field, that it would require a *Volume* of itself, to detail every thing that may be said, even with Advantage to the suffering Patient on this Head. But my Design is not to instruct the Patient in every Particular, but to give a general *Scheme* of *Nervous* Disorders, founded upon Reason, Philosophy, and Experience; and it being both absurd and even impossible for any one to undertake so *obstinate*, so *various*, and so *deplorable* a Distemper, of his own Head in its eminent Degrees, without the Assistance of a judicious, experienced, and honest *Physician:* All the Reader, who is not such, will be able to learn from hence, is, whether he is treated in the Manner, that such an one will always deal with his Patients. So that having said so much and so fully in the general Doctrine of *Nervous* Distempers, I shall have little further to add, but some Limitations and Conditions with regard to particular Cases, which I must suppose applicable only to such individual Cases by the *Physician* in ordinary.

§. II. All the Symptoms and Disorders of a *splenetick* Person will naturally and readily be deduced from too thick and glewy or sharp Juices, some great Bowel spoil'd, or strong Obstructions form'd, and the regorging Fluids thereby brought on, struggling and labouring under the *Animal Functions*, in relaxed feeble, and unelastick Solids. Perfect Health, free Spirits, Ease, and Chearfulness consist in the easy, pleasant and uniform Performance of the *Animal Functions*, in a full *Circulation*, free *Perspiration*, and *regular Secretions*. When by the mentioned Circumstances, all these become forced, labour'd, and uneasy,

easy, the Symptoms we commonly ascribe to the *Spleen*, must necessarily arise: even tho' they be attended with no really form'd Disease, or no noble Organ entirely spoil'd; and the true Reason of the Multiplicity, Variety, and Inconstancy of these Symptoms, is the vast Multitude of the Combinations possible, of these natural Functions, every one of which makes a new *Symptom*, and whose uniform, equable Performance is so necessary to Health.

§. III. The *Spleen* or *Vapours*, as the Word is used in *England*, is of so general and loose a Signification, that it is a common Subterfuge for meer Ignorance of the Nature of Distempers. All *Lowness of Spirits, Swelling of the Stomach, frequent Eructation, Noise in the Bowels or Ears, frequent Yawning, Inappetency, Restlesness, Inquietude, Fidgeting, Anxiety, Peevishness, Discontent, Melancholy, Grief, Vexation, Ill-Humour, Inconstancy, lethargick* or *watchful Disorders,* in short, every Symptom, not already classed under some particular limited Distemper, is called by the general Name of *Spleen* and *Vapours*: of which there are various and different Symptoms, according to the different Constitutions, Tempers of Mind, and common Diseases, Persons subject to such Symptoms labour under. In general, *Vapours* (as it is a Distemper subject to the Rules of *Art*) are bad, sharp, thick, and viscid Juices, attended with weak and relaxed *Nerves, Fibres,* or *Solids*: Where-ever these mentioned Symptoms are, in any eminent Degree, these *Conditions* must be. And on the other Hand, where-ever these *Conditions* are, some more or fewer of these mentioned Symptoms must be, according to the Degree of these Conditions. *Vapours* therefore are either *original* and simple, or not attended with any other real Disease or Malady, as yet apparent (except the Conditions or Causes mentioned) or *Symptomatick*, being caused or produced by some other real determined Distemper, which is attended with,

with, or produces those mentioned Conditions, of which Distemper this Kind of *Vapours* is only a *Symptom* or Effect, and in which they always terminate in their last Stage or Degree. From whence it is pretty evident, that this last Kind of Vapours can never be cured, unless the original Distemper, on which they depend, be cured, when it is become manifest. It is well known, that every bodily Distemper is attended with, or produces Lowness of Spirits, and some others of the *Symptoms* I have mentioned. When the Distemper is removed, these Symptoms gradually vanish, and *Health* and *Freedom of Spirits* return: So that my present Affair is not with these *Symptomatick Vapours*, unless they subsist too long after the original Distemper is removed, and then they are to be treated in the same manner with these genuine, simple, and original *Vapours*, whereof I am treating.

§. IV. To enumerate all the almost infinite Symptoms, Degrees, and Kinds of *Vapours* is impossible, and perhaps very little to the Purpose. In general, when the Symptoms are *many, various*, changeable, shifting from one Place to another, and imitating the *Symptoms* of almost every other Distemper described, if they are attended with no other apparent, real, determined original Distemper (though they be generally the Beginnings of a real Distemper, and, if neglected, terminating in one always.) Then they may be properly called *Vapours*; for Distinction's Sake, I will divide them into three Degrees, though the Reader is neither here to expect Accuracy nor Certainty, that may be depended upon, in such a *Proteus-like* Distemper, because some of the Symptoms of what I call the *second Degree*, may happen in the *first*, and so on the contrary; and though in general they grow and rise in their *Degrees*, as naturally and gradually as Plants or Vegetables do, yet we are not possessed of proper Names and Measures for these Degrees, any more than we are of the Degrees of Heat that cause Flame or Light, it being for Brevity's Sake that I chiefly make the Distinction.

§. V. The *first Degree*, which ought only to be called *Vapours* (if that Name be proper at all) is when the Cause and Disorder is chiefly confined to the *Stomach* and *Bowels*, or the *Alimentary Ducts*, and the Blood and Juices are in a pretty tolerable Condition, but the Solids somewhat relaxed, loose, and flabby: the *Alimentary Tubes* being the first sensible Sufferers in all bodily Maladies whatsoever. The Symptoms then, besides Lowness of Spirits, are *Wind, Belching, Yawning, Heart-burning, Croaking of the Bowels*, (like the Noise of *Frogs*) a *Pain* in the *Pit of the Stomach* (which is sometimes mistaken for a Lung Case, especially if attended with *Shortness of Breath*, and a tickling Cough, from a Wind in the Cavity pressing on the Diaphragm, and thereby pressing on the *Lungs*, which is common, and goes very justly by the Name of an *Hysterick*, or *Nervous* Cough) and sometimes there is an *Inflation*, and an actual visible Swelling, to a very considerable Bigness, in the Stomach to be seen, especially in the *Sex*; a *Coldness* or *Chilliness* upon the Extremities, and sometimes Flushing (especially after a full Meal) and Burning in the Hands and Feet, *Cold damp Sweats, Faintings*, and *Sickness* (especially before a Solution of the Bowels) the Stools being sometimes very *costive*, sometimes *loose* and slimy, a *Feeling* like that of *cold Water* poured over several Parts of the Body, *Head-Aches* either behind or over the Eyes, like a *Puncturation, Flies* and *Atoms* dancing before the Eyes, a *Noise* like the *dying* Sounds of Bells, or a Fall of Water, in the Ears; *Yawning*, and *Stretching*, and sometimes a Drowsiness or *Lethargy*, at other times *Watching* and Restlessness, and several other *Symptoms*, which it is impossible to enumerate. Some have but a few of these *Symptoms*, and some all of them, and a great many more; but a Tendency

dency to *Spitting*, *Ptyalism*, or a Discharge of Phlegm from the Glands of the Throat, seldom fails to attend all the *Symptoms* of it, especially towards the Decline of the *Fit*, if it is not shut up by a high Diet, hot Liquors, some constant Drams, or too great Exercise, (which, by the bye, shews the *Alimentary Tubes*, and their numerous Glands, the Weakness of the Digestion, or unnatural cramming, at least, relative or in Proportion to the Want or Weakness of the Patient, to be the true Seat and Cause of the present Symptoms). I have also observed, both in my self and most of my Patients, one tolerable good Day, and another worse, almost constantly following one another regularly: which suggested a Reason to me, of the great Benefit of the *Bark* in *Nervous* Distempers : *Nature* being uniform in her Productions, and taking, as it were, a regular and equal Time to fill, and discharge the turgid and inflated Cavities and Glands, which is the general Cause of all *Periods* in Diseases. I have also observed something like monthly Periods, especially towards the *Conjunctions* of the *Sun* and *Moon*. Those of the great Seasons, to wit, *Spring* and *Fall*, the *well* Half of the Year, from Midsummer to Midwinter, and *bad* Half from Midwinter to Midsummer, are more certain and regular, especially if they are not joined with other *Chronical* Distempers, which alter their *Periods*; but in this various and inconstant Climate, *Periods* and *Crises* are so uncertain and irregular, that we have nothing but *Miniatures* and *Models* of them, to what they were observ'd in *Eastern* Climates, and orderly People. I only suggest these Things to awaken the Attention of others, and shew the Uniformity of Nature in all Things.

§. VI. The *second* Stage of this Distemper is attended with all these Symptoms, in a much higher and more eminent Degree, and some new ones, which were not felt, and consequently not described under

under the *first* Stage: such as are instead of Lowness of Spirits: a deep and fixed *Melancholy*, *wandering and delusory Images* on the Brain, and *Instability* and *Unsettledness* in all the intellectual Operations, *Loss of Memory*, *Despondency*, *Horror* and *Despair*, a *Vertigo*, *Giddiness* or *Staggering*, *Vomitings* of *Yellow*, *Green*, or *Black Choler*: sometimes unaccountable Fits of *Laughing*, apparent *Joy*, *Leaping* and *dancing*; at other Times, of *Crying*, *Grief* and *Anguish*; and these generally terminate in *Hypochondriacal* or *Hysterical Fits* (I mean *Convulsive* ones) and *Faintings*, which leave a Drowsiness, *Lethargy*, and extream Lowness of Spirits for some Time afterwards. Perhaps the *Fits* return often, if they be weak and partial ones; or if they are strong and severe, their Intervals are longer: The State of the Blood is generally viscid (if the Symptoms are not occasion'd by Accident, or spoil'd Bowels) with all the Consequences which I remark'd when I spoke of what I called the second State of that Fluid. I think this *second* Degree of *Vapours* may always be denominated from *Fits*, *Convulsions*, or violent *Paroxysms* of the Kind mentioned: and from the antecedent or subsequent *bilious* Vomitings that attend such; and indeed when they are come to this Degree, there is generally a beginning Obstruction, or spoiling of some of the great Bowels, such as the *Liver*, the *Lungs*, the *Kidneys*, the *Mesentery*, the *Cawl*, the *Spleen*, or some other Part necessary towards the Animal Functions, attending them; and so a real Distemper immediately follows: of which, the *first* Degree I have mentioned is the *first* Step, this last is the *second*: and if not cured in either of these two, by the struggling and Efforts of Nature, joined with *Art*; the *third* State begins, which is generally some *mortal* and incurable Distemper, such as *Dropsy*, *Black Jaundice*, *Consumption*, *Palsy*, *Epilepsy*, or *Apoplexy*, &c. To make which more plain, let us consider the Tendency

dency of Nature in its whole Progress, with this View.

§. VII. When, by *Food* of *ill* Qualities, or an immoderate Quantity of even wholsome *Food*, the *Humours* are vitiated, the Structure of the *Animal Machine* is such, that Nature (*i.e.* the *Mechanism of the Body*) is presently rouz'd to struggle with all its Might, to attenuate (or concoct, as we commonly say) the gross and vitious Humours, and so bring them to an healthy State (*i. e.* one agreeable to Nature) and drive out, by the most proper *Outlets* of the Body, what cannot be reduc'd to that State. This *Struggle* is the one only proper and real Disease of the Body, arising from the Habit (for I say nothing of those from external Injuries) the vast Variety of particular Diseases, spoken of by *Physicians*, being only so many particular or various *Issues* of this general Struggle of Nature. The State of the *Fibres* or *Solids* of the Body in Strength and Firmness, at the Beginning, is the Foundation of the grand Division of Diseases into *acute* and *chronical*: But, Strength being a relative Thing, it is impossible to settle precisely the Bounds of these two *Classes*. When the Conflict it self is very *hot, brisk* and *eager*, we all agree to call it a *Fever*; when it is slow and languid, I know no receiv'd Name for it, but the Name of *Vapours*, or *Nervous Disorders*, (a Word us'd in a very indistinct Manner, being ascrib'd to all or each of the Appearances that arise in the Progress of this slower Conflict). It were not amiss to restrain the undetermin'd Meaning of this *Word*, to signify all the Disorders of Nature under the Conflict of the Disease when the Solids are weak, as the Name of *Fever* is appropriated to all the *Symptoms* that appear during the Conflict, in a strong State of the *Solids*. This suppos'd, let us next consider the several Events of this *Conflict*, which must be either an intire, or a partial Victory of Nature, or a partial or total Prevalency of the Disease.

Difeafe. The Events are call'd *Crifes*, or Solutions of the Difeafe, by *Phyficians*. The *firft* Sort is *Health*, the laft *Death*, the middle ones are called *Difeafes*; of which again there are many Divifions very different from the two *primary* ones, to wit, *Vapours* and a *Fever*. For 1*ft*, it is very common for Nature to get an intire Conqueft over the Difeafe in a few Days, when the Solids are ftrong, that is, for the *Fever* to end by a *Critical* Difcharge, fuch as *Sweating*, a *Diurfis*, or *Diarrhœa*, and the like; fo that there remains nothing but to recruit the Solids weaken'd in the Struggle. 2*dly*, At other Times when the *Fibres* are tolerably firm, tho' Nature carries on the Conflict with Vigour at firft, to make a quick End, yet it is fometimes oblig'd to compound with the Difeafe, by giving up a *Poft* which was not tenable, that is, to throw the Difeafe upon fome particular *Organ*, and so the *Fever* terminates in a critical *Abfcefs*, &c. 3*dly*, When the Solids are so weak, that Nature carries on the Struggle but faintly for a long Time, without tending to either of thefe two mention'd *Crifes*, and the morbid Matter, thro' the Feeblenefs of the Conflict, is never sufficiently broken and divided, or fitted to be carried out of the Habit, by either of the two mention'd Ways, the Difeafe ends in an univerfal Weaknefs and Feeblenefs of Nature, a general *Cachexy*, or a continued bad State of the Juices and relax'd Solids, if not in *Death* it felf; and this gives ground for the Diftinction between *Nervous* and *Acute Fevers*. But *laftly*, if the Solids are so weak, and the Fluids so bad, that the Struggle is but very faint, imperfect, or scarce difcernable, at leaft compared with the former, the firft Attempts and Beginnings of this Struggle produce thofe Symptoms, which are properly call'd *Vapours* of the firft Kind: And if proper Means or Remedies be not ufed in due Time, they may grow higher and ftronger, with many additional Symptoms of the fame Kind.

§. VIII.

Of the Cure of Vapours, &c. 141

§. VIII. From this Deduction, it is evident, that *Vapours* are the *first* Symptoms of a real chronical Disease, which, if neglected, will terminate in spoiling some of the great Bowels, and so in putting a Period to Animal Life. Some may be born with such a Constitution; but if by no Mismanagement they increase or exasperate these *Symptoms,* Nature may thus go on to its common Period, as well as an Animal may with a broken or wasted Limb: But neglecting the Means, or fuelling the Disease by a *Mal-regimen,* it will certainly terminate sooner or later in those real Distempers, which have Names and Determinations, such as a *Dropsy, Asthma,* or *Consumption,* and so may be attended with the Symptoms that these mortal Distempers are describ'd by, and at last end in *Death.* So that it is needless to enumerate the *Symptoms* of this *Stage,* they being commonly known and described by the *Physicians,* that treat of such mortal Distempers, for being irremediable, as they are in *this* Stage; they admit of nothing but a *palliative* Cure, to make the Symptoms easy; which how it is to be done, I shall shew in the next *Chapter.*

CHAP. IX.

Of the Cure of the Symptoms of Vapours, Hysterical and Hypochondriacal Disorders.

§. I. WHAT I have formerly said about the general Cure of *Nervous* Distempers by a *Regimen of Diet, Exercise,* and the three Classes of Medicines mentioned, is not only the solid Foundation of a substantial and lasting Cure, but is also the most effectual Means for weakening the Symptoms, and making their Intervals longer, and without which all the other Attempts for that Purpose will be ineffectual, at least procure only temporary Relief,

lief, since these Symptoms will return more frequently, and with greater Violence, as the State of the Fluids and Solids grow worse, which they must necessarily do, under a Neglect of these Means, alone sufficient to establish a solid and perfect Cure. So that they would effectually relieve or lessen the Symptoms of *Nervous* Disorders, have nothing more to do, but to accommodate these general Directions to particular Constitutions and Circumstances. But because, while this general Cure is going forward, the Symptoms may be so *dispiriting* and *painful*, that Life becomes an useless Burthen, it is absolutely necessary by all Means possible, to gain a *Reprieve*, from these Symptoms, if not for a long Time, at least for as long a Time as can be, to give Room for these universal Means to operate.

§. II. I know not in Nature a more universal and effectual Remedy for most, if not all the Symptoms of these Disorders when they rise to any high Degree, than gentle *Vomits* suited to the Strength and Constitution of the Patient, not only as they discharge the *Choler*, or *Bile*, and *Phlegm* from the *Liver* and *Alimentary Ducts*, but as by their *Successions* and Action, they open the Obstructions of that vast Number of *Glands* situated in the inner Side of these Ducts, (which too are either the Cause of, or certainly attend most of the violent *Nervous* Symptoms) and promote the Circulation and Perspiration. These *Vomits*, in weak Persons, may be effected by a Decoction or Tea of *Carduus*, *Chamomile Flowers*, *Horse Radish*, or any bitter or acrid Plant; or by *Ipecacuanha* or its Tincture alone; but in the stronger Constitutions nothing is to be depended on without joining some Preparation of Antimony. I never found either in my own Case, or my Practice on others, that I could so quickly and effectually relieve either violent Paroxysms of *Nervous* Distempers, or the other sinking Symptoms attending them, as by such an Evacuation; and I have been

always

Of the Cure of Vapours, &c. 143

always forc'd to repeat it as often as thefe Symptoms return'd, till the Diftemper was quite overcome. I have extremely reliev'd fome, and have totally cur'd others by every Morning drinking large Draughts of *Chamomile* Flower Tea, to throw off the Phlegm, and then drinking *Bath* Waters after the Stomach was fettled, and purfuing a *Regimen* and *Exercife* in the Day-time. Thofe who are young and ftrong, and to whom thefe Symptoms are not become habitual, and whofe Conftitution is yet found, and not loaded with grofs Humours, may fometimes get them off at a leffer Expence, as by frequent Dofes of *Hiera Picra*, *Tincture* of *Rhubarb*, the *Ruffi* or the *Stomach* Pills, but chiefly the *Pilul. Gummos cum Aloe-lota*, in equal Quantities, frequently, if not every Night, repeated, or as Occafion requires. I have never found any great Relief from Blifters, Iffues, or even Bleeding it felf, in this Cafe, unlefs it was in very full Habits, or when premis'd to a general Courfe for the Cure, becaufe the *Cachexy* was univerfal; much lefs is any thing to be expected from lying a-bed and fweating (a late celebrated Method in the Cure of *Vapours*) which I have always found to relax much more.

§. III. Reftleffnefs, *Inquietude* of Spirits, and Want of natural *Sleep*, is one of the moft troublefome and difpiriting Symptoms attending this Diftemper. When it is extreme, nothing is to be done without *Laudanum* or *Opiates*, but thefe ought always to be blended with fome fmall Proportion of the *Volatile* and *Aromatick* Medicines, which increafe their benign, and poffibly may hinder their deftructive Effects, if they have any, however Recourfe is never to be had to them, but in extreme Cafes, and when other Things will not do, becaufe of their *deleterious* Effects on the Solids, which very poffibly they may relax more and more. There are fome with whom doubtlefly *Opiates* agree much better than others; and they are fuch, I think, whofe Solids

lids are yet pretty firm, and where the Fluids are most in Fault, or some of the great Bowels only weakened. There are others, to whom they give a little *dôsing* or dead Sleep, yet when their Force is worn off, they leave a *Lowness*, *Dispiritedness*, and *Anxiety*, that even over-ballances the Relief or Quiet they bring; and they are those who are entirely *Cachectick*, as well as subject to *Nervous* Disorders, such I should perswade to use *Assa-fœtida* in Pills, Morning and Night, or the *Gum Pills* of the *London* or *Edinburgh* Dispensatory, (both which are excellent Medicines for this Purpose) they having often all the good Effects of *Opium*, without the bad ones, though both are but temporary *Reliefs* and not *Cures*: and whose Virtues will be worn out by long Use, and therefore ought to be continued no longer than absolute Necessity requires, and not repeated upon too slight Occasions, for both *Opiates* and *Volatiles* or *Fœtids* are of the Nature of *Drams* and *Cordials*; and Exercise will procure Sleep better than either of these Medicines, no *Opiate* being like that of the *Day-Labourers*.

§. III. Meer Lowness and Dispiritedness, not attended with Sickness or Pain, arises from the Want of a brisk *Circulation* and *Perspiration*. These will always be promoted by *volatile Spirits*, an *Aromatick Cordial*, and generous Wines, or any thing that will *stimulate*, *rouze*, and *spur* the dead and languishing Solids, to push forwards the sluggish *Circulation* and *Perspiration*; but the Force of these Remedies, like all other Helps and Reliefs of this Nature, is soon spent and worn out; and they will often leave the same Effects with *Opiates*, the Nature of which they partake: and therefore, nothing is to be expected from them, but as a present *Relief* in Extremities, nor are they to be used but then only. The most solid and lasting Relief I ever found, for Lowness of Spirits, comes from the astringent Class of Medicines, *Steel*, *Bark*, *Japan Earth*, &c. with *Mineral* and

Cha-

Of the Cure of Vapours, &c.

Chalybeat Waters, the *Bath* especially in the temperate and cold Seasons, and the *cold Steel Waters*, as *Spaw*, *Pyrmont*, or *Tunbridge*, in the hot Weather; but where none of these Waters can be had, from the Necessity of the Patient's Circumstances, *Steel Rust* with the *Extract* or *Powder* of the *Quinquina*, *Pulvis ad Guttetam*, *&c.* joined with Aromaticks, such as the *Species Diambræ*, and wash'd down with an agreeable Bitter, fitted to the Patient's Strength and Constitution: *Elixir of Vitriol*, or *Tincture of Steel*, with *Elixir Proprietatis* in common Water; these will in a great measure supply the Want of *Mineral Waters*, and give a due *Reprieve*, to carry on the Cure, which is only to be attained by the general Methods already described, without which nothing effectual is to be done, nor the Return of these Disorders prevented; and indeed the *Paroxysms* of this Distemper, when deep rooted, are so many or so frequent, and the general Methods require so long Time, that all these Medicines, and *Mineral Waters* also, will be wanted in their Turns.

§. IV. One of the most *dispiriting* Symptoms of this Distemper, and one of the most certain Signs of it, is a frequent Discharge of thin, limpid, pale Water, by *Urine:* which, when in great Quantities, and frequently discharged, does so sink and dispirit the poor Patient, that Life is insupportable, at least, if he is not otherwise strong and hearty. Some, to explain this Appearance, have run into I don't know what *Fusion* of the Blood, and *Relaxation* of the Glands of the *Kidneys*. But having now done with *Theory*, I shall say nothing directly to confute this absurd *Hypothesis*, it being, I think, pretty evident, and confirmed by many Experiments, especially those of *Sanctorius* and Dr. *Kiel*, that it is principally owing to a partial or total Obstruction of the *Perspiration*, which is so common in this Case, from the Weakness of the *Nerves* and *Solids:* and that consequently nothing else can possibly cure its returning Fits, or remove it, but what makes the *Perspiration* good: and accordingly this Symptom is always relieved by those of the *warm, cordial,* and *diaphoretick* Kind, such as *Gascoign Powder, Species Diambræ, Aromaticum Cariophyllatum, Confectio Alkermes, Diascordium, Venice Treacle, Sir Walter Raleigh's Cordial,* and the like, or by a Combination of these, with *Volatiles* and *fœtid Gums,* and appropriated *Juleps*; these Medicines however ought not to be given, so as to raise an actual *Diaphoresis* or Sweating, for that will be to carry on the Expence, Lowness, and Sinking by other Conduits: but only to procure a little Breathing or freer *Perspiration,* and to divide the Evacuation more equally through the whole Habit.

§. V. As to the *Spitting* or *Salivation,* so common in *Nervous* Distempers (especially of a *Scorbutick* Origin, as is commonly said) and cold Diseases, though it generally arises from the same Causes, and may be relieved by the same Medicines, as the Symptom last mentioned, yet since it is generally a critical Discharge, or follows some Excess in the Diet or Nourishment, it ought never to be stopped at first by astringent or warm Medicines, no more than a critical *Diarrhœa,* but ought rather to be promoted and encouraged by some gentle *Masticatory* (such as *Mastick, Pellitory, Tobacco,* or the like) as the Patient can bear it, or has been accustomed. If it is exceeding plentiful, with Sickness, Reaching, and Head-aches, nothing will carry it off so effectually as a gentle *Vomit,* both as this will promote the Discharge, and quicken the *Circulation* and *Perspiration*: or by gentle Stomach Purges, that may be frequently repeated, such as *Rhubarb,* the *Stomach Pills,* and the like. And thus after this Discharge has been sufficiently carried off, the Solids may be strengthened with Astringents, Bitters, or an Infusion of the *Bark,* with *Aromaticks,* especially if made on Lime

Water;

Water; and after that, a Course of *Chalybeats* and *Aromaticks*, such as I have mentioned in the former *Section*, with Mineral Waters of one Kind or another.

§. VI. There are some other Symptoms exceedingly troublesome in *Vapours* or *Nervous* Distempers, to wit, *Choaking* and *Gulping*, the *Symptomatick Asthma*, *Swelling of the Throat and Stomach, Inflation of the Bowels with Rumbling and Noise*. The *Young* are not so much troubled with these Symptoms as the Old and Declining, but they all proceed from one Cause, to wit, the Weakness and Obstruction of the *Perspiration* from the Imperfection of the *Digestions*, whereby the insensible Steams and Vapours, which ought to pass through the Skin freely, are thrown back into the Cavities of the Body, and where high and strong Foods are used, these Steams acquire such an *Acrimony* and Stimulation, as to produce several other more violent Symptoms. The Cure of these is the same with that of the already mentioned Symptoms, to wit, gentle and repeated *Vomits* and Stomach *Purges*, especially of the *Aloetick* Kind, (which in *Nervous* Cases are by far preferable to all other Purgatives, because of their active astringent Bitter) *Aromaticks*, *Bitters*, warm *cordial* Medicines, *Astringents*, and whatever else will carry off the offending Matter, forward the Perspiration, and strengthen the *Digestion* and *Solids*.

§. VII. There is a transient Spice of *Vapours*, which very commonly seizes even young and temperate Persons, otherwise strong and healthy, of pretty sound Juices and firm Solids, which affects with a Disgust of every thing that used to please or amuse them, a certain *Tediousness of Life*, a *Lowness of Spirits*, *Restlessness*, *Heaviness* and *Anxiety*, an Aversion to *Exercise*, either of the Mind or Body, and sometimes with a violent *Head ach*, and Dimness of Sight, which Symptoms, as they will come on unaccountably, without any imaginable or discoverable Cause, so they will go off as unaccountably, in some short Time, without any Medicine or Means used for their Cure: though in Strictness of Reasoning, they have a real material Cause, either from catching of Cold, and thereby stopping the Perspiration suddenly, from the Moisture of the Weather, relaxing the Solids, or from some Intemperance or Excess that they had not heeded, or were not aware of, or from taking some Food too hard for their digestive Powers. The common and ordinary Way of treating such *transitory Symptoms*, is, the eating next Meal some salt, savoury, and relishing Delicacy, and drinking a good large Dose of some scarce, active, generous, and spirituous Liquor, that may briskly rouze and stimulate the sluggish and unactive Solids, and rarefy, warm, and enliven the heavy and dull Fluids, (or, as the Expression is, to give Nature a *Fillip*) to quicken the Circulation, forward the Perspiration, and carry on all the necessary Secretions in their due Degree and Order. The Fact and Experiment is undeniable, (and has been too often tried and repeated, to admit of a Doubt) and I think the Reason of the Success is pretty plain from what has been said, and, I am afraid, has given Occasion to some *unphilosophical* and unexperienced Persons to advise it as a certain and never-failing Remedy, even in more frequent, deeper, and more habitual Symptoms of these Disorders: and I fear has been the Cause of the common Advice to Persons of *weak Nerves* and low Spirits, *to drink a Bottle heartily every Day*, to take frequent *Drams*, or a *Bowl of Punch*, and to the Use of *salt Sturgeon, red Herring, Anchovies, pickled Oysters, Salmon-gundy, Ham, pickled* and *potted Foods* of all Kinds, for a *Provocative*. All I shall say on this Head, is, to caution People not to use this Cure too frequently, or to expect any great Feats from it, when such Symptoms grow stronger, more frequent, or more deeply rooted in the Constitution,

ſtitution, or towards the *Decline* of Life; for tho' it may give a ſhort *temporary* Relief, and laſh the ſluggiſh and reſty Solids to perform their Functions for a ſhort Time, yet it will infallibly aggravate and increaſe their future *Symptoms*, and at laſt render them dangerous and incurable. The much ſafer, and even more infallible, tho' perhaps, leſs quick Remedy, would be to take ſome gentle *Stomach* Purge, that might not interrupt Buſineſs, and, the next Night, ſome eaſy *Diaphoretick*, a lighter Diet than ordinary, for a few Days, or uſe a greater Degree of Exerciſe, by a Journey, Hunting, and the like.

§. VIII. Theſe are the moſt material, moſt troubleſome, and oppreſſing *Symptoms* of *Vapours*. Others leſs material may be reduc'd to theſe mention'd, or are ſome Appendages of them; or, if omitted here, perhaps may be taken notice of in treating of the higher Degrees of *Nervous* Diſorders, or may be entirely neglected as inſignificant. I have ſuggeſted nothing in treating theſe, but the common and well known Medicines, not only becauſe by long Experience, I have found them the moſt effectual, but even becauſe they are common, and univerſally known and approved. For it is in *Medicines* as in *Food*, (Medicines being only a more *rare* and leſs natural Kind of Food) that which is *common* to the middling Sort of every Country, and which has the Approbation of the Generality of the Inhabitants, and is ſuited to the Conſtitution of the Community, is generally the moſt *beneficial*; ſince it is the Experience and Obſervation of the Generality that makes them common: and ſpecial or particular Things, or Rarities, are juſtly to be ſuſpected.

CHAP. X.

Of the Nervous Disorders of the Convulsive Tribe, particularly of Hysterical and Hypochondriacal Fits, and those other Paroxysms that attend Nervous Disorders.

§. I. AS most of those Disorders which are commonly called *Nervous*, *Hysterical*, or *Hypochondriacal*, are attended with some *Convulsive* Motions, *Fits*, or *Paroxysms*, especially when they arrive to their higher and more eminent Degrees, and to the *second* Stage of *Vapours*, which I have denominated or distinguished by these Symptoms chiefly: I shall here treat of these Disorders in general, shewing the Nature of all *Convulsions*, but particularly those incident to such Constitutions, and attending these Distempers that I am principally treating of, and laying down the proper and peculiar Method of Cure, for each Kind or Degree.

§. II. It is well known, that whatever will prick, wound, tear, or violently stimulate the Solids, will thereby produce *Spasms*, *Convulsions*, and violent *Contractions*, first and chiefly in the Part affected: which, by Consent, and the *Mechanism* of the Parts, may be communicated further and further over the whole *Machine*; and, when vehement and continu'd, may be propagated through all the *Limbs*, *Muscles*, *Tendons* and *Membranes* of the Body, and this where-ever the Wound, or whatever Part of the Solids the Puncture or Stimulation happens to be made in; but most readily where there is the greatest Collection of *Nerves*. This is evident from the Effects of a Fall, a Blow, a Bruise, the Puncture of a *Lancet*, a *Thorn*, a *Pin*, a *Nail*, or any other wounding Instrument, or from sharp and corroding Steams, Humours, or Matter (which are as it were a Collection of small Pins, Needles, Lancets, *&c.*)

upon

upon any of the more sensible Solids. I have before shew'd, that there is in all Animal *Fibres* an innate Power of Contraction, or an original *Mechanism* of *Elasticity* or *Spring*, by which they exert a natural Power of Contraction, however they are stimulated or solicited thereto, whether by the Command of the Will, (beginning the Motion by an inexplicable Effort) or self-motive Power; or by the Action of some material appropriated Agent on them, and this in every *Muscular* as well as *Nervous Fibre* of the Body. I have seen a *fistulous Tube*, of a very considerable Length, holding some Quarts of *Pus* or *Matter*, opening only towards the Middle of the Back, and passing down from thence between the Interstices of the *Muscles*, to the Thigh; which when the Matter contain'd in it, was arriv'd to its full Degree of *Quantity* and *Acrimony*, so as to produce a *Symptomatick* Fever; the Solids of the whole Machine, but particularly those near the *fistulous Canal*, were stimulated and put in Action, so that it threw out that vast Quantity of its Contents, upwards and against the Force of their own Gravity; though such a *Canal* was not made naturally, or with the greatest Advantage for such an Action: From whence it is evident, that every Point and Particle of the *Solids* is *elastick*, and acts for the Relief of the *Whole*.

§. III. This being premised, it is evident, that any acrid, sharp, or corroding Juice, *Vapour*, or *Steam* that will stimulate and vellicate the *Fibres* wherever placed, may occasion *Convulsions, Spasms, Gripes* or Pains on that Part first and chiefly, and may be communicated (according to its Force and Strength) by Contact and Consent, to all the adjacent Parts, and even through the whole Habit, continuing till the offending Matter is by such violent Action or Motion worked off, or removed: in the same Manner as the *Fœtus*, by its Motion or Pressure, raises those *Throws* and *Convulsions* in the Mother, that bring it into the World; or as the Stone or Gravel, stimulating the *Kidneys* or *Ureters*, raises those Vomitings and Reachings that promote its Exclusion. Thus *Choler, Wind, sharp* and *porracious* Juices, occasion those *Fits* and *Convulsions* in the Bowels, (like *Verjuice, Vitriol,* or *Poison* swallow'd down) being the Struggle of Nature to throw them out, which are commonly call'd *Hysterick Fits*; and thus any *irritating, acrid,* or *sharp* Humour or Steam, according to the Place wherein they are lodged, or the Sensibility of the Part affected, occasions all the various and different Degrees or Kinds of * *Convulsions* that are common in *Nervous* Disorders.

§. IV. As to *Childrens Convulsions*, if they proceed from the shooting the Teeth, whereby the *Gums* and their *Membranes* are distended, torn, and lacerated, they are easily cured by *Incision*; but if they arise from sharp Juices in the Stomach or Bowels, (as they most commonly do) and the Child is about the first Year of its Age, they may be cur'd by a *Blister* between the Shoulders; gentle *Rhubarb* Purges, frequently repeated; and the *Testaceous Powders* taken two or three times a day in a little black Cherry Water or Breast Milk, but especially by *Cinnabar* in Powders, with the *testaceous* Powders and *Rhubarb* interchangeably: Sometimes a few Drops of *Spirit* of *Hartshorn,* or *Goddards Drops,* taken two or three times a day in common Water, if the Constitution, Juices, and Solids are pretty sound, will do the Business. But if their *Fits* be stronger, and they further advanc'd in Life, they must be overcome by gentle *Vomits* fitted to their Age and Strength. *Cinnabar of Antimony,* with the *Pulvis ad Guttetam,* and these *Rhubarb* Purges, interchangeably us'd, as has been said. But it is to be observ'd during the whole Course, that if the

---

* Vide Boneti Sepulchret. Anatomii Lib. I. Sect. 12, 13.

Of Convulsive Disorders, &c.

Child is on the Breast, it ought to be fed with nothing but its *Nurse's Milk*, or, if wean'd, with nothing but thin *Pap*, at least till it has gone over its *Teething*; and, to give a due Force and Strength afterwards, the *Quinquina* ought to be us'd either in *Extract* or *Decoction*, especially after it has acquir'd some Years. This Method will not only cure their *Fits*, but their *Rickets* likewise, both proceeding from the same Cause, to wit, *acrid Humours* lodged in the Stomach or Bowels, or some other Part of the Body, and a *Relaxation* of the Solids.

§. V. If such *Convulsions* happen to the younger Part of the Sex about a certain Time of their Lives (as they often do) then they generally proceed from some Disorder in that great Affair, which ought, if possible, to be set to Rights. But since, before that can be any ways executed, there generally happens a great Quantity of *Choler*, either generated through the Defect of that Evacuation, or in whatever other Manner: or from whatever Cause: this is by all possible Means to be first remov'd; which is only or most readily and effectually to be performed by frequent *Vomits* fitted to the Strength of the Patient, and of the Disease. While that is doing, the *volatile active Gums*, with the *volatile alcaline Salts*, are to be combin'd with *Cinnabar* of Antimony in some Form or other. This Method is to be carried on till the Fits are weakened, the Quantity of the *Bile* lessen'd, and the *primæ Viæ* pretty clear; and then, and not till then, will proper *Emmenagogues*, with *Steel, Chalybeat Mineral Waters, Bitters*, and *Aromaticks* take Place. In the Fits themselves there is little to be done but by *Volatiles* and *Opiates*, in appropriated *Juleps* to lessen their Violence, and to quiet their *Spasms*; but by a steady Continuance in this Method, and a proper *Regimen of Diet*, I scarce ever saw the Patient miscarry.

§. VI.

§. VI. As to the *Fits* of grown Perſons, *Hyſterical* or *Hypochondriacal*, though they proceed generally from the general Cauſes mention'd, and are to be treated much after the ſame Manner, yet they are infinitely more obſtinate and difficult to be remov'd: the Habit of Body being more deprav'd, and the Diſeaſes more rooted and confirm'd, thro' a long Train of *Miſmanagement*, and Neglect of the Means by which Health is to be preſerv'd; and in the higher Degrees of theſe, there are commonly ſome one or other of the great Bowels (as the *Liver* and its Appendages, the *Meſentery*, the *Cawl*, the *Spleen* or the *Stomach*) if not quite ſpoil'd, yet much weaken'd and obſtructed, and all the *Glands* ſtuff'd and render'd uſeleſs. To leſſen the Violence of the *Fits*, at leaſt in the firſt Inſtance, all the great Evacuations are to be attempted, eſpecially *Bleeding*, *Vomiting*, *Bliſters*, *Glyſters*, and the like; and then the *Spaſms* and *Convulſions* are to be quieted by *Opiates*, with warm and *volatile* Medicines and *Fœtid Gums*, according to the Strength of the Patient and the Neceſſity of the Diſeaſe. If theſe Evacuations cannot be conveniently made, or do not ſoon enough take Effect, there is nothing elſe to be done under the *Fits*, but by theſe mention'd *Opiates*, with the *volatile Gums* and *Salts*, *Pulvis ad Guttetam*, *Aromaticks* and *Alcaline Spirits* in proper *Juleps*, till a convenient Interval be obtain'd, or the Violence of the *Convulſions* ceaſes, and then rouzing *Vomits* are to be thrown down, and after that ſharp *Glyſters* (with *Emetick* Wine, and *volatile Spirits* in them, which will check their further Return for ſome time.) This Method is to be repeated as often as theſe *Paroxyſms* return. During the Intervals *Cinnabarine Medicines*, or *Æthiops Mineral*, the *Mercurius Dulcis*, or *Alcaliſatus*, with the *volatile Gums* and *Salts*, are to be taken once or twice a Day, with *Chalybeat* Waters, and *Aromatick* Bitters, and at Night the *Gum Pills* compounded with the *volatile Salts*, the

general

general Method already laid down, being at the same time regularly pursued. Which Method and Medicines, if duly continu'd for a sufficient Time, cannot fail of Success, if any thing will succeed, and the Patient not too far advanc'd in Life, or some of the great *Organs* are not quite spoiled. But in my Judgment and Observation, the greatest Stress is to be laid (especially in gross Habits, or Symptoms produced even by *relative* Intemperance only) in the Medicinal Way upon *Vomits* often repeated, *Quinquina Bitters*, *Aloetick Purges*, and *Mineral* or *Chalybeat* Waters; which not succeeding, little is to be expected from *Art*, the other less effectual Methods being too weak for such Cases and Constitutions, and therefore they must be entirely left to the *Palliative* Remedies of warm *Opiates*, such as *Venice Treacle*, the *Philonium Romanum*, with high and strong *Cordial Juleps* and *Volatiles*, such as I have already mention'd. Those who are of thinner Habits, and whose Bowels therefore are not probably so much *stuff'd* and *obstructed*, will have a fairer Chance, and be restored with gentler Evacuations, smaller Doses of *Opiates*, *volatile*, or *cordial* Medicines, and more easily recover'd by *Diet*, *Air*, *Exercise*, *Chalybeat* and *Mineral* Waters, with *Aromatick* and *Quinquina* Bitters, and those other Things I have so often mentioned.

§. VII. As to the *Fits* attending other *Nervous* Disorders, as the *Apoplexy*, *Epilepsy*, and the like, that Part of them which is *convulsive* depending entirely on the *primary* Distemper, being the Struggle of Nature to throw off the peccant Cause, if it were possible to separate them, they were to be treated in the same Manner, and by the same Medicines: But intending to say something of them in particular, I shall here pass them by, and only add, that the several *Forms*, *Doses*, and other Circumstances in using these Medicines, I have already mentioned in the proper Cases, requires the Attention of
the

the wisest and most experienced Physician, to whom these Means and Medicines may be familiar, and are never to be trusted to any one not duly and regularly instructed and educated in these Matters, much less to the Patient himself, who, let his Knowledge and even Experience be ever so great, yet under them he is not capable to judge for himself, and therefore there will be no Occasion for being more particular and circumstantial.

CHAP. XI.

Of Nervous Fevers, Cholicks, Gouts, Asthma's, Rheumatisms, and other Distempers denominated Nervous.

§. I. HAVING, I hope, solidly and justly established the Causes and Principles, on which the Differences between *Nervous* and humorous or inflammatory Disorders (as they are called) are founded, it will be no difficult Matter to apply this general Doctrine to particular Distempers, to shew wherein their true and essential Nature and Difference consists, and thereby the Solid Intention to be followed in their particular Cure. For the only real Difference lies in the Firmness or Laxity of the Solids; to wit, that these Distempers are or ought to be called *Nervous* only, when they are attended with a loose and relaxed State of the *Fibres*, which is chiefly manifested by some few or more of those Symptoms I have assigned to *Spleen* and *Vapours*. And on the contrary, that they are or ought to be deemed humourous, hot, or inflammatory, when the Solids are as yet tense and firm, the Symptoms high, and the State of the Blood inflammatory; for tho' in both Cases, the great differential Marks of the Distemper will appear, yet the Symptoms will be higher and more acute,

acute, or weaker and flower, and will be attended with some other Appearances, consequent upon the Strength or Weakness of the Constitution, tho' in both of them, the same Materials should be thrown in, to produce the Disease, which shews the true Foundation of the Distinction between the *Strictum* and *Laxum*, or the strait and loose of the antient *Methodists*, and between the *hot* and *cold* Diseases among the *Moderns*.

§. II. According to this *Plan* or *Idea*, it will be easy to determine the Nature and Constitution of a *Nervous* (or as it is sometimes called, *Malignant*) *Fever*; it generally attacking those of *originally* or *occasionally* weak Solids or Constitutions, who have formerly had some of the Symptoms and Marks which I have assigned in a former *Chapter*, to belong to weak *Nerves* or *Fibres*: The Symptoms of such a *Fever* are these following; the *Rigour* and *Chilliness*, tho' not so strong or violent at first, yet is longer, more slow and imperceptible; the *Burning Heat* afterwards is not so intense, nor the *Head-ach* and Sickness so great, nor with such frequent *Vomitings*, but rather a continued Sickishness; the *Pulse* is neither so quick, strong, or full, as in the *inflammatory* Kinds, but small, oppressed, and sometimes interrupted; the *Sleep* resembles a *Lethargick* Dosing or Dreaming, with Startings; the *Water* sometimes crude, commonly *limpid*, pale, and in great Quantity, without any great *Sediment* at first; In short, the *Fever* rather creeps in, than attacks or surprizes, and the whole Duration of the *Exordium* or first Stage, is more slow and tedious, that in acute, inflammatory, or depuratory *Fevers*, insomuch that it is sometimes six, seven, or perhaps nine Days before it comes to its *State*, by which any one may judge of the *Duration* of the whole (for the sooner a *Fever* comes to its *State*, the shorter is its *Duration*) and of its Danger, which is always greater from its Nature, and also because it is long before

Assistance

Affistance is called, or Means ufed, or the latent Enemy difcovered; In its *State* (efpecially the middle Time of that) the *Head* is ftupid, confufed, and incapable, rather than delirious; the *Tongue* is feldom *black*, till towards the very End of the *Fever*, at leaft, not *parched*, but covered with a thick, white, or brownifh Cruft, and generally moift; the *Thirft* is fo far from being intenfe, that Drink is fcarce called for, or fwallowed with Ardour; the *Breathing* difficult, with *Glutting*, *Gulping*, or *Choaking*; the *Pulfe*, tho' quick, yet fmall and threedy; the *Water* now fometimes limpid and much, fometimes *broken* and in fmall Quantities, by turns, but never with a grofs or full lateritious Sediment; the *Tendons* leaping and jumping: and Pulfations from Flatulency, like what is vulgarly called the *Life-Blood*, in feveral Parts of the Body; and during this whole *Period*, uncertain Fits of Coldnefs and Rigour, with fucceeding Glowings, and broken, coldifh, faint Sweats, and conftant *Exacerbations* towards Night, or after Sun-fet; the *Belly*, tho' perhaps it might be open, and tending towards a *Diarrhœa* at firft, becomes now quite conftipate and tumified with Flatulencies; the *Tip* of the Nofe and Ears often cold with an *Ichor*, and fometimes an Ulcer in thefe laft; a carelefs and unnatural Pofture of the Body, with fimple childifh *Gefticulations*; and, by Turns, a *lethargick* Dofing, or watching *Coma*, with ftaring Eyes, or their White turn'd outwards. This State continues, or grows worfe, from the *fifteenth* to the *twentieth*, or *thirtieth*, or fometime the *fortieth* Day, if they live fo long (as generally the Time of the *Crife* of all Fevers is as long as the *Exordium*, and the *Duration* of the *State*, is equal to that of both firft and laft Periods together). Towards the End of this *Fever*, they either fleep, as it were, into the Arms of Death, or if a *Crife* happens, it is either into a meer *Languor* and *Infenfibility*, a confirmed *Cachexy*, with deep *Nervous* Symptoms, or fettled *Melancholy*,

Of Nervous Fevers, &c.

lancholy, a *Palsy*, some *mortified* Limb, a violent lasting *Diarrhœa*; and sometimes those of the more benign Kinds terminate in *Intermittents*. This Fever (which always arises from a *Cachexy* and great Obstructions, as well as weak Solids, and which enters, in some Degree into our *Malignant Fevers* of all Kinds) has infinite Degrees and Variety, according to the original Strength of the *Fibres*, or the Time of the Patient's Life, but those I have described are the most common, and perhaps the worst Symptoms, as any one who has seen and observed them must know.

§. III. From this Description of the Disease, and what I have already said about the Symptoms of *Vapours*, it is pretty evident, what will be the principal *Intention*, and the best manner of treating it, viz. the Grinding, Breaking, and Dissolving the Cohesion, Viscidity, and Sharpness of the Fluids, and throwing them off by the safest and most patent Outlets. All the Evacuations must be gentle, except *Vomiting*, which may be repeated freely thro' all the Stages (if the Symptoms require, and Strength permit, but especially in the Beginning) and *Blistering*, which necessarily must be as extensive and universal as possible, tho' not violent, or all at once, but gradually applying one or more Blisters on different Parts, as the others dry up: As to *Bleeding*, I think it ought to be done once, and but cautiously repeated, be the Blood ever so *sizy* and *Rheumatick*, because the Vessels must be kept full, tho' not turgid, in order to preserve their *Tension*, for grinding or concocting the Morbid Matter. The much better Way is to endeavour by all the Means possible in *Art*, to thin and dilute, to remove the Obstructions, and to rouse the weak and languishing Solids into a more hearty Struggle, both by *Diet* and Medicine, to conquer the Disease. This is to be done by the *Cinnabarin*, *Antimonial*, and *Mineral* Medicines chiefly, such as *Antimony Diaphoretick*,

retick, *Bezoar*, *Mineral*, *Cinnabar*, and the like, joined with volatile and urinous Salts, such as that of *Hartshorn*, *Amber*, &c. and these again compounded with gentle *Diaphoreticks*, as *Saffron*, *Contrayerva*, *Goa Stone*, *Oriental Bezoar*, *Gascoign Powder*, or the warmer Compounds, as *Confectio Alkermes*, *Venice Treacle*, *Diascordium* without *Opium*, *Confectio Rawleiana*, *Electuarium de Sassafras*, &c. wash'd down with appropriated Juleps, and quickened with volatile Spirits, as those of *Hartshorn*, *Sal-volatile*, or *Goddard*'s Drops, for here universally Liquid Forms are to be preferred to Solid ones; and thus to try to overcome the Viscidity of the Juices, and to rouze the Sluggishness of the Solids to a brisker *Circulation* and Struggle, for which Purpose the *Diet*, at least, the Liquids are allowed commonly a little stronger and higher than in *inflammatory Fevers*; tho' I shall ever be of Opinion, where there is any Degree of quick Pulse or præternatural Heat, *Diluents* and *Coolers* are directly indicated, whether in *Fevers inflammatory* or *nervous* : and *Cordials* and high Food only as the Pulse and Spirits sink too low. I allow that if *Art* could always *prompt*, *whip*, *spur*, and *stimulate* the *Animal Oeconomy* to grind the sizy Juices by a strong and brisk Circulation, the *Fever* would be shorter, and the *Crise* more complete, and the *diluting*, *cooling* Method of Cure less necessary: But as that is both uncertain and unsafe, because none alive can ascertain the precise Degree of Strength in the Patient, nor of the Malignity in the Disease, and that the *Crise*, (if attainable) under such a Method, is almost ever with the quite Destruction of the whole *System* of the *Nerves*, the *Brain*, the *Faculties*, the *Limbs*, or the whole rational *Man* : and therefore the cool Method, tho' tedious, yet is ever without Danger, and the Recovery, when obtained (which the cool Method will always obtain at last, if the Distemper is not stronger than the Patient, as well in *Acute* as
Chronical

Chronical Cases) always complete, full and productive of strong Health after. This is all I need to say of *Nervous Fevers*, as distinguished from hot and depuratory ones. How to fetch up the Patient, if he recovers to Health and Spirits, I have shewn already.

§. IV. The *Nervous Cholick*, as distinguished from the *Bilious*, arising chiefly in such Constitutions as I have described, differs principally, if not only, from that, in the Violence and Duration of its *Paroxysms*, and there being more of the *Convulsive* or *Spasmotick* Kind in them: produced chiefly by the same Kind of acrid and sharp Juices; but as the Solids, in the *first* Case, are more sensible and irritable, a less Quantity of this irritating Matter throws them into more violent *Tumults* and *Convulsions*, which lasts sometimes two or three Days with violent *Tortures*, *Reachings*, and *Vomitings*, throwing up every thing that is taken down, till at last the Morbifick Matter being quite spent and ejected for this Time, Nature, almost overlaid and worn out, sinks down into a *lethargick* Dosing, which leaves the Patient quite feeble and dispirited. A Coldness upon the Extremities, *Yawning*, *Anxiety*, a *Nausea*, and Sickishness, are the Signs of the Approach of this Kind of *Cholick*, and such recover but slowly, and at first their Intervals are but short. I generally suspect that the *Liver* of such is beginning to be faulty, bigger and larger than ordinary, or obstructed: because of the great Quantity of *Bile* that is constantly thrown off, and the *Jaundice*, that always succeeds it for some Days, which probably might have been occasioned by a *Mal-Regimen*, or too great a Quantity of high Food, at least, for such Constitutions: for it is well known, that Cramming and Over-feeding with higher than a natural Food, as I have said, will swell and increase the *Livers* of all Animals.

§. V. The Cure of this Distemper is almost intirely the same with that mentioned in a former *Chapter* of the Symptoms of Vapours. If the *Fits* are not prevented by frequent *Vomits*, proportioned to the Strength of the Patient, or gentle *Stomach Purges* to throw off the peccant bilious Humour, as collected, nothing can be done in the Fit, but by repeated Doses of *Opiates*, with proper *Cordials*, as often as they are thrown up, either in a solid or liquid Form: to stop and allay the *Torture* till the Fit is quite spent; and a gentle Stomach Purge, (if the Bowels can bear it without too much Irritation) with a Dose of *Laudanum* to quiet them afterwards; the Intervals are to be filled up with *Chalybeats, Aromaticks, Bitters, Mineral Waters*, a strict Regimen of Diet, and much Exercise, or a *total* * *Milk Diet*, which seldom fails to cure this Disorder, if the Patient is not too far gone in Life, or some of the great *Viscera* spoiled, and irremediably ruined, in which Case, it terminates in one of the incurable Distempers I have so often mentioned.

§. VI. As to Nervous *Gouts, Rheumatisms*, and *Asthma*'s, they being generally denominated thus from those Constitutions I have mentioned to be most subject to *Nervous* Distempers, it were a needless Repetition to say any thing of these Diseases; in general, they being to be met with in those Authors that have treated professedly of them, and what regards them specially as they are *Nervous*, being easily deduced from the general Doctrine of *Nervous* Distempers, and what has been said of the several Symptoms in particular: only in *Nervous Asthma*'s with Flegm, or perhaps, (as I have already insinuated) in *Humorous Asthma*'s, both of Persons of firm and lax Solids, Liquid Quicksilver, (or *Bellost*'s Pills made with *Gum Ammoniac*) will be found a sovereign Remedy, if discreetly managed, half an Ounce taken once or twice a Day, with a

---

* Vide Sydenham Dissert. Epist. de Affectione Hysterica.

thin,

thin, light, fluid Diet, will do more than *Ammoniacum* alone, and all the Class of the *Volatile* and *Fœtid* Medicines, to diſſolve the Flegm, aſſiſt Expectoration, and to make the Expiration and Inſpiration eaſy; whether this be done by the Weight of the *Mercury* in the Guts, opening all their *Glands* and *Valves*, but eſpecially by this *Clump* of Weight, turning the Mouths of the *Lacteals* from *circular* to *oval*, and thereby driving out all their thick *flegmy* Doſſils that obſtructed them, whereby they becoming pervious, the Steams and Particles of the Quickſilver may pervade the whole Habit, diſſolve the Viſcidity, and ſcour all the Veſſels. I ſay, however this happens, the *Fact* is undeniable, and aggreeable to innumerable Experiences, in the moſt atrocious and obſtinate Caſes of this Complaint. All that can be further ſuggeſted, without manifeſt *Tautology*, will be comprehended in theſe two Particulars, *firſt*, that in treating the particular Diſtempers of ſuch, beſides the Medicines proper and peculiar to them, which are commonly ſucceſsful or uſual in ſtrong Conſtitutions, theſe others are to be combined with them now, which I have ſuggeſted in the Cure of the Symptoms of weak *Nerves*, or, at leaſt, they are to be then uſed when the *Nervous* Symptoms have the Predominance. The *other* Thing is, that the *Doſes* of the Medicines, and the *Regimen of the Diet*, ought to be proportioned to the Weakneſs of ſuch Conſtitutions. The ſame Things are to be underſtood of all other Diſtempers, of whatever Denomination, that are called *Nervous*.

CHAP. XII.

Of the Palsy, St. Vitus's Dance, and other Paralytick Disorders.

§. I. THERE is no Disorder incident to the Inhabitants of this Island and Climate more common, of late especially, than the *Palsy,* or *Paralytick Symptoms,* nor of a more difficult Cure, when they happen to People of original or acquired weak *Nerves,* or upon the Decline of Life. A Cold, or being exposed to a sharp freezing *North-East* Wind, continuing long in an unnatural Posture, so as to stop some great Blood Vessels: hard and excessive Labour, a moist and damp Situation *Antimonial* or *Mercurial* external Steams, a *Blow* or *Contusion* upon some Parts of the Body, where there are the greatest Collections of *Nerves;* all these, I say are sufficient Causes to produce *partial* or temporary *Palsies*: but these arising chiefly from some Obstruction of the Blood Vessels, where by the Passage of that Balsamick Liquor necessary to cherish the Muscles, is intercepted, and the *Nerves,* hurt only by Accident, yield generally to Bleeding, active and ponderous Remedies of the *Mineral Kind,* to break the coagulated Blood, and open Obstructions, joined with Astringents, towards the End of the Cure, such as the *Quinquina, Oak Bark, Misletoe,* and the like; Blistering, and warm, caustic, outward Applications, as Fomentations, with a Decoction of *Mustard Seed, Horse Radish, Pellitory, Zedoary, Juniper Berries, &c.* with an Addition of *camphorated Spirit of Wine,* Active and penetrating Ointments and Epithemes, as the *Nervous Ointment,* an Ointment made with *Horse Radish,* the *Opodeldoc,* and the like, or *Friction* with the Flesh-Brush, and anointing with *Opodeldoc,* dissolved in camphorated Spirit of Wine after, or with the other warm Oils,

as

as those of *Amber, Cloves, Vitriol diluted,* &c. and drinking the *Bath Waters,* bathing in the same, or *pumping* on the Part affected. These Kinds, I say, are not the Palsies I intended principally to treat of here, since they happen generally to good sound Constitutions and firm *Nerves,* and are thus easily remedied.

§. II. These I am principally concerned about, are such as happen in the *Decline of Life,* to Persons of vitiated Juices and weak *Nerves,* where *Nervous* Disorders have preceded, or in which *Vapours* commonly terminate, who have spoiled their Habits, at least, by *relative Intemperance* (which is always to be understood when I speak of Excesses producing Diseases) such *Palsies* are either a general Seizure of most, if not all the *Muscles* and *Nerves* of the whole Machine, or of one half of the Body only, as of the right or left Side, or of the upper Part of the Body on one Side, with the lower Part on the other Side, or lastly, of some particular *Limb* or *Muscle.* There is generally Reason to conclude from the Appearances, that besides a Laxity of the *Nerves,* or a Defect in their innate Power of Contraction and *Tonical* Nature, there are likewise Obstructions of the Capillary Blood Vessels, from some Fault in the Animal Juices, which, when rectified, cures the *Palsy.* This is manifest, from the Cure of a great many inveterate Palsies, while the Patient is strong, by *Salivation* or *Mercurial* Medicines, and yet there is nothing more evident, than that much *Mercury* or *frequent Salivations,* in weak Constitutions, will give *Paralytick Symptoms;* witness the *Tremor Mercurialis,* so common in Persons of weak *Nerves,* under such an Operation, from whence is further confirmed (what was pretty manifest before, from other Appearances) that towards animal Motion, the Influx of a sound balsamick Blood, to moisten and cherish the fleshy Fibres, is as much or more necessary, even than the Integrity and innate Action of the *Nerves,* or *animal Spirits* (if you please). And as the Faultiness of both concurs towards producing all *nervous* Distempers, so more especially to those call'd *Paralytick*. There can be no Difficulty to one, acquainted with Nature, and the *animal Oeconomy*, why the same Cause, *Mercury* for Example, should cure, and yet cause and produce in different Degrees and Quantities, the very same Disease, to wit, a *Palsy*. We know, a certain Degree of Heat, which will only produce *Smoak*, rais'd to a higher Degree, will produce *Light* and *Flame*: A certain Degree of Heat, in the same *Fomentation*, will dissolve and dissipate a *Tumor*, and a higher Degree of it will harden and make it *schirrous*; and thus, *Mercury*, in moderate Doses, will break, dissolve, and attenuate the Blood and Juices, whose Viscidity and consequent *Compression* on the *Nerves*, interrupt their Vibrations and Action, and so produce a *Palsy*, which a gentle Salivation will remedy and antidote. But when the *active Steams* and small *ponderous Particles* of *Mercury* have penetrated and saturated the Substance of the *Nerves* and *Solids*, they will spoil and alter their whole Substance and Action, and so cause an universal *Palsy*. But the Juices seem to be the principal Cause of the Difficulty of the Cure of *Palsies* in the Decline of Life; because towards old Age the Solids stiffen and harden at a greater Rate, than in the younger Part of Life, so the spoil'd Juices are then more hard to be remedied.

§. III. If a Person, at or about the *Meridian* of Life, be seiz'd with such *Paralytick* Disorders, and they are not cur'd, or at least prevented from settling or confirming at first, they are seldom ever afterwards totally freed from them, whatever Methods be tried with them: And therefore, as soon as the Disease is discover'd, *Bleeding* at first, if the Patient is strong, and the Pulse full, and then *Blisters*, first over all the Head, then on the Nape of the

Of Paralytick Disorders. 167

the Neck, the Legs and Arms, and especially on the Parts affected, and in the Intervals, or when the Effects of these are pretty much worn off; active warm Purges, especially of *Hellebore* and *Sena*, on a vinous *Menstruum*, ought to be used and repeated as often as the Strength of the Patient will bear, with some *cordial* Medicines, as that of Sir *Walter Raleigh*, *Electuarium de Saffafras*, &c. (at Night, after the Operation is over) wash'd down with a *nervous Julep*, mix'd with *Volatile Spirits*. When these Evacuations have thus been duly made, a Course of *Chalybeats*, *Aromaticks* and *Bitters*, is to be prescrib'd, to recruit the Strength of the Solids, and warm and active *Oils* and *Ointments*, especially the *Opodeldoc*: and stimulating Fomentations applied to the Parts affected, they being first well curried with a *Flesh Brush*. *Cold Bathing* may be also tried on sound Constitutions, but *hot Bathing* of any Sort or Kind, will, I fear, be of little Use, and may, in some deep rooted Cases, do hurt by a temporary, at least greater Relaxation, unless the Juices be extremely well thinn'd by *ponderous* Medicines first.

§. IV. If these Medicines are duly and effectually tried, under the Direction of a proper Person, and with little or no Success, the Case may be deem'd incurable. Not that it is always mortal, for I have known them last as many Years under a *paralytick* Stroke, as under an Amputation, especially if the *Palsy* had not followed after an *Apoplectick*, *Epileptick*, or some strong *nervous* Paroxysm or Fit: And even then, if the Constitution was tolerable, and the general Method of Cure of *nervous* Distempers has been duly and steadily pursued, seldom any thing worse has happen'd from it than the Loss of that Organ or Limb, which the Distemper had seiz'd, and disabled: Life in other Respects, and under such a Management, having gone on pretty tolerably.

§. V.

§. V. Saint *Vitus's Dance*, (as it is call'd) the *mimicking Diftemper*, and all such irregular and equivocal *nervous* Diforders, may be eafily reduced under fome of the general Heads I have affigned. The *firft* is certainly a Mixture of *paralytick* and *convulfive* Diforders. It very often arifes out of an *Epilepfy*, efpecially in young People, when the original Diftemper is overcome, and a greater Degree of Strength is obtain'd, though fometimes it is only a *Prelude* to that fevere Diftemper, and may it felf fometimes be an original Difeafe; I have cur'd it, as I mention'd in my Book of the *Gout*, in young Perfons, by repeated *antimonial Vomits, mercurial Purges, Steel*, and *Aromaticks*, and the other general Methods fo often mention'd.

CHAP. XIII.

Of the Apoplexy and Epilepfy.

§. I. THE *Apoplexy*, in its *Fit* and *Paroxyfm*, is one of the moft frightful and fatal Diftempers belonging to the *nervous* Clafs of Difeafes, few out-living the firft Fit, fewer the fecond, and, as it is commonly faid, none at all the *third:* though this Obfervation is not altogether without Exceptions; for it is in this, as in all other bodily Diftempers, thofe who are ftrong and robuft, and in whom the Caufe is but juft beginning to operate, and meets with a greater Refiftance from the State of the Solids, will hold it longer, and ftruggle more than the weak and tender. Few are ever feiz'd with this Diftemper, if it comes naturally, and without an Accident, till towards the *Decline of Life*, unlefs they have been much troubled with violent and acute *Head-aches*, or Inflammations upon the *Brain*, or its *Membranes*, or have fome inflammatory Diftemper tranflated from the Extremities upon the Head,

Head, such as the *Gout, Rheumatism, Erysipelas,* and the like: those who are seiz'd with a deep Stroak of it, have scarce any Warning, but a sudden violent *Head-ach,* a Sickness at the Stomach, or a *Cholick,* and drop down immediately, without Sense or Motion, and have scarce any Sign of Life, except now and then an uncertain Twitch or Twinkle in the Pulse, (if it is not from Flatulence) and scarce any Breathing that can be discover'd, even on the Surface of a Glass, but a constant *Snorting* and *Snoring* in the Throat and Nostrils. Those in whom it comes naturally, are observ'd generally to be either *gross Feeders,* or those who deal too plentifully in strong and *spirituous Liquors,* of a gross and full Habit, *short and thick neck'd,* voluptuous and lazy; though some thinner Habits may suffer under it, but they are those who have formerly been subject to violent *Head-aches,* or are worn out by *Lechery.*

§. II. There are three Kinds of *Apoplexies,* distinguish'd by the different Causes that produce them; as *first,* a *Symptomatick Apoplexy,* such as I have mention'd, from a Translation of the *Gout, Rheumatism,* &c. 2*dly,* An accidental one, from a *Fall, Bruise, Wound,* or the like: and 3*dly,* an *acquir'd one,* arising from an *Apoplectick* Disposition or *Discrasy,* proceeding from Intemperance and Excesses, Laziness, and Neglect of the *Non-naturals* in Persons of the abovemention'd particular Make and Constitution of Body. It is of this *last* chiefly that I intend to say any thing here, the Treatment of the others being obvious. As to the immediate *Cause* of the *Apoplectick Fit,* I think it must be one of these two, *viz.* * either a *Rupture* of the Blood-Vessels in the *Brain,* whereby a great Quantity of *Blood* being extravasated upon its including *Membranes,* or

---

* Vide Philosoph. Transact. No. 313.

into its *Cavities*, presses upon the *Origin* of the *Nerves*, so as to intercept their Operation and *Functions*, from whence the mention'd Appearances may be easily deduc'd. And this may be either occasion'd by a *Fall*, a *Bruise*, a *Wound*, or any other violent Accident upon the *Skull*, or by too great a Quantity of *Blood*, or its being overheated by strong Liquors, violent Exercise, or immoderate sensual Pleasures, in those who have the Configuration I have described. This seems to be the Case of those *Apoplexies* that happen in *Southern Countries*, where, though the *Climate* confines them to a very moderate *Diet*, yet as they wallow in *sensual Pleasures* of another Nature, and deal sometimes pretty freely with *spirituous* Liquors, and *Opiates*, (which have the same *deleterious* Effects) these things in a scorching *Climate*, may kindle a Flame in the Blood sufficient to produce these mention'd Effects.

§. III. The other Kind of *Apoplexy*, which happens naturally, and is most frequent in *Northern Countries* and colder *Climates*, seems to arise chiefly from an *Extravasation*, or rather *Ouzing* out through the Sides of the relax'd and worn out Capillary Blood-Vessels, of a thin *putrid Serum*, upon the mention'd Parts, which I have hinted in the former Case. This chiefly happens to *gross* and *full Feeders*, to those who are too free with strong and *spirituous* Liquors, and are consequently very unactive and lazy. I have formerly shewn how such a *Course* and *Regimen* will almost, or altogether, destroy the red or grumous Part of the *Blood*, and turn the whole Mass of the Fluids into a *dirty Puddle* of thin *alcaline saltish Serum*, which corrodes or *ouzes* through the flabby and relax'd Capillaries. That this is pretty near the Truth, is evident from opening the *Heads* [*] of those who have died of a natural *Apoplexy*, the

---

[*] Vide Boneti Sepulchret. Anatom. Lib. I.

Cavities of the Brain having been found generally quite filled, either with *extravafated Blood*, or such a *Serum* as I have mention'd. Those who want further Light in this Affair may confult *Wepfer*. The mildeſt apoplectick Fits, of all, where the Patient efcapes for once or twice, feem to arife only from an Obſtruction or *Tumefaction* of the Blood-Veſſels, or *Glands* in the Cavity of the *Skull*, upon the Removal of which Obſtruction, by the Struggle and Effort of Nature, in the *Paroxyſm*, it ceaſes. This Degree is what feems only capable of being cured; but if it is ſuffer'd to go on without any effectual Method, us'd to remove the *apoplectick* Difpofition by rectifying the Juices, two or three more ſuch *Paroxyſms* burſt the Veſſels, and bring on the incurable Kinds mention'd.

§. IV. If the Account here given of this terrible Diſtemper be juſt, there will be no Difficulty in forming the true *Indications*, and the moſt effectual Method of *Cure*, as far as it is poſſible. Which of theſe Cauſes have the Prevalency in a particular Caſe, will be evident, from the Manner of Life, the Age and Conſtitution of the Patient, and the Symptoms of the *Fit*. There is very little Hope of Succeſs in either Caſe, unleſs the Cauſe be but juſt beginning and very weak; or the Perſon very ſtrong and young, and otherwiſe ſound. To rouze them out of the preſent Fit; in the *firſt Caſe*, the moſt plentiful *Bleeding* that can poſſibly be ventur'd upon, is to be attempted at the Arm, in the *temporal* Artery, or the *jugular* Vein, in the Foot, and by Cupping on the Nape of the Neck, together with ſharp, cooling and acid *Glyſters*, while Bliſtirs are laid on in every Place where they can conveniently be. In thoſe *Fits* produced by ſuch a *Serum* as I have mention'd, or from an Obſtruction in the *Glands*, *Vomits* are alſo immediately to be forc'd down, (but avoided in thoſe occaſion'd by a *Hæmorrhage*, becauſe in this laſt, the great Affair is to ſtop the Violence of
the

the *Hæmorrhage*, and to draw it off by all possible Means from the *Brain*) : And Care is likewise to be taken, neither by inward Medicines nor outward Application, to increase the Hurry, Heat, or *Inflammation* of the Blood : and therefore the Solids are not to be stimulated to too violent Efforts. Whereas, in the *other Case*, neither of these can be done too much : and therefore, not only sharp *Sternutatories*, *fœtid Smells*, and *volatile Spirits*, may be applied to the *Nose*, but (other Things not succeeding) even actual *Cauteries* are to be applied to the Soles of the Feet, and Crown of the Head, as far as it can be done safely, to raise *Sensibility* and Pain : besides the warmest *cordial* Medicines, in a liquid Form, if they can be thrust down any how.

§. V. As to the *Apoplectick* Disposition, in those of the inflammatory Kind, all proper Means are to be used that tend to cool the Blood, and allay its *Fermentation* and Heat, such as *Acids*, *acidulated* Draughts, mild *Balsamicks*, gentle *Catharticks*, with an extremely cool, moderate, and spare *Diet*, abstaining from violent Exercise, and every thing that may heat and inflame the Blood. The other *Apoplectick* Disposition must be treated much after the same Manner, with this Difference only, that the Medicines must be stronger and warmer, the Exercise greater and more constant, that continual Drains, by *Blisters*, *Issues*, *Setons*, and the like, be set a going, and that the *Diet* be somewhat higher in Quality, though not in Quantity, and the other general Methods for the Cure of the *Nervous* Symptoms that succeed upon it, be pursued according to the Directions formerly given.

§. VI. Next to the *Apoplexy*, the *Epilepsy* is the most dangerous, terrible, and disheartning Distemper that belongs to the *Nervous* or *cold* Class of Diseases ; seldom any, or, at least very few, escape from it, unless they be otherwise very strong and vigorous, without a Stroke of an *Apoplexy*, which generally ends their

Of the Apoplexy and Epilepsy. 173

their Lives: a *partial* or *half-Body Palsy*, or a total Demolition of the *Intellectual Faculties*. Young Children, well treated, may be recovered, and get strong and lusty, by stronger *Doses*, and a longer Course of the same Medicines and Methods I have advised for their *Convulsive* Fits. The Symptoms that attend grown Persons are, their *dropping down* suddenly, as if shot; but sometimes with violent *Convulsions* and *Throws* in the *Belly*, *Breast*, and *Limbs*; beating and tearing themselves, *clinching* their *Fists*, *biting* their *Tongues*, *grinding* their *Teeth*, and *foaming* at the Mouth, with a small *Trembling*, *unequal* and sometimes *interrupted Pulse*, and an involuntary Secretion of all the natural Discharges: having scarce any Sense or Knowledge of what they do, or what is done to them: but the most dangerous of all, are the violent *Convulsions* and involuntary Motions, by which they would tear, bruise, and destroy themselves, if not with-held: the *Fit* generally terminates in a Dosing or *Lethargy*, which continues longer or shorter, according to the Violence of the *Paroxysm*, and then by Degrees their Spirits and Strength return, though with a greater Degree of Lowness and Confusion, or Stupidity. This Distemper sometimes follows the Periods of the * *Luminaries*, especially their *Conjunctions* and *Oppositions*; but this is uncertain, and in some Cases only, as all *Periods* are in our inconstant *Climate*.

§. VII. From this Account of the Symptoms of this Distemper, I think it is pretty evident, that it differs very little, or not at all, or at most, in a few Circumstances only, from *Hypochondriacal* and *Hysterick Fits:* which last, when violent, terminate always in these *Epileptick* Fits, as they, on the other hand, when they become weak, dwindle

---

* Vide Mead de Imperio Solis & Lunæ.

into

into on *Hysterick* Kind: So that having treated of these last so fully, it will be needless to say any thing further about these others; only this, that the Diet must be much more strict, cool, and moderate, and the Medicines stronger and oftner repeated, especially *Vomits*, *Steel*, and *Bitters*. Dr. *Taylor* of *Croydon* cured himself intirely and absolutely, of the most violent, constant, and habitual *Epilepsy* that perhaps ever was known, after having, in vain, tried all the Methods and Medicines advised by the most eminent *Physicians* of his Time, by a *total Diet of Milk*, without Bread, or any other Vegetable, or any thing, (besides a Spoonful of compound *Peony Water* sometimes, to prevent its Curdling) confining himself to a *Pint* in a Morning, a *Quart* at Noon, and a *Pint* at Night, of the Milk of *Grass-fed* Cows in the *Summer*, and of those fed with *Hay* in the *Winter*, the *Milk* of Cows fed with *Grains* always inflating him, and lying uneasy on his Stomach. He had continued in perfect Health and Vigour (having had several Children) seventeen Years when I saw him, and received this Account from him, insomuch that he could have play'd four or five Hours at *Cricket*, on *Banstead Downs*, without Weariness or profuse Sweating, and probably might have continued many Years longer in perfect Health (as he did seven or eight Years more) had he not entred upon a different *Regimen of Diet* (as I am informed since I first wrote this History, in my *Treatise of the Gout*, by a Person of great Credit) and come to eat *Animal Food*, by which, in a *short* Time, he was destroyed. Some others have been cured by me, by a *Regimen of Diet* less strict, and the Medicines already suggested; but I believe none ever were cured who have been come to *Maturity*, without a very exact *low Regimen*, continued during all their Lives, the transgressing it for any long Time, always bringing their Disorders back, if not something worse: and I believe a total Milk, and Vegetable

table Diet, as absolutely necessary for the total Cure of the *Epilepsy*, as it is for the Gout or a *Consumption*. Here were the proper Place to say something of *Lunacy* and *Madness*, being satisfied that the Methods here laid down are sufficient, and the most effectual for these Distempers; but designing this principally for common intelligent Readers, and those who suffer under *Nervous* Distempers, though not regularly bred to the Practice of *Physick*: and People under these mentioned Distempers being incapable of Reading, or at least, of serious and close Application, and these Disorders being the Province of particular *Physicians*, or those appointed by the Publick for that Purpose, I shall here put a *Period* to this Part of the Treatise.

THE
English Malady:
OR, A
TREATISE
OF
Nervous Diseases of all Kinds,
AS
Spleen, Vapours, Lowness of Spirits, Hypochondriacal and Hysterical Distempers, &c.

PART III.

CONTAINING

Variety of CASES *that illustrate and confirm the foregoing Method of Cure.*

With the AUTHOR'S *own* CASE *at large.*

Γλακτόφαγων, ἀϐίων τε, δικαιοτάτων ἀνθρώπων.   Homer.

By *GEORGE CHEYNE*, M.D.
Fellow of the *College of Physicians* at *Edinburg*, and F.R.S.

DUBLIN:
Printed in the Year, MDCCXXXIII.

ADVERTISEMENT.

*T*HIS *Laſt, has been by far the moſt difficult and unpleaſant* Part *of my* Work. *The obvious* Sneer *of its being a* Quack's Bill, *has been the leaſt* Part *of that* Difficulty; *for when I ſet about finiſhing this* Work, *for the Benefit of the Sedentary, Tender and Decay'd, I made a* Sacrifice *of ſome part of my Vanity and Intereſt. But among the very many Inſtances I could have adduced, I was obliged to lay aſide all thoſe whoſe* Caſes *were pretty much alike, and to pick out ſuch only, as ſeem'd to me to be more particular, or which were moſt proper to illuſtrate and confirm the ſeveral Steps of the preceding Doctrine, and to direct the* Valetudinarian *in the leſs obvious and uncommon Symptoms. But that which diſtreſs'd me moſt, was, the* Names *of the Perſons, whoſe* Caſes *I was oblig'd to mention, moſt of them being ſtill alive, and few caring to be made Examples of in any Reſpect. The* Diſtempers *of Patients are ſacred,* (Res ſacra miſer) *and nervous* Diſtempers *eſpecially, are under ſome Kind of* Diſgrace *and* Imputation, *in the Opinion of the* Vulgar *and* Unlearned; *they paſs among the Multitude, for a lower Degree of* Lunacy, *and the firſt Step towards a* diſtemper'd Brain; *and the beſt*

Construction is Whim, Ill-humour, Peevishness *or* Particularity; *and in the* Sex, Daintiness, Fantasticalness *or* Coquetry. *So that often when I have been consulted in a Case, before I was acquainted with the* Character *and* Temper *of the* Patient, *and found it to be what is commonly call'd* Nervous, *I have been in the utmost Difficulty, when desir'd to define or name the Distemper, for fear of affronting them, or fixing a Reproach on a* Family *or* Person. *If I call'd the Case* Glandular *with nervous* Symptoms, *they concluded I thought them* pox'd, *or had the* King's-Evil. *If I said it was* Vapours, Hysterick *or* Hypochondriacal *Disorders, they thought I call'd them* Mad *or* Fantastical: *and if they were such as valued themselves, on fearing neither* God *nor* Devil, *I was in Hazard of a* Drubbing *for seeming to impeach their* Courage: *and was thought as rude as if I had given them the* Lie; *and even the very best has been, I my self was thought a* Fool, *a weak and ignorant* Coxcomb, *and perhaps dismiss'd in Scorn; and some I have actually lost by it. Notwithstanding all this, the Disease is as much a bodily Distemper (as I have demonstrated) as the* Small-Pox *or a* Fever; *and the Truth is, it seldom, and I think never happens or can happen, to any but those of the liveliest and quickest natural* Parts, *whose Faculties are the brightest and most spiritual, and whose Genius is most keen and penetrating, and particularly where there is the most delicate Sensation and Taste, both of Pleasure and Pain. So equally are the good and bad Things of this mortal State distributed! For I seldom ever observ'd a* heavy, dull, earthy, clod-pated Clown, *much troubled with* nervous *Disorders, or at least, not to any eminent Degree; and I scarce believe the Thing possible, from the* animal Oeconomy *and the present Laws of Nature.*

But besides this, when I was determin'd to publish this Work, the Persons whose Cases *I had*
pick'd

ADVERTISEMENT.

pick'd out for my present Purpose, were all scatter'd and at great Distances from me, some being in other Kingdoms and Foreign Parts, and most of them were in such Circumstances and Situation, that it was by no means convenient or proper to publish their Names *without Leave; and I was unwilling to put my* Friends *and* Patients *to the Pain, either of a Consent or Refusal, and resolved even to bear the Slur of* Forgery, *and let the Whole rest on my own Credit, rather than contend with such Difficulties. I have therefore mentioned their Names, only in those Cases where I was absolutely at Liberty; but solemnly declare, that the others were such in the main, as I have represented them; and in any particular* Case, *if called upon, I am ready to assign the* Person, *under proper Conditions, and have always describ'd the* Case *from the* Name *and Character of the* Patient, *and the* History *of the Distemper placed before my Eyes.*

I have classed the Cases, *as I had done the several Stages of this Distemper in the* former Part, *viz. into the* three *different Orders. The* first Class *and* Chapter *contains Examples of those whose nervous Disorders being chiefly confin'd to the* alimentary Tube, *the Juices being tolerably sound and good, and the Solids pretty firm, a Regulation only of common Diet, as to Quantity and Quality, and a general Course of* nervous Evacuants, *for Prevention, and* Volatiles *on Paroxysms, has been sufficient. The* second Class *and* Chapter *contains Instances of those whose* Cases *being deeper and more obstinate, where the Juices have been either* sizy, *thick or inflam'd, or some noble* Organ *beginning to be spoil'd: more powerful* Evacuants *and* Alteratives, *especially of the* ponderous Medicines, *have been necessary; and a* trimming middling Diet, *of alternate Days of young tender Flesh Meat, and Milk and Vegetables, with Wine and Water for Drink, were requir'd. The* last Class *and* third

Chapter *is of such, where the Case being almost incurable otherwise, extremely frightful and painful, from some of the necessary* Organs *visibly spoil'd and decay'd, and the Juices verging towards* Putrefaction: *the strongest* Evacuants *and* Alteratives, *with a total* Milk and Vegetable Diet, *long persisted in, was indispensably necessary. The Medicines I have only hinted at, to prevent the* Quacking of Patients themselves, *but have pointed them out so clearly, in general, that no body of common Sense and liberal Education can mistake them, in any thing but the* compounding and doseing: *and that none but a regularly-bred* Physician *can be sufficient for; and of the Medicines, I have mentioned only the preventive or extirpative ones. It had been endless to have set down all those prescrib'd under the Fits; these I have sufficiently describ'd in the former Part.*

THE

THE
English Malady.

PART III.

CHAP. I.

Of those whose Nervous Complaints were cured by Medicine, under a common, though temperate Diet.

CASE I.

A Tender *young Gentleman*, of great Worth and Ingenuity, here in our *Neighbourhood*, had from his Infancy been troubled with a most violent *Nervous Headach*, which returning at certain *Periods*, overcame and sunk him to Extremity; and even sometimes approached near to *Epileptick* Fits. I advised him, when seized with them or it, to go to Bed as soon as he could conveniently, and to take four or five of the *Pilul. Gummos.* and *de Aloe Lotâ a æ. p.* and to drink plentifully of small Sack Whey, or Water-Gruel, with *Spt. C. C. Vol.* Gutt. x in each

each Draught, repeating the *Pills* every Night till well, and after weekly, or as often as his Illnesseever returned; by which alone he has been constantly relieved. I advised him also to keep a very temperate (though a common) Diet of *Animal Foods*, at Dinner only, and not to drink above half a Pint, or at most a Pint of Wine a Day, using constant Exercise on Horseback, or otherwise. He has continued this Method ever since, is in the main well, and has grown yearly better and stronger now for above these twenty Years, and in all Probability will grow stronger and heartier to a great old Age.

CASE II.

A Lady of *great Fortune* in this Town, *eminent* for her great *Charity*, *Piety*, and *fine Breeding*, was originally of very weak *Nerves*; her chief Complaints were, tender *Bowels*, extreme low Spirits, with great Sinking, and sometimes *Hysterick Paroxysms* to an eminent Degree. Upon these last Occasions, I have given her several Medicines, as the Case indicated; but for Prevention, I prescribed only gentle *Emeticks*, when her Stomach was loaded, *Rhabarbarat* and *Carminative* Catharticks, Bath Waters almost constantly now for near these twenty Years, (for the Benefit of which she chose to live here) with constant Exercise, especially on Horseback, and a *Diet* of the plainest, lightest, and most simple *Animal Foods*, at Noon only, and a little of the best *French Wines*; and by these Means she has yearly grown better and stronger, and continues to do so; her Disorders returning now seldom, and being easily removed.

CASE III.

A Gentleman *of Scotland*, eminent in the *Law*, and of great *Honour*, *Probity*, *and fine Parts*, had been long troubled with a *Nervous Head-ach*; and having neglected it many Years, it came to such a Height as was no longer tolerable. Besides this almost incessant *Head-ach*, he had constant extreme
Lowness,

Lowness, Oppression, and at last the greatest Difficulty to attend his Studies, or to apply to the Business of his Profession; and the Disorder terminated in *Want of Sleep,* Loss of Appetite, and Inquietude; and all these *Symptoms* brought him to such a State as to render his Condition most miserable. He came here, to *Bath,* in this Condition. His Disorders were the most distinctly *Periodical* of any *Nervous* Case I had ever met with, (though in most I have observed something of that Nature.) One Night it was extreme, so as to make him pass it almost entirely without Sleep; next Day an unexpressible Lowness, and a constant *Ptyalism* or spitting thin *Rheum* ensued, by which the following Night was more tolerable, and thus alternately. I prescribed several *Vomits, Quinquina-Bitters,* the *fœtid Gums,* with the *Extract of the Bark,* and the *Animal Salts, Aloetick Purges,* together with liquid *Steel* in the *Bath* Waters. But above all, a light, sparing Diet of tender *Animal* Food, and at Noon only, and a very little *Wine,* with constant *Exercise* on Horseback, or otherwise: By these he was much relieved, while here; and pursuing the same Method at home, for several Years: drinking in the hot Weather the *Mineral Chalybeat* Waters of his own Country, by slow Degrees he grew perfectly well, and has for many Years enjoyed a compleat State of Health, which he preserves by great *Temperance* and *Exercise*.

CASE IV.

A Lady of the first *Quality,* and of *eminent Virtues,* was so much oppressed with these *Sinkings, Anxiety,* and *Hysterick* Disorders, together with violent *Cholicks, Watchings,* and *Inflation,* as to be extreamly miserable. She had drank the Waters, and taken Medicines a long Time here, without any Relief, and was just desponding, and about leaving the Place. Being called, I ordered her to repeat some *Vomits,* gave her *Quinquina-Bitters with* and *without Rhubarb* daily, made her drink the *Bath* in the

the Morning, and *Pyrmont* Waters with her Meals; regulated her Diet both in Quantity and Quality, confining it to the lighteſt, youngeſt *Animal* Foods, and the leaſt Wine poſſible; and by continuing her in this Way ſome Time, ſhe was recover'd to perfect *Health, Vivacity,* and *Activity.*

CASE V.

An Officer's Lady of *fine Parts* and *great Worth,* was ſent here to drink the Waters, for a conſtant *Bilious* Vomiting, and *Hyſterick Lowneſs*: She had been ordered by her *Phyſician* to take an *Ipecacohana* Vomit every Morning, (without any *Reſtrictions* on her *Diet*) which ſhe had taken for ſome Time. Being called, I told her, I thought it was ſufficient to repeat the *Vomits* when ſhe had an Urging and Sickneſs; and that when the *Choler* was actually derived from the *Liver* into the *Stomach,* that *Symptom* would infallibly happen, and then, and only then, was a *Vomit* uſeful or neceſſary. I adviſed her a *Quinquinated and Rhabarbarated* bitter Wine, to be taken every Night, with a weak liquid *Steel* in the Morning, and at the ſame time regulated her Diet, and by Degrees ſhe recover'd perfectly.

CASE VI.

A young *Lady* from the Weſt, had for ſeveral Years ſo frequent *Hyſterick* Fits and *Cholicks,* and to ſuch a Degree, that they had made her extremely miſerable, and at laſt crippled her both in *Hands* and *Feet,* (which is common to *Nervous* Cholicks) ſo that they were of no more Uſe to her, than if they had been cut off. I repeated ſeveral *Vomits* in the Courſe of the Waters; regulated her Diet with Exactneſs to young Meats at Noon only; gave her a *Quinquinated Bitter* before Meals, and a *Quinquinated and Rhabarbarated* Tincture daily at Night; and, in a proper Time, gave her *Steel* in the Waters, and made her pump both Hands and Legs, rubbing them often after with the *Opodeldoc* diſſolved in *Spirit of Wine camphorated*; by theſe Means only, in ſix Months,

Months, she perfectly recover'd both her Limbs and her Health.

When 'the *Case* was obstinate, and the Patient young, firm or strong, and I was left to my own Liberty, I always began with the *ponderous* Medicines, continuing them for Months, and finish'd with the *Quinquinated Bitters*, or with *Rhubarb* and *Bark* compounded with other Bitters, in liquid Steel: And even in common, slight, *Scorbutical*, *Colical* and *Nervous*, but especially *Rheumatic*, *Scrophulous* or *Cutaneous* Cases, of such as came here for the Benefit of the Waters, if not constrain'd, I always began with the *ponderous* Medicines, or some one *Preparation of Mercury*, or another, continued for some Time, and only finish'd with the *Bitter*, *Astringent*, and *Chalybeat* ones; but still regulated their Diet, without which I scarce ever succeeded, even in the very slightest Cases.

CHAP. II.

Of Nervous Cases, requiring a mix'd or trimming Regimen of Diet, viz. of tender, young Animal Food, and a little Wine and Water one Day, and the other only Milk, Seeds, and Vegetables.

CASE I.

A Gentleman well known, and as much belov'd by all that know him, for his *fine Parts*, great *Probity*, and the distinguish'd Figure he has constantly made in the *Senate*; having been long troubled with *bilious Vomitings*, constant *Heart-burnings*, *Lowness* and *Oppression*, for which, after all the *Nervous* and *Stomachick* Medicines, prescrib'd by the most eminent *Physicians* in *England*, together with the whole Circle of *Mineral Waters* at different Times, and at last a *Tour* (when he was near Sixty) thro'

thro' the *Southern Climates*, came hither to *Bath*, once and again; but without any lasting Benefit or Relief, the same Miseries of this sinking Distemper still persecuting him. I at last persuaded him to enter upon a *Trimming Diet*, one Day light Pudding or *Milk and Vegetables* dress'd, especially of the *farinaceous and seed* Kind; the other, a little *young, tender*, plain *Animal Food* for *Dinner* only, and not to exceed two or three Glasses of Wine a Day, taking sometimes *Quinquinated* and *Rhabarbarated Bitters*, and sometimes *Mineral Waters*, as his Case required, to wit, the *Bath* in temperate or cold Weather, and the *Cold* (as *Tunbridge, Spa*, or *Pyrmont*) in hot Weather. By persisting in this Method, he has recovered and grown better every Year, and is now (at Seventy-three) one of the healthiest, halest Gentlemen of his *Age* in *England*, being from *Lean*, grown *Plump, Full* and *Active*, without Oppression or Lowness, and is in great likelihood to hold it many Years; to which, no doubt, his having given up Business has greatly contributed; though, I think, his *Regimen* has had the far largest Share in his *perfect Recovery*.

CASE II.

A *Gentleman* of *Scotland*, of an *Antient* and *Honourable* Family, loving, and belov'd of all Mankind, was early in Life subject to *Nervous* Disorders, which tho' universal, did chiefly affect his *Auditory Organs*, so as to impair his Hearing. For this he had try'd a great many *Active* and *Dangerous* Remedies, which I think, had damag'd an otherwise naturally clean and firm Constitution. After having serv'd his Country long in Eminent Employments, he was seiz'd about the Sixty-seventh Year of his Age, with *Nervous, Hypochondriacal*, and *Convulsive Fits* and *Paroxysms*, the most severe, terrible, and obstinate that I had ever seen. At first, they return'd three or four times every Day, *shaking* and *convulsing* every *Limb, Muscle*, and *Organ*, of the whole Machine,

chine, tho' all the Time his *Senses* and *Faculties* were found and entire; only at their going off, they left him *languid*, *low*, and *exhausted*. He had try'd various Remedies, and run through the whole *Circle* of the *nervous*, *volatile*, and *fœtid* Medicines, prescrib'd by the most eminent *Physicians* of the whole Island. He came at last to *Bath*, and was under my Care, and drank *Bath*, *Bristol*, and *Pyrmont* Waters occasionally, for the Space of almost two Years: The effectual Medicines, were *Antimonial* and *Ipecacuhana* Vomits mix'd, which always weaken'd or stopp'd the *Fits*, (the Case, in my Opinion, being chiefly an obstructed *schirrous Liver*, with *Calomel* Purges, *Gum* and *Aloetick Pills*, *Quinquinated Bitters*, and sometimes *Fœtids* and *Volatiles*, only as a present Relief. These were the principal Remedies which reliev'd, and, at last, cur'd him; but what chiefly accomplish'd the Cure, was that (of his own Accord, I not daring to offer such an Advice to one who was so far advanc'd in Life) he enter'd into a *Trimming Diet*, chiefly of *Milk* and *Vegetables*, with weak Broths and Fish but sometimes, and two or three Glasses of Wine at Dinner only, which *Regimen* I much approv'd of and encourag'd. After he had recover'd a tolerable good State of Health, I advis'd him, both on his own, and the Account of some others of his Honourable Family, to finish the *Cure*, by spending a Season or two at *Spa*, and wintering in *Italy*; and now, by the Divine Blessing, he is as Stout and Healthy as any Man of his Age can possibly be, being free from all his *Nervous Symptoms*, unless on Accidents, and then by the same Method and Medicines easily reliev'd.

CASE III.

A *Knight Baronet* of an *Antient Family*, by keeping bad Hours, in attending upon the Business of the *Parliament*, and living freely about Town, had so worn down his Constitution, that he run into an habitual *Diarrhœa*, attended with extreme *Flatulence*,

lence, Lowness, Oppression, Watchfulness, and *Indigestion.* These constantly returning upon the least Excess, or catching Cold, had quite enfeebled and enervated a formerly robust and healthy Constitution, even into almost a *Nervous Atrophy.* He had consulted again and again the most eminent of the Profession, but all the Benefit he reap'd was only a *temporary* Relief, or having a *Drag* put upon the Wheel, to prevent its running too fast down the Hill. He at last came to *Bath,* and was for a considerable Time under my Direction, to try if he cou'd by any Means be assisted to a *lasting Cure,* he being then not far past the *Meridian* of Life, tho' wasted and reduced from a *round, muscular,* and *brawny* Natural Frame, almost to a *Skeleton;* and his *Alimentary Tube* being so much relax'd, that the most moderate common Meal of Butcher's Meat was too much for him, and run off *Crude,* leaving him quite sunk and flat. I was unwilling to advise him to a total *Milk and Vegetable Diet,* being uncertain if he would persevere, and knowing well the Danger of a sudden Return; but put him into a *Trimming* one, allowing him *white Meats* some Days, and only light Pudding, with Milk and Seeds other Days, with two or three Glasses of Claret at *Noon,* and *Bath* Waters tepid in a Morning, but *Bristol* Waters at Meals, and only *Vegetable Seed Meats,* with Milk for Breakfast and Supper; giving him, at the same Time, *Vegetable* Astringent Medicines, and sometimes gentle *Vomits, Testaceous* Powders, and *toasted Rhubarb* with *Diascordium.* Under this *Regimen and Medicines,* (with constant riding a Horseback in the Forenoon,) he grew better by Degrees, his *Diarrhœa* became more moderate, his *Spirits* brisker, and his *Sleep* longer and sounder. He continued thus the whole *Winter,* and next *Summer,* tho' thin and low, yet not to such a Degree as before; in the *hot* Weather he drank *Spa* Water, with a liquid weak *Quinquinated Chalybeat.* Next *Winter* I advis'd him to go to the *South of France,*

where

Of Nervous Cases, &c.

where he continued a Year or two, under the same *Regimen* and Medicines, came Home much mended in *Flesh* and *Spirits*, and by Degrees acquir'd an *Athletick* State of Health; and has been these twenty Years a hale, strong, fine Gentleman, on common plain Diet, with due Temperance.

C A S E IV.

A *Worthy* Merchant of the *North of England*, came here to *Bath* for my Advice, in a most deplorable State, *viz.* a total Loss of Appetite, exceeding low Spirits: he had *Rigors* and Night Sweats, a fix'd *Melancholy*, *Terror*, and *Dread*, a violent *Headach*, and a want of Natural Sleep, with *Faintings* and *Paralytick* Numbnesses, and in a Word, all the Symptoms of the mentioned *second Stage* of these *Nervous* Disorders. I repeated *Vomits* often, gave him *Quinquinated Bitter Wines*, *Liquid Chalybeats*, sometimes *Hiera Picra*, *Tincture of Rhubarb* with *Bark Aromaticks* and *Bitters* of several Sorts, sometimes the *Gum* with *Aloetick Pills*; *Bath* Waters in a Morning, and *Pyrmont*, with but a little Wine at Meals, and especially a rigid, *alternate*, vegetable, and young *Animal* Food Diet, with constant *Exercise* of one Kind or other. Under this Method he got perfectly well and chearful in five or six Months, and has continued so these several Years.

C A S E V.

A young Lady from the *Western Sea-Coast* came here miserably oppress'd with *Sinking*, *Lowness*, and *Porraceous* Vomitings, frequent *Rigors* and Chills, succeeded by *feverish* Heats, *Restlesness* and *Anxiety*. I try'd gentle *Vomits*, *Quinquinated Bitters*, with and without *Rhubarb*, several Kinds of the slightest *Chalybeats*, as *Lac. Mart. Vitriol. Mart. Elixir Vitrioli*, and *Tinctura Antiphthisica*, *Spa* and *Pyrmont Waters*, *Vin Chalybeatum*, with *Volatiles* and *Fœtids*, and various Kinds of Bitters, but all without Success. I found, upon Observation, that she was always worst about five or six in the Afternoon, to wit, after the

great

great Meal, and that her *feverish Paroxysms* came on as the Day wore out, and rose higher in the Course of the Digestion, till towards the Morning. I learned likewise, that she eat and drank too heartily and fully for one of her Constitution and Complaints, three times a Day, (the *Bath* Waters, and the *mention'd Medicines* giving her a *Craving*.) Upon this, being satisfied that all her Symptoms proceeded from her Difficulty in Digestion, (as almost all such *hysteric* Cases do) I confin'd her to Broths, with light Pudding, and the small fresh River Fish, and at *Dinner* only, and *Milk* and *Vegetable* Food for Breakfast and Supper, allowing her little or no Wine, but *Spa* or *Pyrmont* Waters for Drink at Meals; for I have always found *Bath* in the Morning, and *Spa* or *Pyrmont* at Dinner, a most effectual Method in such Cases. By continuing the mention'd Diet and Medicines, as the *Symptoms* indicated, in two Months she became perfectly well and free of all her *Lowness, Faintings, Fits,* and *feverish Heats,* and went away fresh, chearful and strong.

CASE VI.

A *Gentleman* of fine Parts, grievously afflicted with the *Gout,* and with a perpetual *Lowness, Sinking,* and *Oppression,* both in Fits and the *Intervals:* to wit a constant Sickness and Reaching before the Formation, and after the Fit was over; and for a long time after, a much longer (than is common) *Sickness, Inappetency,* Weakness, and greater Lameness: so as to be one half of the Year almost under its Effects; and being weary of a Life under such Miseries, he was willing to attempt any thing probable to mitigate them. But being justly afraid of a *total Milk and Vegetable Diet,* lest by relaxing and cooling too fast, the thus inflamed Solids, he might give occasion to the *Bilious* and *Goutish* Humours and Salts, to flow too fast upon the common *Shoar* of the *Stomach and Bowels,* and there to beget *Sickness, Pain,* and *Danger;* therefore a *trimming* and middling Diet being

ing propos'd, chiefly of light, fresh River Fish, (as least inflaming, and not over enriching the Juices) alternately with Milk and Vegetables: and every Day the Value of a *Pint* of some generous, soft, balsamick Wine, (as *Sack, Canary*, or *Palm*) he readily and chearfully enter'd upon it. This *Method* abated both the *Violence, Duration,* and Frequency of his *Fits* in a few Years, without any Danger; and by Degrees effectually remov'd these Vomitings and Sicknesses with which the Fits began and terminated: especially, by almost every Night taking a few Spoonfuls of a *Rhubarb* and *Bark* Bitter, made on Wine with Aromaticks, in the Intervals; and he has now only a very tolerable, short, regular Fit once a Year, and soon gets about his Business again, and is in likelihood to go on with Health and Strength to a great Age.

I cannot omit here to observe, that if any Person designs, either for the Sake of *Health, Long-Life,* or Freedom from Diseases, to regulate his Diet, I universally prefer to all others this *trimming* Method, of an *alternate* Diet of *Milk* and *Vegetables* one Day, and the other plain or young *Animal* Food, and a moderate Portion of *Wine*; for if his Case requires his descending still lower, yet this *trimming Diet* will be the best and safest first Step to begin with; and if his Recovery thereby be so perfect, that he may rise to a higher Diet, this will make the *Transition* safer; and even those who love palatable and delicious Foods, to a great Degree, will bear a *Meagre* Day more easily, when they know they shall have a *Gaudy* one the next; and I have known those, who from a weak *Nervous* and *Cachectic* Habit have arriv'd to a confirm'd State of Health, noble Spirits, and great Age, by this *Trick* alone; so that Fasting and Abstinence in this Manner, might seem not more a *religious* than it ought to be reckon'd a *medical* Institution.

O CHAP.

CHAP. III.

Of Nervous Cases, requiring a strict and total Milk, Seed, and Vegetable Diet.

CASE I.

A Young *Lady* under my Direction, being naturally of a *tender* and *delicate* Constitution, had by a *Mal-Regimen*, and too *strong* and high *Food* while at a *Boarding* School at *London*, fallen into *hysterick* Disorders of all the Forms and Shapes were ever observ'd or describ'd; sometimes *Laughing, Dancing,* and all *Jollity*, at other times *Weeping, Crying, Sighing*, and *Melancholy*; often she was taken with *Fainting Fits* and *Convulsions:* now in great *Chills*, again *Hot* and *Feverish*; sometimes great Quantities of *pale*, at other times but a little *high-colour'd* Water; sometimes *Costiveness* to an Extremity, at other times purging and *slippery* Bowels; and most, if not all these Symptoms, sometimes three or four times in twenty-four Hours, insomuch that ignorant People thought it *Witchcraft* and *Inchantment*. Various *Nervous* and *Antihysterical* Medicines had been prescrib'd by the *Physician* in Ordinary at *London*, which had reliev'd and eas'd her for a Time, but still she relaps'd in a Month or two; and *Riding, Country Air,* and even Changes of that *Air* were try'd with little or no Success. At last, her Parents being under the greatest Concern about her, and fearing lest her Faculties (which were above *Mediocrity*) might be impair'd by so tedious and unaccountable a Distemper, put her intirely under my Care, with an absolute Power to do by her, both in *Diet* and *Medicines,* as I should think best. I first try'd all the common *Nervous* and *Antihysterical* Medicines over again, under a common Diet, with no Manner of Benefit. But tir'd out at last, I resolv'd to put her upon an

entire

entire *Vegetable Diet*, without *Flesh*, *Fish*, or *fermented Liquors*; Milk she lik'd not, besides, by its Curdling on a *bilious Stomach*, it both inflated and made her more sick; the only Medicines I ever after used in the whole Course, were gentle *Vomits*, when the *Bile* seem'd to be gathered or flow (which she always found by a greater Degree of Sickness, Oppression, and a greater than ordinary *Headach* that recurred *Monthly*) and a constant Course of *Cinnabar*, fresh and finely levigated, half a Dram Morning and Night for a long Time, and once a Week the *Pilul. Gummos. & de Aloe lota ā p. æ*, with *Bath Waters* in a Morning in the temperate, and *Pyrmont* in the hot Weather: sometimes *Riding* a *Horseback*, other times *Walking*, as she could best like, or could bear them. After the first *Month* of this *Diet* and *Medicines*, she never had any one Fit more to be observed; sometimes indeed she had a good deal of *Lowness*, *Headach*, or *Sickness*, but a *Vomit* always relieved her. By going on steadily in this Course, she grew sensibly better every two or three Months, and in less than two Years was perfectly cured of all her Complaints, and then returned to common Life, though with great *Care, Caution, and exact Temperance*, drinking not above a Glass or two of Wine a Day, and for most part eating only the tender, young *Animal Foods*, being but of a tender Fabrick and weak Constitution by Nature, though now she is perfectly *Well, Chearful, and Healthy*.

CASE II.

A *Young Lady* of an Honourable and Opulent Family, and of the most distinguish'd Merit, and the finest Parts I ever knew in the Sex, had from her *Parents* inherited *weak Nerves*, which for want of due Care and proper Management, brought on at last the most violent, extreme, and obstinate *Nervous Paroxysms*, (with their whole Circle of *Symptoms*) I had ever seen. She had been naturally of a *thin Habit*, but of a sudden had grown excessively fat; and had had often Threatnings, and sometimes pretty long Seizures of the same Class of Disorders before; which from time to time other Physicians, and often I, had cured by the common Medicines, *viz. Vomits, Volatiles, Chalybeats, Bitters, Pyrmont and Bath Waters,* with gentle *Evacuations.* But at last all these *Nervous Symptoms* became so extreamly obstinate, frightful, and painful, that neither I, nor any of her *Physicians* (of whom she had consulted many) could procure her any lasting Reprieve. She came at last to *Bath,* where I had often had the Honour to direct her, and the rest of the Family for many Years; the Waters with *Quinquinated Bitters,* and *Pilul. Gummos. cum Aloe lotâ,* at first gave her the most sensible and longest Relief, but at last they fail'd also. I afterwards try'd the greatest and most extensive Variety of *Nervous* Medicines, I had ever us'd in any such Case, since I first practised Physick. I try'd over and over all the Tribe of the *Nervous Antihysterical,* and *De-obstruent* Medicines, *Bitters, Volatiles, Chalybeats, Fœtids, Alteratives;* all Kinds of *Evacuations,* as *Bleeding, Blistering, Vomiting* again and again) together with the *Ponderous, Mineral* and *Mercurial* Medicines of all the proper Preparations, and at last even *Opiates* themselves, combined with all the *Antihystericks*: Indeed every thing I had ever used, heard of, or read in approv'd Authors, and each of these for a time sufficient for Trial. Notwithstanding all this, her torturing *Headachs,* her constant *screaming Fits, burning Heats, sleepless Nights, Terrors,* and other inexpressible Sufferings, were intolerable and insupportable. I was in the utmost Concern and Anxiety about her, and knew not what Hand to turn me: for tho' other *Physicians* had been join'd, yet I having been hitherto always successful in the Family, they did me the Honour to place a particular Confidence in me, and I was as heartily and warmly desirous of serving them successfully. At last (after above a Year spent under this Method

and

and these Medicines) I told them and her, that I had but one thing more to propose, which I had done long before, but that she had been often and strongly caution'd and warn'd against it, and I was afraid neither she nor her Friends would willingly come into it, after so many, so weighty Remonstrances against it, and from those whose Duty it was to direct her, so that I was willing to have effected the Cure by the common Means and Medicines, but found they would not do; and therefore I told her at last plainly, that the only Hopes of her Recovery was from a total *Milk* and *Vegetable* Diet, and Abstinence from all fermented Liquors, but as a *Cordial*. I met indeed with a readier Compliance on all sides than I had expected; and accordingly the *Lady* went chearfully into a total *Milk* and *Vegetable* Diet, and in less than three Months she was much better, in six Months tolerably well, and in nine Months almost perfectly well; this chiefly by her cool Diet, for after she enter'd upon it, she had occasion to take very few Medicines, so that she went away with no other Directions, but the Continuance of *gentle Vomits* when required, *Pyrmont* Waters for her common Drink, and Perseverance in her *Diet*: with the *Gum and Alœtick Pills* on transient Disorders. The *ponderous* Medicines she had long taken at first, had made the *Liver* pervious, (which had been evidently obstructed before,) so that there was constantly *Choler* poured out into the Stomach for a long Time after, which made *Vomits* sometimes necessary to discharge it. I hear she continues extremely well, without any means but her *Diet* and these few Medicines on Occasions with Exercise, and grows more hardy, active, and chearful, as I was certain she would, and doubt not she will long continue so.

CASE III.

A *Gentleman of Fortune*, and an *Officer* of *Distinction* in the *Army*, was afflicted with the most painful and frightful *Colicks* I had ever known, which often terminated in *Epileptick Fits*. Some of his Family about the same Time (*viz.* the *Meridian*) of Life, had died of the same Sort of *convulsive* and *nervous Colick*, which had justly made him the more cautious and careful. He came here to *Bath*, to put himself under my Direction: I at first try'd with the Waters, all the common *Nervous* Medicines, as *Quinquinated Bitters, Volatiles, Fœtids*, and *Alteratives* of the *mineral* Tribe of all Kinds, and in all the Shapes I could contrive; besides constant riding, on *Chalybeats* (which always makes them more effectual) but all without Success: So that I have often seen him rolling on the Ground in *Agonies*, crying out to put an End to his Pains any how. Nothing gave him Ease, except great Doses of warm *Opiates* in strong *Nervous Cordials*, and they always left him dispirited, low, and restless, even to Extremity. I was willing to try every thing first, before I proposed the *last Remedy*; for I never found any one would come into it till their Sufferings were *extreme*, and that they found nothing else would do, and so were brought to be willing to purchase Ease at any Rate. *Gold may be bought too dear*; and as long as *common Remedies*, and *common Life* will do, I own, it is not reasonable to expect that any should submit to *uncommon and extraordinary Methods*. *Dying* alone, is not so terrible to an honest and good Man; tho' all the *Bounces* about it, I have sometimes heard, seem really *unnatural*, and pass with me for nothing; the *Author* of our *Nature* has wisely implanted the *Terror of Death* in us, to support our Endeavours of living under the many Miseries and Misfortunes of our present Imprisonment; the only Misfortune is, when we come too late in the Application of this *last Remedy*, and the Time is elaps'd for a perfect Recovery. This *Gentleman*, being one of finely *cultivated Parts*, as well as of good, sound natural Sense, comply'd more readily than I expected from a Gentleman of his *Profession*: when I propos'd a *Milk and Vegetable*

Vegetable Diet, as the *sole Means* left for his total Recovery from all his Complaints, and for a firm State of future Health. When he enter'd upon it at first, his *Appetite* was quite gone, so that he lived in it for some time on the least I ever knew a Man do. I have known him pass *many Weeks*, and *some Months*, with a little *Bohea Tea*, and a small Cup of *Milk*, with about half a Penny Roll, without Butter, for *Breakfast*: and about a *Pint* of boil'd Milk, with scarce a whole *Roll* for *Dinner*; and his *Supper* (if any) was two or three Spoonfuls of *Honey* boil'd and skim'd in a *Pint* of Water, with a Slice or two of a *Penny Roll* toasted; and he told me, he found *Honey* thus boil'd in Water, and thus *skim'd* and *defæcated*, one of the most *heartening* and enlivening Meals he could then take; and certainly this is an excellent Method to take off the *Rawness*, *Crudity*, and *Colicking* Quality of *Honey*, which being a Kind of Natural Balsam or *inspissated Juice* of the Meal of young *Vegetables* on the *Blossoms of Plants*; is consequently, when thus boil'd, skim'd, and diluted, a most excellent tender Food for weak Stomachs. After passing a *Winter* at *Bath*, to inure him to this *Regimen*, repeating *Vomits* and *warm Opiates* on *Paroxysms*, Riding, and Drinking the *Bath* Waters, I sent him through the *South of France* into *Italy*, where, being out of the Way of Temptation, and an *ingenious, well-educated Gentleman*, he passed his Time both agreeably and usefully; and after about two Years stay, he brought Home with him a sound, firm *Vegetable* Constitution, and a Stock of useful Knowledge, for the Ornament of the Country he resides in, and has been now Healthy for many Years; (and Father of fine Children,) by continuing his *Vegetable Diet*.

CASE IV.

A *Gentleman of Wales*, of strong *natural Parts* and great *Ingenuity*, but descended of a *Gouty* Family, was early in Life seized with that Disorder, which in a few

few Years rose to such Height, that he was almost constantly confined to his Bed by it, at least for *eight* or *ten* Months in the Year; and when his *Hands, Feet, Knees, Hips* or *Shoulder Joints* were not affected, it was in his *Head, Stomach,* or *Bowels,* so that he had no Ease but from pouring down constantly great *Doses* of strong *Wines, Drams,* or *Cordials.* Thus wearied out, crippled, and crucified, he came here to *Bath,* to be under my Direction; ready and willing to submit to any *Discipline* or *Self-denial* I should prescribe, to get, at least Ease, if not rid, of so tormenting a Distemper. As he was in this Disposition, I put him immediately on a *Vegetable Diet,* (it being in Summer, and he then in his *lucid Interval*.) Besides the *Diet,* I gave him a medicated opening Wine, with *Rhubarb, Quinquina, Aromaticks* and *Bitters*; (or a Kind of *Lower's Tincture,* without *Steel*) this, with the Waters, I designed should cleanse the *Primæ Viæ* thoroughly, and lessen the Quantity and *Acrimony* of the *Arthritick Salts* by Degrees. He continued here four or five Months, drinking the Waters, and using this Medicine, by which his next *Fit* was less painful and durable; and he has kept to this *Regimen,* and these Medicines, under some Form or other, at times, ever since. In the *Fit* I ordered him to drink plentifully of *small Sack Whey* or *Sage Posset,* with *Hartshorn* Drops, and to live mostly on the Seed and Meal Meats then, (as *Bread, Pudding, Water-Gruel, Panada, Rice,* and *Sago,* with or without Milk;) in the *Intervals* of the *Fits,* on *Milk, Fruit, Roots,* and *Herbs,* and to take often the *medicated Wine* I have mentioned, and on Occasions the *Bath* Waters, with the constant Use of the *Flesh Brush.* By this Method he has not only recover'd the Use of his Limbs in a great Degree, but in the long Intervals, is as *lightsome, chearful,* and *happy* as any Man can be, after having been so long *crippled* by so violent *hereditary* a Distemper. His *Fits* are with very moderate Pain and little *Inflammation,*

flammation, and their coming on and going off, is with little or no Sickness. He looks *healthy*, *hearty*, and *chearful*, and, I believe, would not change his present Life, for his past, for the greatest sensual Gratifications; he is now yearly growing better, and is like to hold it out to a *great* and *green old Age*; whereas formerly, under the Management he was forced to use for Relief, he could have held it out but a very few miserable Years.

CASE V.

A *dignified Clergyman*, of great *Learning* and *Worth*, well known by his *excellent Works*, had naturally a great deal of *Spirit* and *Fire*, but by a *sedentary* and *studious* Life, had brought on *Flatulence*, *Giddiness*, Oppression, Lowness, and Anxiety to a great Degree, by which he had been long oppressed. He had been always very temperate, of a slight, tender Make, but of late had grown very thin, dry, and was running almost into a *Scorbutical* and *Nervous Atrophy*. I had advis'd him formerly in the best Manner I could, sometimes the *Gum Pills*, with an *Aloetick*, sometimes *Sylphium*, or *Steel and Bitters*, and sometimes *Spa*, *Pyrmont*, or *Bath* Waters, by which he had been much reliev'd; but at last none of these, nor any thing I could suggest, would have any durable Effect. In fine, I told him, that nothing, in my Opinion, but a total *Milk* and *Vegetable* Diet could effectually and entirely cure and restore him; which he readily and chearfully complied with, and entered upon directly, being, as I said, *thin* and *temperate*, and without *gross Humours*. So he had no Reason to expect any *Dispumatory* Fits by this Method: And with no other Assistance from *Art*, but sometimes an *Aloetick Pill*, or the *Rheum Quinquinatum*, he got in a very short Time *easy*, *chearful*, of full and free Spirits, and capable of any Degree of Application and Study, without Weariness and Oppression, and without the Necessity of that *Posting* Life of *Horse-Service*, so necessary to carry

carry off the superfluous Load in others, under the same Kind of Complaints, and in a full and free *Diet*. He is now like to continue long healthy, chearful, and lively.

CASE VI.

A *Gentleman*'s *Lady of Oxfordshire*, of as much *Virtue*, *Piety*, *Charity*, and good Sense, as any one I ever was acquainted with, came here to *Bath*, for *schirrous Knots* and *Tumors* in her Breast, which both I and other *Physicians* believed to be a threatening or beginning *Cancer*. I tried here with her *Cinnabar*, *Milliped*, *Lenitive Electuary*, *Diacassia cum Manna*, and other cooling and soft *Openers*, with a regulated young *Animal Food Diet*, and a very little *Wine*, under the Course of the *Bath* Waters, which she pursued here for many Weeks with great Exactness and considerable Benefit. I advised her to continue the same Medicines at home, with *Asses Milk* and *Bristol Waters*, which she persisted in all that *Winter*; but towards *Spring* her *Pains* and *Shootings* became more intense and frequent, being attended with a Cough, by which she began to be alarmed, as far as one of her admirable *Patience* and *Resignation* could be. I then told her plainly, that nothing but a *total Milk* and *Vegetable Diet* could save her from a *Cancer*, which she most implicitly submitted to, and has continued in ever since, and is now become the most *lively*, *easy*, and *chearful Lady* alive, being a publick Blessing to her Neighbours and poor *Tenants*, and a Happiness to all her Friends and Acquaintances.

CHAP.

CHAP. IV.

The Objections against a Regimen, especially a Milk, Seed, and Vegetable Diet, considered.

I. MANY more Cases I could mention, of such as, in the like *Distempers* with these here specified, have actually obtained under my Direction a *lasting and solid Cure*, by a Regimen of *Diet* and such *Medicines*, as I have hinted. But if these will not satisfy my Reader, *Volumes* of *Cases* would not; they will be sufficient for the *Candid Miserable* and *Sincere*; the *Captious Healthy*, and the *Diffident*, nothing I can say will satisfy. It is certain none will undertake such a *Method*, till they have found all others vain and ineffectual; nor can I blame any one for so doing: If the Gratification of their *Palate* and *Taste* be of greater Pleasure to them than their Sufferings are of Pain, they are as yet unfit for any such Regimen or *Method*; they must be *worse*, before they can be *better*. I think it pretty certain from the Way of Living of the *lower* Rank of all Nations, that such a *Regimen* will not directly *kill* or *starve* any thing but *Distempers:* Unless the *Wound* be actually *mortal* and *incurable* in its own Nature and Degree: and even then it will prolong their *Days*, and make their *Passage* less miserable and painful, than any other Method; and I daily see many wretched Persons *complaining, grumbling*, and inwardly cursing the *Creator* of the *Universe* for their Miseries and Sufferings, who I am *morally* and *medically* certain, bring all their Wretchedness on themselves, by constantly over-loading, bursting and cramming the *poor passive Machine:* and who, by the Methods and Medicines I have mentioned, might be made *easy, chearful*, and *happy*, though not perhaps always at *first*, (unless they have few *Humours* or *Salts* in their Juices) yet surely in *some Time*. A

vege-

vegetable Patient of mine, very juftly obferv'd to me, that whereas before, he could never truft his Appetite's Longings or Craving, while on an *animal high Diet*, without fuffering to Extremity: Now he found, he might fafely and fecurely truft Nature and Appetite, without Danger, Fear or Suffering. Others I have known, who having entered upon, and being in fome Degree recovered by this Method and thefe Medicines, yet have continued weak, poor, and valetudinary all their Days, for Want of *Refolution* and *Perfeverance* in it, by being divided and frightened by the unexperienced *Gainfayers*. But in about thirty Years *Practice*, in which I have in fome Degree or other, advifed this Method in proper Cafes, I have had but two *Patients*, in whofe total Recovery I have been miftaken; and theirs were both *fcrophulous Cafes*, where the *Glands* and *Tubercules* were fo many, fo *hard* and *impervious*, that even the *ponderous* Remedies and *Diet* joined, could not difcufs them, and they were *both* alfo too far gone before they entered upon them; and I have found deep *fcrophulous* Vapours, the moft obftinate and perverfe of any of this *Tribe* of thefe Diftempers: and indeed nothing can poffibly reach fuch, but the *ponderous* Medicines, joined with a *liquid, cool, foft Milk and Seed Regimen*; and if thefe *two* do not in due Time, I can boldly affirm it, nothing ever will.

II. One of the moft terrible Objections, fome weak Perfons make againft this *Regimen* and *Method*, is, that upon accidental *Trials*, they have always found *Milk, Fruit*, and *Vegetables* fo inflate, blow them up, and raife fuch *Tumults* and *Tempefts* in their Stomach and Bowels, that they have been terrified and affrighted from going on. I own the *Truth* and *Fact* to be fuch in fome as is reprefented: And that in *Stomachs* and *Entrails* inured only to hot and high Meats and Drinks, and confequently in an *inflammatory* State, and full of *Choler* and *Phlegm*, this Senfation *sation* will sometimes happen; just as a Bottle of *Cyder* or *fretting Wine*, when the Cork is pulled out, will fly up, fume, and rage: And if you throw in a little *Ferment* or *Acid*, (such are *Milk, Seeds, Fruit* and *Vegetables* to them) the *Effervescence* and *Tempest* will exasperate to a *Hurricane*. But what is Wind, Flatulence, Flegm, and Choler? But stopp'd *Perspiration*, superfluous Nourishment, inconcocted *Chyle* of high Food and strong Liquors, fermenting and putrifying? And when these are shut up and cork'd, with still more and more solid, strong, hot, and *styptick* Meats and Drinks, is the Corruption and Putrefaction thereby lessened? Will it not then at last either burst the Vessel or throw out the Cork or Stoples, and raise more lasting and cruel *Tempests* and *Tumults*? Are *Milk and Vegetables*, Seeds and Fruits, harder of Digestion, more *Corrosive*, or more capable of producing *Chyle*, *Blood*, and Juices, less fit to *circulate*, to *perspire*, and be *secreted*? But what is to be done? The *Cure* is obvious. Begin by Degrees, Eat less *Animal* Food: the most tender and young, and drink less strong fermented Liquors for a Month or two; then proceed to a *trimming* Diet, of one Day Seed and *Vegetables*, and another, tender young *Animal* Food; in the mean Time take frequent gentle *Wash-Vomits*, and *Rhubarb* and *Bark* Stomach Purges; drink *Mineral* and *Chalybeat* Waters, and *Aqueous Bitters*; take *Testaceous* Powders and *Alkaline Earths*, and then by Degrees slide into a total *Milk, Seed, and Vegetable Diet*: Cooling the *Stomach* and *Entrails* gradually, to fit them for this soft, mild, sweetening *Regimen*; and in Time your Diet will give you all the *Gratification* you ever had from *strong*, *high*, and *rank* Foods and *spirituous* Liquors: And you will enjoy to the Bargain at last, *Ease*, *free Spirits*, *perfect Health*, and *Long Life*. *Milk* of all Kinds, and *Seeds*, are fittest to begin with in such Cases, when dried, finely ground and dress'd, and consequently the least *flatulent*. Lessen the Quantity

tity even of these, under what your Appetite would require, at least for a Time. *Bear a little, and forbear.* *Virtue* and *good Health* are not to be obtained without some Labour and Pains against contrary Habits. It was a wild *Bounce* of a *Pythagorean*, who defy'd any one, to produce an Instance of a Person who had long lived on *Milk and Vegetables:* who ever *cut* his own *Throat*, *hang'd* or *made away* with himself; who had ever suffer'd at *Tyburn*, gone to *Newgate*, or to *Moorfields*, (and he added profanely) or would go to *Hell* hereafter.

III. Another *doughty* Objection against a *Vegetable Diet*, I have heard has been made by *learned Gentlemen:* And is, that *Vegetables* require great *Labour*, strong *Exercise*, and much *Action*, to digest and turn them into proper *Nutriment*, as (say they) is evident from its being the common *Diet* of *Day-Labourers, Handy-Craftsmen,* and *Farmers:* This Objection I should have been asham'd to mention, but that I have heard it came from the Men of Learning; and they might have as justly said, that *Freestone* is harder than *Marble*, and that the Juice of *Vegetables* makes stronger Glew than that of *Fish* or *Beef!* Do not *Children* and young Persons, *that is,* tender Persons, live on *Milk* and *Seeds,* even before they are capable of much Labour and Exercise? Do not all the *Eastern* and *Southern* People live intirely almost on them? The *Asiaticks, Moors,* and *Indians,* whose *Climates* incapacitate them for much Labour, and whose *Indolence* is so justly a Reproach to them? Are there lazier and less laborious Men than the *Highlanders* and *Native Irish?* The Truth is, *Hardness* of *Digestion* does principally depend on the Minuteness of the component *Particles:* as is evident in *Marble* and *precious Stones;* and *Animal* Substances being made of Particles that pass through innumerable, very little, or *infinitely small excretory Ducts,* must be of a much finer *Texture,* and consequently harder and tougher in their Composition, than any

Vege-

Vegetable Substance can be: And the *Flesh* of *Animals* that live on *Animals* are like double distill'd Spirits, and so require much more Labour to break, grind and digest them: And indeed, if *Day-Labourers* and *Handy-Craftsmen* were allowed the high, strong Food of Men of *Condition:* and the *quick* and much *thinking* Persons were confined to the *Farmer* and *Ploughmen*'s Food, it would be much happier for both.

IV. The *last Objection* I shall take notice of against a *Milk and Vegetable Diet*, is, that it breeds *Phlegm*, and so is unfit for tender Persons of cold Constitutions, especially those whose predominant Failing is too much *Phlegm*: But this Objection has as little Foundation as any of the precedent; *Phlegm* is nothing but superfluous *Chyle* and Nourishment, or the taking down more Food, than the *Expences* of Living, and the *Waste* of the *Solids* and *Fluids* require; the People that live most on such Foods, (the *Eastern* and *Southern* People, and those of the *Northern* I have mentioned) breed less *Phlegm* than any others. *Superfluity* will always produce *Redundancy*, whether it be of *Phlegm* or *Choler*; and that which will digest the most readily, will breed the least *Phlegm*, (as is evident from infinite *Experiment*, and the best *Philosophy*) such are *Milk*, *Seeds*, and *Vegetables*. Generally speaking, the *Phlegm* in the *Glands*, in the *Lungs*, and on the *Stomach*, is nothing but the *Viscosity* of the *Serum* of the Blood, and that which will least produce *Viscosity*, will produce least *Phlegm*; it is true, by cooling and relaxing the Solids, the *Phlegm* will be more readily thrown up and discharged; more, I say, by such a *Diet*, than by a hot, high, *caustick*, and restringent one; but that Discharge is a Benefit to the Constitution, and will help it the sooner and faster to *dispumate* and *purify*, and so to get into perfect good Health; whereas by shutting these up, the *Case* or Cask must fly and burst so much the sooner.

V. The only material and solid Objections against a *Milk*, *Seed*, and *Vegetable* Diet are, *First*, that it is *particular* and *unsocial*, in a Country where the common Diet is of another Nature: But I am sure *Sickness*, *Lowness*, and *Oppression* is much more so; and I should never advise any one to such a *Diet*, who can do tolerably under a *common* one: Tho' these Difficulties happen only at first, while the *Cure* is about: for when good Health comes, these *Oddnesses* and *Specialities* will vanish, and then all the contrary to these will be the Case. *Secondly*, That it is *weakening*, and gives a Man less Strength and Force than common Diet. It is true, that may happen at first also, while the *Cure* is imperfect; but then the greater *Activity* and *Gaiety* which will ensue on Health, under a *Milk* and *Vegetable Diet*, will liberally supply that Defect, if real; and I should never advise any one to such a *Diet*, whose Manner of Living and *Occupation* requires great *Mechanical* Force, Labour, and Strength; for they seldom or never can want so poor and low a *Diet* for this Distemper, because their *Labour* and *Exercise* drawing off and *antidoting* the Faults and Inconveniencies of a full, strong, and free Manner of Living, will preserve them; so it will never be required or be necessary or fit for the *governed*, but the *governing*; never for those whose Excellence lies in their *Limbs*, but those whose Superiority lies in their *Heads* and *thinking Faculties*; never for the *Active*, but for the *Sedentary*. But *Thirdly*, The most material Objection against such a Diet, is, that it *cools*, *relaxes*, *softens*, and *unbends* the Solids at first, faster than it *corrects*, *thins*, and *sweetens* the Juices, and so brings on greater Degrees of Lowness, than it is designed to cure, and so sinks instead of raising. But this Objection is not universally true, for there are many I have treated, who without any *Rub*, *Inconvenience*, or consequent *Lowness*, have gone into this *Regimen*, and have been free from any *Oppression*, *Sinking*, or any Degree of Weakness ever after; and they

they were not only those who have been generally temperate and *clean*, free from Humours and Sharpnesses; but who on the *Decline* of Life, or from a naturally weak Constitution or Frame, have been oppress'd and sunk, from their Weakness and their Incapacity to *digest* common *Animal Food*, and *fermented* Liquors. Those who have been very *voluptuous*, or very *gross*, when this cooling *Diet* has loosened their gross *Humours*, *acrid Bile* and *sharp Serum*, must suffer in throwing these off; but I have suggested Means constantly to relieve these Symptoms. *Bark, Rhubarb, Bitters, Steel*, and *Chalybeat Mineral Waters*, will always keep up the Tension of the Solids in a Degree sufficient for such a Diet; and I very much question if any *Diet*, either *hot* or *cool*, has any great Influence on the *Solids*, after the Fluids have been intirely sweetened and *balmified*. For then I have always found the *Solids* return to much the same State of *Strength* and *Spring*, they were in before the Distemper; and all the Functions return to the same *Tenor*: *Sweeten but and thin the Juicies, the rest will follow of Course*.

The Case of the Honourable Colonel Townshend.

Colonel *Townshend*, a Gentleman of excellent natural Parts, and of great *Honour* and *Integrity*, had for many Years been afflicted with a *Nephritick* Complaint, attended with constant *Vomitings*, which had made his Life painful and miserable. During the whole Time of his Illness, he had observed the strictest *Regimen*, living on the softest Vegetables and lightest *Animal Foods*, drinking *Asses Milk* daily, even in the Camp: and for common Drink *Bristol* Water, which, the Summer before his *Death*, he had drank on the *Spot*. But his Illness increasing, and his Strength decaying, he came from *Bristol* to *Bath* in a Litter, in Autumn, and lay at the *Bell-Inn*. Dr. *Baynard* (who is since dead) and I were called to him, and attended him twice a Day for about the Space of a Week, but his *Vomitings* continuing still incessant, and obstinate against all Remedies, we despaired of his *Recovery*. While he was in this Condition, he sent for us early one Morning: we waited on him, with Mr. *Skrine* his *Apothecary* (since dead also); we found his *Senses* clear, and his *Mind* calm, his Nurse and several Servants were about him. He had made his *Will*, and settled his Affairs. He told us, he had sent for us to give him some Account of an *odd Sensation*, he had for some Time observed and felt in himself: which was, that composing himself, he could *die* or *expire* when he pleas'd, and yet by an *Effort*, or some how, he could come to Life again: which it seems he had sometimes tried before he had sent for *us*. We heard this with *Surprize*, but as it was not to be accounted for from now *common Principles*, we could hardly believe the *Fact* as he related it, much less give any Account of it: unless he should please to make the *Experiment* before us, which we were unwilling he should do, least, in his weak Condition, he might carry it too far. He had continued to talk very distinctly and sensibly above a Quarter of an Hour, about this (to Him) surprizing *Sensation*, and insisted so much on our seeing the *Trial* made, that we were at last forced to comply. We all three felt his Pulse first: it was distinct, though small and *threedy*: and his *Heart* had its usual Beating. He compos'd himself on his Back, and lay in a still Posture some Time: while I held his right Hand, Dr. *Baynard* laid his Hand on his Heart, and Mr. *Skrine* held a clean Lookinging-glafs to his Mouth. I found his *Pulfe* fink gradually, till at laft I could not feel any, by the moft exact and nice Touch. Dr. *Baynard* could not feel the leaft Motion in his *Heart*, nor Mr. *Skrine* the leaft Soil of Breath on the bright *Mirror* he held to his Mouth; then each of us by *Turns* examin'd his *Arm, Heart*, and *Breath*, but could not by the niceft *Scrutiny* difcover the leaft *Symptom* of *Life* in him. We reafon'd a long Time about this odd *Appearance* as well as we could, and all of us judging it inexplicable and unaccountable, and finding he ftill continued in that Condition, we began to conclude that he had indeed carried the *Experiment* too far, and at laft were fatisfied he was actually dead, and were juft ready to leave him. This continued about half an Hour, by Nine o' Clock in the Morning in *Autumn*. As we were going away, we obferv'd fome Motion about the Body, and upon Examination, found his *Pulfe* and the *Motion* of his *Heart* gradually returning: he began to *breath* gently and fpeak foftly: we were all aftonifh'd to the laft Degree at this unexpected Change, and after fome further Converfation with him, and among ourfelves, went away fully fatisfy'd as to all the Particulars of this Fact, but confounded and puzzled, and not able to form any rational *Scheme* that might account for it. He afterwards called for his *Attorney*, added a *Codicil* to his *Will*, fettled Legacies on his Servants, received the *Sacrament*, and calmly and compofedly expir'd about five or fix o' Clock that Evening. Next Day he was opened, (as he had ordered) his Body was the foundeft and beft made I had ever feen; his *Lungs* were fair, large, and found, his *Heart* big and ftrong, and his *Inteftines* fweet and clean; his *Stomach* was of a due Proportion, the *Coats* found and thick, and the villous

lous *Membrane* quite entire. But when we came to examine the *Kidneys*, though the *left* was perfectly found and of a just *Size*, the *right* was about four Times as big, distended like a blown *Bladder*, and yielding as if full of Pap; he having often pass'd a *Wheyish* Liquor after his Urine, during his Illness. Upon opening this *Kidney*, we found it quite full of a white *Chalky* Matter, like *Plaister of Paris*, and all the fleshy Substance dissolved and worn away, by what I called a *Nephritick Cancer*. This had been the Source of all his Misery; and the *symptomatick* Vomitings from the Irritation on the consentient *Nerves*, had quite starved and worn him down. I have narrated the *Facts*, as I saw and observed them deliberately and distinctly, and shall leave to the *Philosophick Reader* to make what Inferences he thinks fit; the Truth of the material Circumstances I will warrant.

The Case of the learned and ingenious Dr. Cranstoun, *in a Letter to the Author at his Desire, in Dr.* Cranstoun's *own Words.*

Jedburgh, Sept. 20. 1732.

DEAR SIR,

YOURS of *May* last was most agreeable: I am much oblig'd to, and at the same Time charm'd with, that *masterly* Reasoning in such *massy* Expressions, as brings the most subtile *Speculations* in a manner to the Senses, in plain Conceptions, vastly like the *Simplicity* of *Nature*, which is never perplex'd, however much so our Accounts of of it may be. What you are pleased to communicate, of a *Treatise* you design for the Press, gives me great Pleasure. A *Class* of Diseases so universally frequent, and so peculiarly the *Cloud* and *Bane* of the most worthy and valuable *Lives*; deep set in the *Oeconomy*, and so little gained upon by *Medicine*: *superficially* treated by its *Professors*, and *carelesly* or *weakly* trifled with by the Patients; demands and well deserves a *Master's Hand*. I rejoice to find the Task undertaken, by one equally qualified to do Justice to the Subject, and Good to Mankind. For my own Part, I shall never reflect upon the miserable *Distress* I have suffer'd, but with grateful Remembrance of that kind Humanity, wherewith you communicated your frank and friendly Advice. The clear distinct Knowledge, from small imperfect *Hints*, you had at first of my Distemper, was equally surprizing, with the positive Assurance of Success, with which you pressed to persuade and encourage my following your *Method of Cure*; nothing but mature Experience and well-taken Observations, upon certain Principles of *Science*, cou'd have warranted, or supported a Prediction more like *prophetick Security*, than *physical Prognostick*, which hitherto has answer'd; as I have faithfully the Condition. And now Dr. Dr. *Infandum!* ―― *Jubes renovare dolorem*. But as so good a Friend's Commands are sacred, if it may in the least be serviceable to your Purpose, I shall, beside what you know already, give a short *Abstract*, as I can now recollect, of the Origin and Progress of my Disease, wherein, without the least Reasoning, Conjecture or Term of *Art*, I shall confine it to a simple Narration of most essential Matters of *Fact*, without troubling you with every Circumstance and *Symptom*, which however proper to the true *History of a Disease*, would

would be too tedious, and perhaps superfluous here. And though, at best, I'm always at a vast Loss for Language and Expression, I must beg you'll forgive my careless Freedom in this: While I write with Ease and Openness to a Friend: if you can but take the Meaning, I hope whatever Use you please to make of it, you'll be so kind as to treat me and it as your own.

(1.) A Constitution rather *tractable* than strong, nor subject to considerable Disorders, except such transient *Symptoms* of a *Colluvies Serosa*, upon Cold or Errors in Life, as commonly denominate a *scorbutick Habit*, never afflicted since Childhood with any formed Disease, till at *Leyden*, I got an *autumnal Quartan* in 1719, then Epidemical in *Holland*; which gave easy Way to the *Cortex*, and the whole succeeding Winter had no Relapse; but that same Winter I first suffer'd by Gripes and Purging, which always seiz'd me early in the Morning, without the least further Trouble through the Day. The following Spring Season, a Return of the *Ague* in a tertian *Type*, carried off that *Symptom*, which never return'd more for several Years, to interrupt good Health, in pursuing my Business with considerable Fatigue, careless altogether of either *Diet*, or Exposures to all Airs in all Seasons without much Inconvenience.

(2.) About *Spring* Time 1727, I began to be visited now and then with an odd uneasy Sensation in the right Side, between the false Ribs and *Spine* of the *Ilium*, or, as I judged, at the Seat of the *Cæcum*, which seldom came up to acute Pain: but of various Feelings, sometimes of Coldness, at other Times of Heat, and often it felt like *vermicular* Motions, or *spasmodick* Workings in that Part; and these *Symptoms* would sometimes be commu-

communicated to the external *Teguments*, at other Times spread inward to the *Bowels* in different Commotions. This Trouble, without much further affecting the Body, came and went at first a long Time, but, always irritated by Cold, became at last more constant through the whole Summer, when I *dragg'd* about with a great deal of Trouble; now become more universal, as frequent *chilly cold Horrors*, sick *Periods*, with a quick small Pulse and dry Mouth, insuperable Coldness in the *Extremities*, even in the hottest Days, &c.

The Beginning of *Autumn* 1727, after being much expos'd to cold rainy Weather, my former Complaints formed more directly into *Gripes*, and sick *Throws* in the Guts; which often arose from, or at least most affected that first Seat of Trouble in the right Side, and settled into *periodical* Returns, which were about the Evening Sun-set: and the same Hours in the Morning: which *Periods*, or I may call them *Paroxysms*, continued always till by repeated Evacuations of crude *Fæces* and glutinous *Lentor* the *Intestines* were throughly evacuated. But retaining an Appetite sharp enough, and being tolerable easy in the Intervals, without minding its Progress or Consequence, I persisted in my ordinary Course of Living and Business, though with severe Incommodement, and daily Aggravations from Cold: till the Middle of *October*, when the Season turning bitter Cold and wet, all the *Symptoms* increased, attended with a *Latent Fever*, I was disabled at once and confin'd.

(3.) Thus, though better and worse, I continued after the same Manner all the *Winter* in great Distress; oppress'd with innumerable *Symptoms*, which partly arose from the *Genius* of the Disease, and partly from its Effects on the *Oeconomy*,

nomy, and so more common to an exhausted Constitution and debilitated *Nerves*; which need not be enumerated here. When the Disease was not diverted from its Course by *Medicine*, *Management* or an excessive *Fever*, that sometimes made its Violence continual without Regularity; the *Dysenterick Symptoms* seem'd generally inclined to periodical *Exacerbations*, which commonly began in the Morning early about four or five, and kept near the same Evening Hours. The *Gripes* and *Purging* were usher'd in with a *mortified* Coldness, especially in the Extremities; deep felt in the *tendenous* Parts: the *Gripes* through all the *Guts*, but chiefly the *Colon*, and that on the right Side, which soon after affected the *Rectum* with wringing Violence, and rigid *Pressure* on Dejection; after one Motion, no more quiet, but by repeated Irritation all the *mucous* and crude Contents were discharged, after which the succeeding Stools were surprizingly different, at different Times: liquid purely, or *Crass*, in all the malignant Variety of Colours and Consistence that has ever been observed in that Discharge: and while that Matter was moving in its Descent through the *Guts*, the horrid Sensations, *Rigors*, Heartsick Throws, &c. which attended its Progress, always *prognosticated* the virulent Appearance.

After this Course of several Hours was finished, there was some Respite till the *Intestines* were again replete, or the new Time of Access approached, when the same *Scene* was repeated. In the mean time the *Urine* was variable, of a deep *saturate* Colour, when the *Fever* was sensibly high, with a *lateritious*, dusky or dark Sediment sometimes, especially when the Purging was retarded or abated; good Quantities of crude, limpid, or greenish tinctur'd *Urine*, of a bitter acrid Pungency; often attended with *nervous* Affections,

Dr. Cranſtoun's Caſe.

for ordinary about ten or twelve o' Clock of the Day, the *Urine* would come to ſome Separation: towards the Evening more crude and limpid, and the ſame again at the Morning *Period*.

For ordinary, when the Fever was moderate, and no immediate *Nauſea* affecting the Stomach, the Appetite was tolerable; ſometimes ſharp and an unnatural Craving, with an ungrateful acid Taſte in the Mouth; but eating was but laying in a new Load, rather to be preſſed down in new Commotions than digeſted. Little Thirſt, except ſometimes, when a *Dryneſs* of the Mouth, *&c.* or *feveriſh* internal Heat, made it unquenchable. Commonly a rigid Dryneſs of the Skin, though oft-times *Symptomatick* Fluſhes of Sweat, rarely univerſal and natural: which when it happen'd of a *critical* kindly Sort with gentle urinous Diſcharge, ſeldom fail'd of doing Service. By labouring thus through the whole Winter, you may believe I was pretty much exhauſted and emaciated, with conſiderable Swelling of the Legs, *&c.*

Medicines, I us'd ſeveral to little Effect, *Rhubarb*, or the gentleſt *Stimulus* enraged all the *Symptoms*; all eaſy gentle Aſtringents of every kind had no Effect, and ſtrong ones, as *Decoct. Diaſcord.* with *Terra Japonica*, proved violent *Cathartics*; *Injections* of any kind, when the Diſeaſe rag'd, promoted it; *Opiates* only, though not always, check'd the Purging; but only by ſiſting the Action of irritate *Fibres*, the Load was accumulated for a redoubled Diſcharge: and in the mean time moſt always produced a *Nauſea*, Vomiting, with many other *nervous Symptoms*, till their retentive Power was gone, and never failed effectually to debar Sleep, though by quieting Pain, it gave eaſy *watching Reſt*.

(4) About

(4) About *March* 1728, with the Assistance of *Opiates*, the Disease began to abate, and at last the Purging went off, but left the *System* vastly debilitated; and subject to many Disorders, proper to such a State; however I pass'd the *Summer* and next *Winter* without the *Dysentery*; but in continual Hazard of a *Relapse*, and little Confirmation of Health or Strength. All that Time I made choice of the most *drying* Food, and red Wines in small Quantities; with a simple Intention to abstract from the *Materies Morbi*, and corroborate the *primæ Viæ*, abstaining from whatever might be said to moisten or relax.

(5) Towards the End of *Summer* 1729, the old *Symptoms* (2) began to recur. I neglected them, still exposing to the *autumnal* Colds, till all came to the same Heights as before; (3) went through the same Course of Distress that Winter with little essential Variation, save what might arise from the greater Violence of the Disease, and less equal Strength in the Subject. Except a few Weeks of Respite from the *Dysentery* that *Spring*, without which it is likely Nature had yielded. I had no more Intermission all the *Summer* 1730, the Disease rag'd with more Heat and Thirst, *&c.*

But the warm Season allow'd me to drag a feeble and distressed Body abroad, and that as far as *Tunbridge*; I made tryal of the Waters there, you know without any Success, returning to *London* in as great Distress as ever; I wanted much to be determin'd, doubtful if I should be carried towards *Bath* or Home: I then first made free with a *Character* I was a little acquainted with by the *Press*, and asked your Opinion: by a speedy and kind Return, you dissuaded me from *Bath*, upon good Reasons, confirmed by Experience, and with a *friendly Warmth*, advis'd a *Method*

thod of *Living*, as the only Cure remaining, pressed by most encouraging Assurance of Success, if I was not beyond the Power of *natural Agents*. I obey'd, came Home through a Journey of the greatest Distress ever one travelled, and immediately began *your Method*, of a *Milk* and *vegetable Diet*, but the Disease rag'd with such Violence, and natural Strength was so far gone, that I was not able to observe any *Rules* with Exactness. All the *Symptoms* (3) formerly mentioned were aggravated with several Changes, which I cannot particularly relate, only, in general, more sensible Heat, Thirst, and evident *Fever*, than had ever been before.

At this Time, *Jan.* 1731. when exhausted more than ever, the Purging, by a little Assistance of *Opiates*, after a Day's *Nausea* and *Vomiting*, was abated, which preserved the remaining Life. I then began to be exact in *Diet*, restricting it only to *Milk* and *Grains of Rice*, *Millet*, &c. and abdicated all *animal* Food; in about six Weeks or two Months, the *Dysentery* gave Truce, in which Time I was often fretted with *strangurious Symptoms*. I sometimes took Notice of one *Phœnomenon* in the *Urine*, which I never remember to have seen, or heard, or observ'd before, which was the *Pellicle*, which it commonly carry'd on the Top, was powdered with exceeding small *shining Particles*, like *Gold-dust*; the Sides of the Glass beset with the same, and the *mucous* Cloud in the *Centre* wrought full of them: These glittering *Atoms*, when gathered on the Finger, had the Feeling of fine hard Dust, and the *Urine* saturate with these at its first Evacuation, would sparkle and rise in the *Glass*; at such Times there was deep Disorder in the *Oeconomy* and *nervous System*.

(6) The Beginning of next *March* 1731. the Season being a sharp Frost, after some Days of chilly mortify'd Cold, I was seiz'd with a heavy *Stupor* and *feverish* Heat, with a Return of the *Dysentery*; by this Time, feeble, and little able to stand the Shock: the *Stomach* felt loaded, which came to a Vomiting of a heavy *Pituit*: the Sense of a stuffing Load still remaining, I took a Vomit which discharg'd a vast Quantity of *crude Flegm*, clear and glassy, just as the unbroken White of Eggs; still the Weight at *Stomach* continued, the *Fever* increased with biting Heat and great Thirst, a *Pulse* feeble, unequal, and quick; at the same time a languid Inflammation seized my Throat, and Parts about it: A little after appeared an Erruption of *Apthæ* in the Mouth, especially on the Tongue, which was all over thick set, with very small *pellucid Pearl-coloured Pustles*: these were attended with a great *Salivation* of crude, insipid crass Stuff, such as I had vomited; the *Apthæ* remained constant, the Sinking and Rising as the *Fever* varied, most Part highest at Night. After about a Week, the *Apthæ* changed their Colour to pale-red, then darker, sometimes livid, and at last a black Depression on the Top of every one of them. By this Time, natural Strength was just a going, mostly supported by *Asses Milk*, which too I was restrained from by reason of the great Effusion of Urine, which it provok'd. Scarce able to move out of Bed, after two or three Weeks thus on the Brink of Dissolution, it pleased God to set the Bounds! The *Symptoms* all gradually, slowly, and insensibly declined, and the *Dysentery* went off at the same Time.

VII. I resolutely, as soon as capable of a Diet, held myself close to your Rules of *bland vegetable Food*, and *elementary Drink*; and without any other Medicine, save frequent chewing of *Rhubarb*, and

and sometimes a little *Cortex*. I passed last Winter and this Summer without a *Relapse* of the *Dysentery*; and, tho' by a very slow Advance, I find now more Restitution of the Body, and Regularity in the *Oeconomy*, on this *primitive Aliment*, than ever I knew from the Beginning of this Trouble. This encourages much my Perseverance in the same *Method*, and that so religiously, as to my Knowledge, now for more than a Year and half, I have not tasted any thing that had *animal Life*. There is Plenty in the *vegetable* Kingdom, and *Milk* taken itself, affords Variety: And, say it were otherwise, *Health* should be thought an easy *Purchase* at a little Restriction of *Taste*, did not its principal Enjoyment shamefully consist in *Pleasure of Sense*.

Every one, upon the most obvious Considerations, may be convinced of the great Influence that *Aliment* must have on the *Crasis* and Constitution of our Bodies, which it daily supplies, and of which, at last, it becomes *constituent Materials*. And yet for want of due Attention to this *noble Branch* of *Medicine*, or from a vicious Indulgence, and Weakness of Resolution, how often is our *Practice* rendered `miserably unsuccessful? and in many, the most considerable *chronical* Distempers, degenerates into meer *Trifling* or *Quackery*.

I have too much tried your Patience with an unpolished but faithful Relation of *Facts*, and must leave such Speculations to more Experience and a better Judgment.

When it is not mispending your Time, you'll believe, I hope, it is real Pleasure, as well as improving, to have a Letter from my good Friend; being most sincerely, *Dear Doctor,*
Your most affectionate,
and obliged humble Servant,
W. CRANSTOUN.

I chose to give this *Case* in the *Doctor's* own Words, thinking it would be more satisfactory in its *native Dress*; for tho' *He* modestly thinks it might want a little of the modern polishing, yet the strong good Sense, the nice Observations, and unaffected Simplicity, is infinitely preferable to all *Varnish*, and shews *him* equally an *excellent Physician*, and a Man of *Probity*. Other *Cases* of the same Kind under my Care, I have from several *Gentlemen* of the *Faculty*, which shall be produced (if necessary) in due Time, after obtaining their Permission.

The *CASE* of the *Author*.

§. I. I Was born of healthy Parents, in the *Prime* of their Days, but dispos'd to *Corpulence*, by the whole Race of one Side of my *Family*. I passed my *Youth* in close Study, and almost constant Application to the *abstracted Sciences*, (wherein my chief Pleasure consisted) and consequently in great *Temperance* and a *sedentary Life*; yet not so much but that I sometimes kept *Holiday*, diverted myself with the Works of *Imagination*, and roused *Nature* by agreeable Company and *good Cheer*; but, upon the slightest *Excesses*, I always found slippery Bowels, or a Spitting to be the *Crise*; whence afterwards, on Reflection, I concluded, that my *Glands* were naturally *lax*, and my *Solids feeble*; in which Opinion I was confirmed, by an early *Shaking* of my *Hands*, and a Disposition to be easily rufled on a *Surprize*. Upon my coming to *London*, I all of a sudden changed my whole Manner of Living I found the *Bottle-Companions*, the *younger Gentry*, and *Free-Livers*, to be the most easy of *Access*, and most quickly susceptible

ceptible of *Friendship and Acquaintance*, nothing being necessary for that Purpose, but to be able to *Eat* lustily, and swallow down much *Liquor*; and being naturally of a large *Size*, a cheerful Temper, and tolerable lively *Imagination*, and having, in my Country Retirement, laid in Store of *Ideas* and *Facts*, by these Qualifications I soon became carressed by them, and grew daily in *Bulk*, and in Friendship with these gay Gentlemen and their Acquaintances: I was tempted to continue *this Course*, no doubt from a *Liking*, as well as to force a *Trade*, which Method I had observ'd to succeed with some others; and thus constantly Dineing and Supping in *Taverns*, and in the Houses of my Acquaintances of *Taste* and *Delicacy*, my Health was in a few Years brought into great Distress, by so sudden and violent a Change. I grew excessively *fat*, *short-breath'd*, *Lethargick* and *Listless*.

§. II. The first sensible *Shock* I had, was an *autumnal intermittent Fever*; this I conquer'd in a few Weeks with the *Bark*, which at that time, I found exceeding *fresh*, *thin*, *Cinnamon-coloured*, and *curled*: This sort (as I know from long Experience) greatly contributing to the Speed and certainty of the *Cure* of such Distempers, being more easily digested, and entering more readily into the Mass of Blood, while the Stomach is spoilt by a *Disease*, and the Juices under a *præternatural Ferment*. For one Year I went on tolerably well, tho' as it were *jumbled* and *turbid*, and neither so clear in my Faculties, nor so *gay* in my Temper: But next Autumn I was suddenly seized with a *vertiginous Paroxysm*, so extreamly frightful and terrible, as to approach near to a *Fit* of an *Apoplexy*, and I was forced in it to lay hold on the Posts of my Bed, for fear of tumbling out, as I apprehended. After immediate *Bleeding* and *Vomiting*

miting (whereby its Violence was abated) I thought it might be owing to an *anomalous* Fit of my relapsing *Inmittent*, and thereupon took about four Ounces of this fine *Bark* in 48 Hours, but without any sensible Benefit or Injury. I found after this, some small Returns of my *Vertigo* (in Bed especially) on lying on a particular Side, or pressing upon a particular Part of my Head; but by Degrees it turned to a constant violent *Headach*, *Giddiness*, *Lowness*, *Anxiety* and *Terror*, so that I went about like a *Malefactor* condemn'd, or one who expected every Moment to be crushed by a *ponderous* Instrument of Death, hanging over his Head. At this time I left off *Suppers* of all kinds, and have never resum'd them since; then, even at *Dinner*, eating but a small Quantity of *animal Food*, and drinking very little fermented Liquor, well knowing, that *Diseases* must always be cur'd by their *Contraries*. On this Occasion, all my *Bouncing*, *protesting*, *undertaking* Companions forsook me, and dropt off like *autumnal Leaves*: They could not bear, it seems, to see their Companion in such Misery and Distress, but retired to comfort themselves with a *cheer-upping* Cup, leaving me to pass the melancholy Moments with my own *Apprehensions* and *Remorse*. Even those who had shar'd the best Part of my Profusions, who, in their Necessities, had been assisted by my false Generosity, and in their Disorders relieved by my Care, did now entirely relinquish and abandon me; so that I was forc'd to retire into the Country quite alone, being reduc'd to the State of *Cardinal Wolsey*, when he said, that if he had serv'd his *Maker* as faithfully and warmly as he had his *Prince*, he would not have forsaken him in that Extremity; and so will every one find, when *Union* and *Friendship* is not founded on *solid Virtue*, and in Conformity to the *Divine Order*, but in *sensual Pleasures*

and

and mere *Jollity*. This silly Circumstance I mention, because I thought then, it had some Share in my succeeding *Melancholy*.

§. III. I retir'd, I say, to the Country, into a fine Air, and liv'd very low: I had a *Seton* made in my Neck, which I carried about for many Months; I took frequent *Vomits*, and gentle *Purges*, try'd *Volatiles*, *Fœtids*, *Bitters*, *Chalybeats*, and *Mineral Waters*, and had the Advice of all my *Physical Friends*, but with little or no sensible Benefit; my *Headach*, *Giddiness*, *Watchings*, *Lowness*, and *Melancholy* rather increasing on me. I had by chance heard of the great Benefit, which one of my particular Acquaintances had reap'd from some active *mercurial* Medicines (tho' prescrib'd by a very insufficient *Practitioner*) in a violent stupifying *Head-ach*, which I had Reason to believe came by the same Intemperance; these I resolv'd to try. I *first* took twenty Grains of what is call'd the *Princes Powder*, which gave me twelve *Vomits*, and near twice the Number of Stools; and I had certainly perished under the Operation, but for an *Over-dose* of *Laudanum* after it. In two or three Days more, I took twelve Grains of *Turbith-mineral*, which had not quite so violent an Effect; after that I took ten Grains of *Calomel*, twice a Day, for about ten Days together; this put me into a *Petit Flux de Bouche*: After which in three Weeks Time I got abroad lightsomer indeed, and less confus'd, tho' still very bad, and scarce any thing better, but not worse; but two Months after that, I found an extream Sickness in my *Stomach*, which obliged me to take frequent *Vomits*, these now pumping up *Oceans* of *Choler*, which they had never done in any Degree before: Whence I concluded, that the *ponderous* Remedies I had taken, had opened my obstructed *Liver*, *Gall bladder*, and *Porus*

rus Biliarius, and broken the Cohesion of the viscid Juices.

§. IV. While I was thus (as I have said) forsaken by my *Holiday* Friends, and my Body was, as it were, melting away like a *Snow-ball* in Summer, being dejected, *melancholy*, and much confin'd at home, by my Course of *mineral* Medicines, and Country Retirement, I had a long Season for undisturbed *Meditation* and *Reflection* (my Faculties being then as clear and quick as ever) which I was the more readily led into, that I concluded myself infallibly entering into an *Unknown State of Things*. Having had a *liberal* and *regular Education*, with the Instruction and Example of pious Parents (who, at first, had designed me for the *Church*) I had preserv'd a firm Perswasion of the great and fundamental Principles of all *Virtue* and *Morality*: viz. the *Existence* of a *supreme and infinitely perfect Being*, the *Freedom* of the *Will*, the *Immortality* of the Spirits of all intelligent Beings, and the Certainty of *future Rewards* or *Punishments*. These Doctrines I had examined carefully, and had been confirmed in, from *abstracted* Reasonings, as well as from the best *natural Philosophy*, and some clearer Knowledge of the *material System* of the World in general, and the *Wisdom*, *Fitness* and beautiful Contrivance of particular Things *animated* and *inanimated*; so that the Truth and Necessity of these *Principles* was so riveted in me (which may be seen by the first Edition of my *Philosophical Principles*, published some Years before that happened) as never after to be shaken in all my *Wanderings* and *Follies*: And I had then the Consolation to reflect, that in my loosest Days, I had never pimp'd to the *Vices* or *Infidelity* of any, but was always a determined Adversary to both. But I found, that *these* alone were not sufficient to *quiet my* my Mind at that Juncture, especially when I began to reflect and consider seriously, whether I might not (through *Carelessness* and *Self-sufficiency*, *Voluptuousness* and Love of *Sensuality*, which might have impaired my *Spiritual Nature*) have neglected to examine with sufficient Care: If there might not be more required of those, who had had proper *Opportunities* and *Leisure*; *if* there might not, I say, be higher, more noble, and more enlightening *Principles* revealed to Mankind *somewhere*; and *if* there were not more encouraging and enlivening *Motives* proposed, to form a more extensive and *Heroic* Virtue upon, than those arising from *natural* Religion only (for then I had gone little farther than to have taken *Christianity* and *Revelation* on *Trust*) and *lastly*, *if* there were not likewise some clearer Accounts discoverable of that *State* I was then (I thought) apparently going into, than could be obtained from the mere Light of *Nature* and *Philosophy*. Such were my Reflections in this my *melancholy* Retirement, and this led me to call to Mind, *which*, of all my numerous and various Acquaintances, I could wish to resemble *most*, now in these my (to me seemingly) approaching *last* Moments; and who among all those of my particular Acquaintances, was *He*, who being of sound *natural*, and duly *cultivated* Parts, had most strictly and constantly liv'd up to their Convictions, under the commonly received Principles, and plain Consequences of *Christianity*. In a Word, who it was I could remember to have had received, and lived up to the plain Truths and Precepts contain'd in the *Gospels*, or more particularly in our *Saviour's Sermon* on the *Mount*. At that Time among many whom my Memory suggested to me, I fix'd on one, a worthy and learned *Clergyman* of the *Church of England*, sufficiently known and distinguished in the

Philosophical and *Theological* World (whom I dare not name, because he is still living, tho' now extreamly old); and as in studying *Mathematicks*, and in running over (as I was able) Sir *Isaac Newton*'s *Philosophical* Works, I had always pickt out, and mark'd down the *Authors* and Writings mostly used and recommended by those others, and by him, because I thought they could best judge of such; so in this Case the more quickly to settle my *Mind*, and quiet my *Conscience*, I resolved to purchase, study, and examine carefully such *Spiritual* and *Dogmatic Authors*, as I knew this *venerable Man* did most approve and delight in. In this Manner I collected a *Set of religious Books* and *Writers*, of most of the *first Ages* since *Christianity*, recommended by him, with a few others of the most *Spiritual* of the *Moderns*, which have been my *Study*, *Delight* and *Entertainment* in my Retirements ever since; and on these I have formed my *Ideas*, *Principles* and *Sentiments*: so as, under all the Varieties of *Opinions*, *Sects*, *Disputes* and *Controversies*, that of *late*, and *since* the *Earliest Ages*, have been canvassed and bandyed in the World, I have scarce ever since been the least shaken, or tempted to change my Sentiments or Opinions, or so much as to *hesitate* in any *material Point*. This tedious, perhaps impertinent Circumstance I mention, because the *Fright*, *Anxiety*, *Dread* and *Terror*, which, in Minds of such a Turn as mine (especially under a broken and *cachectick* Constitution, and in so attrocious a *nervous* Case) arises, or, at least, is exasperated from such Reflections, being once settled and quieted, *That* after becomes an excellent *Cordial*, and a constant Source of *Peace*, *Tranquillity* and *Cheerfulness*, and so greatly contributes to forward the Cure of such *nervous* Diseases: For I never found any sensible *Tranquillity* or Amendment, till I came to this firm and
settled

settled *Resolution* in the Main, *viz.* To neglect nothing to secure my eternal Peace, more than if I had been certified I should die within the Day: nor to mind any Thing that my secular Obligations and Duties demanded of me less, than if I had been ensured to live fifty Years more. This, tho' with infinite Weakness, and Imperfection, has been much my settled Intention in the Main since.

§. V. The Spring following I was advised and pressed by all my Friends, and the *Physicians* I consulted, to try the *Bath Waters*. I went there accordingly, for the first Time, as a *Patient*; and, for many Weeks, was much relieved both in my *Stomach* and *Spirits* by them: And tho' in the Opinion of the World, I liv'd very temperately, yet by increasing the Quantity of my *Animal Food*, and *strong* Liquors (my Appetite being now stronger and more craving, and my Spirits brisker, from the drinking of the Waters) in the Space of four or five Months, I was heated so, as to apprehend a *Hectic*. I then changed the *Bath* for *Bristol* Waters, retrenched my *Diet*, and increased my daily Riding and Exercise, and continued sometimes gentle *Vomits*: by which I past that Year better than the former, tho' far from well; but, on the Return of the next Spring, some *Symptoms* were exasperated, insomuch that their Severity, the Continuance of my Miseries, and the constant Complaints, common to *Hypish* People, made Life a Burden to myself, and a Pain to my Friends. I accidentally met with a Clergyman, who told me of a wonderful Cure, which Dr. *Taylor* of *Croydon* had wrought on himself in an *Epileptick Case*, by a total *Milk Diet*. This *Hint* accidentally dropt, wrought so on me, that I began to recollect a great many Things, that before had escaped me without much Reflection. I had read in Dr. *Sydenham*, that in violent and obstinate *Hysterick Fits* and *Colicks*, he had, with great Success, prescribed a *total Milk Diet*, as the last and surest Remedy. Dr. *Pitcairn*, my Master and Friend, in his *Dictates* had recommended it as the only *infallible Cure* in an inveterate *Scurvy*, *Cacochimy* and totally vitiated Juices: And I myself knew it to be the only Remedy in the *Gout*, a confirmed *Hectic* and *Consumption*, and had seen Miracles wrought by it in such Cases; besides, I knew *nervous* Distempers of all Kinds, differed only in Degrees. All these Considerations determined me, next Day, in the Middle of Winter, to ride to *Croydon* to advise with Dr. *Taylor* personally. I found him at home, at his full Quart of Cow's Milk (which was all his Dinner.) He told me, he had had the Advice of all the most eminent *Physicians* of his Time about *London*, and had taken all their Medicines, and all he had ever read or heard of, for his *Epilepsy*, but with so little Success, that he used frequently to be seized with it on the Road, while he was riding in the Country about the Business of his Profession, so that dropping from his Horse, he remained senseless, till by the next Waggoner or Passenger he was carried to the nearest House; and that both his *Life* and *Faculties* had been in the utmost Danger by it; but that, on reading *Sydenham*, he had first dropt all fermented Liquors, whereby his Fits became less violent and frequent, and then, by Degrees, he had given over all *animal Food*, living intirely on *Cow-Milk*, with which, at first, he used only to take a few Drops of *Sal volatile* or *Harts-horn*, or a Spoonful of *compound Pæony* Water, to prevent its curdling; that, in a Year or two his *Fits* had entirely left him: and that now, for *seventeen Years*, he had enjoyed as good Health as human Nature was capable of, except that once in a damp

damp Air and foggy Weather, riding thro' *Essex*, he had been seized with an *Ague*, which he had got over, by chewing the *Bark*. He told me, he could then play six Hours at *Cricket* on *Banstead-Down*, without Fatigue or Lowness, and was more *active* and *clear* in his *Faculties and Senses* than ever he had been in his Life before. He informed me also of a great many Persons he had cured of inveterate Distempers by this *Diet*, and particularly that he had removed the *Barrenness* of some great Families by it, who before had wanted *Heirs*.

§. VI. Having thus fully satisfy'd all my Doubts and Difficulties, I return'd to *London*, fully determin'd to enter upon this Course, for which I was sufficiently before prepared, by the low *Animal Diet*, and small Quantity of fermented Liquors, I had of a long Time been accustomed to. I drank *Cow-Milk* from the *Park* every Morning, and engag'd a Milk Woman at a higher Price than ordinary, to bring me every Day as much pure and unmix'd, as might be sufficient for *Dinner* and *Breakfast*; (for, as I mentioned before, I had given over all Kinds of *Suppers*, and never after resum'd them, having always found myself worse on the slightest Attempts that way at Night, tho' even in Milk and Vegetables.) I used *Seeds*, *Bread*, *mealy Roots*, and *Fruit* with my Milk indifferently, taking them all to be pretty near of the same Nature and Class of Foods: *Milk* being *Vegetables* immediately cook'd by *Animal Heat* and *Organs*, and directly (without going the Circulation) drawn from their *Chyle*, or from an *Emulsion* of Vegetables in the Stomach. I thought scarce any grown Person was so delicately fram'd by Nature, or that I was not reduced to such extreme Weakness, that *infinitesimal* Errors, could do great Hurt; and therefore I continued all these,

these, for a little Variety, lest I should be cloy'd by only one Kind of Food; and ever since have used and prescribed *Milk* and *Vegetables* indifferently, in extream low and dangerous Cases only, when sufficiently prepar'd by *Culinary Heat and Organs*, and am perswaded they differ little in their Nature. In five or six Months I was considerably recovered; only upon the *Glands* being loaded, and the peccant Matter of the old Habit being thrown upon the *chyliferous* Duct, and the constantly ensuing Oppression and Restlesness thereupon; I was forced to cleanse them often by a gentle *Vomit*, or an *Aloetick Pill*, which as constantly restored me to my usual clear and free Spirits, and to a good Appetite for my then Food.

§. VII. By this Time I had been extreamly reduced in my Flesh, and was become Lank, Fleet and Nimble; but still, upon any Error even in this low Diet, I found more or less Oppression and Lowness. Next Spring tho' I began to feel a constant Pain, fix'd in the *Pit* of my *Stomach*, which I mistook for a *Pulmonary* Case, and therefore became still more temperate and abstemious even in this my Milk and Seed Diet. During all this Time, I generally rode a Horseback ten, or fifteen Miles a Day, both Summer and Winter; in Summer on the *Downs* at *Bath*, and in Winter on the *Oxford Road* from *London*. I began more frequently then to take an *Aloetick Pill* once in ten or fourteen Days, (for *Rhubarb* never agreed with me) which always gave me great present Relief in my *Stomach*, and consequently in my *Spirits*. All this Time I followed the Business of my *Profession*, with great Diligence and Attention, in Summer at *Bath*, and in Winter at *London*, applying myself more particularly to *chronical*, and especially to low and nervous *Cases*, they seeming more immediately to concern my self, and

offering

offering more frequently at *Bath*, where all of that Kind, in both *Islands*, arrive first or last, who can afford it.

§. VIII. The Pain in the *Pit* of my *Stomach*, being now constant, violent, and seeming to increase, I began to think of Dr. *Taylor*'s chewing the *Bark* to cure his Ague; and knowing it to be so sovereign a Remedy in *Stomach and Nervous* Cases, I got some of the finest, and chewed about half a *Dram* of it twice or three times a Day, on an empty *Stomach*; and in ten Days or three Weeks at most, I found so wonderful a Change on my whole Man, as to *Spirits*, *Chearfulness*, *Strength* and *Appetite*, by it, that I thought it *Enchantment*, and could scarce believe I was my self; and had I been much *Enthusiastically* given, would have accounted it *miraculous*, being naturally one of these *Quick-Thinkers*, who have a great Sensibility either of Pleasure or Pain. My Juices being thin, sweet, and fluid by the *Diet*, it seems there was nothing wanting to the perfecting Health, but the winding up and bracing the Solids, for which the *Bark* was *specifick*. From that Time forward I encreas'd in *Spirits*, *Strength*, *Appetite*, and *Gaiety*, till I began to find a Craving and insufferable Longing for more solid and toothsome Food, and for higher and stronger Liquors; but being well apprised of the Danger of too sudden and quick a *Transition*, from a low to a high and fuller *Diet*; I proceeded at first with great Caution and Wariness, eating only the Wing of a small Chick, and drinking but one Glass of White Wine (for I found all red, and especially *French*, by a grating on my lax *Stomach* and *Guts*, keep me awake three or four Hours in the Night) all that Summer and the next Winter, (which I pass'd at *London*) I enjoyed perfect good Health and Spirits,

rits, though I had used little or no Exercise; but notwithstanding all my Caution, I had certainly gone too fast and too far into this new *animal Diet*; for the Spring following I was seized with a *depuratory Fever*, which notwithstanding all the Skill and Care of my Brethren, the *Physicians*, lasted above twenty Days, and the Medicine (after the universal Evacuations) that had the greatest Share in my Recovery, was, I think, large Draughts of warm *Barley* Water or small *Sack Whey*, acidulated with *Gas Sulph.* which was advis'd by Dr. *Baynard*, towards the latter End of my *Fever*; this, at last, threw me into a profuse *Sweat*, which lasted above three or four Days, and reduc'd me so extremely low, that for some Time I liv'd chiefly on *French* Claret, with Water and toasted Bread, this being the only Food I could relish; and though I never exceeded half a *Pint*, or at most a *Pint* of Wine a Day, mixed with Water, yet having used my self to so little for a great while before, this small Quantity kept me perpetually *Hectical* and Restless for many Weeks, even after the *Crise*: so that I began to think I had done wrong before, in using my self to so little Wine; and therefore to secure against such an Accident for the future, I began (after my perfect Recovery) to inure my self by Degrees to more Wine, gradually dropping or lessening the Quantity of my *Milk* and *Vegetables*, and by slow Degrees and in moderate Quantities, living only on the lightest and tenderest animal Food for some Time, and at last gradually went into common Life, with great *Freedom*, but exact common *Temperance*.

§. IX. But the long and violent *depuratory Fever*, which I did not get over entirely in less than six Months, had so drain'd, drench'd and wasted

wasted me, that upon my total Recovery, my Appetite being insatiable, I suck'd up and retain'd the *Juices* and *Chyle* of my Food like a *Sponge*, and thereby suddenly grew *plump*, *fat*, and *hale* to a Wonder; but indeed too fast. However, for near twenty Years, I continued *sober*, *moderate*, and *plain* in my Diet, and in my greatest Health drank not above a Quart, or three Pints at most, of *Wine* any Day, (which I then absurdly thought necessary in my Bulk and *Stowage*, though certainly by far an over *Dose*) and that at Dinner only, one half with my Meat, with Water, the other after, but none more that Day, never tasting any Supper, and at Breakfast nothing but Green Tea, without any *Eatable*; but by these Means every Dinner necessarily became a *Surfeit* and a *Debauch*, and in ten or twelve Years, I swell'd to such an enormous Size, that upon my last Weighing I exceeded thirty two *Stone*. My Breath became so short, that upon stepping into my Chariot quickly, and with some Effort, I was ready to faint away, for want of Breath, and my Face turn'd black. At *Ainhoe* (waiting on the late Honourable Mrs. *Cartwright*) and going up only one Pair of Stairs, with high Steps, hastily, by pushing my Breath a little too violently, to make room for those that were following, I was immediately seiz'd with a *Convulsive Asthma*, returning by repeated and strong Inspirations, *Fits* and small Intervals, which lasted above a Quarter of an Hour, so that I thought to have died on the Spot; but by *Evacuations* and *low Living*, I got rid of this Disorder also, in some Degree, though after that, I was not able to walk up above one Pair of Stairs at a Time, without extreme Pain and Blowing, being forced to ride from Door to Door in a Chariot even here at *Bath*; and if I had but an hundred Paces to walk, was oblig'd to have

a Ser-a Servant following me with a Stool to rest on.

§. X. About this Time (twelve Years after my first Recovery) my Legs broke out all over in *scorbutick Ulcers*, the *Ichor* of which corroded the very Skin, where it lay any Time, and the fore Parts of both Legs were one continued Sore. I had the Advice and Care of many of the most eminent *Surgeons* in *England*, none of whom could heal them up even in three Years. Tir'd out at last, I took *Æthiops Mineral* for four Months, in the midst of Winter: half an Ounce at least twice a Day, and a Purge with twelve Grains of *Calomel* once a Week, observing a much lower Diet than before; I found that the *Mercury* had not only colour'd the *Money* in my Pocket, and the *Buttons* in my Shirt; but to all my Observation, the very Substance of the *Æthiops* was transpir'd upon the *Plaister*, every Day, when my Legs were dress'd, *viz.* towards the End of the Cure; at least, the Appearances seem'd to me, on the Plaisters, like a Steam or Smoke from *Sulphur* and *Mercury*, and was quite different from what it had been before I began that Course: This I was perfectly assur'd of, though I did not then think of making such a *critical* Observation, as that *this* Instance might serve as a Proof, that the *Æthiops* passed through the Habit; though I am certain since, from repeated *Observations*, that every Preparation of *Mercury*, and even the *Crude* it self, in Time, and in some lax Habits, will *Salivate* in some Degree or another: and that *Mercury*, in its *minutest Particles* and insensible *Steams*, does penetrate the solid Parts of all *living Animals*, as *inflammable Spirits* most certainly do. After this Course, my Legs healed perfectly, with common Dressings, and have continued sound ever since; my Health was likewise very good for four

or

or five Years after. But continuing the same full, though (commonly accounted) *temperate Diet*, and using little or no Exercise, I became at last *heavy, dull*, and *lethargick* to an extreme Degree, especially after Dinner; and the *Midsummer* 1723. I was seiz'd with a severe *Symptomatick Fever*, which terminated in the most violent *Erisipelas*, and with the largest and fullest Blisters all over my Thighs, that I had ever seen. I suffered extremely in the Symptomatick *Fever*, by violent *Head-aches*, great *Sicknesses* and *Sinking*; and having lately had two full-bodied Patients, who had died of *Mortifications* from that Distemper, I was much frightened at mine. My Blood was then, I found, one continued *impenetrable Mass* of *Glew*, and my *Erisipelatous* Inflammations were so painful, (and attended with *Lowness, Sinking* and *Inquietude*) as reduc'd me to the very last Degree of Misery. I had always resolv'd, upon any great Change in my Health, to return to my *old Friends, Milk* and *Vegetables*, and to abstain from Wine in a great measure, provided I had but sufficient Warning by any *Chronical* Illness. I then made a long Journey in a Coach, and liv'd on *Milk* and *white Meats*, drinking *Bristol* Water, and only a *Pint* of Wine a Day, by which I was somewhat relieved, though not so much as to conquer my Fears or my Sufferings; so that having continued this Method for two Months, I began gradually to lessen the Quantity of my *Animal* Food still more, and at last, to live entirely on *Milk* and *Vegetables:* This, in some Time, made my Spirits vastly better; but still, for two Years, I was regularly and *periodically* seiz'd every third Month, almost to a Day, with this *Erisipelas*, the Symptoms of which were indeed not so grievous as at first, though still attended with violent *Head-aches*, a *Symptomatick Fever* for forty eight Hours before

fore the *Eruption*, large Blisters full of *Scorbutick Ichor*, and great Lowness for the Space of a Week; after which I recovered my *pristine* State. But I was always obliged to *vomit* before the Eruption, to push it out: and relieve the *Head-ach* and *Fever*: and to purge after it was over. Thus I went on for seven or eight Months, wasting daily, but at the same Time recovering Spirits, Activity, and the Use of my Limbs. I had all that Winter had a slight Pain in the back *Tendon* of my left Leg, reaching down to my Heel, which in *March* following terminated in a regular Fit of the *Gout*, in the Joint of my *big Toe*; this confin'd me a Fortnight or three Weeks, and it had no sooner left that Place, than it seiz'd my *Shoulder Joints*, where it continued for above a Month. I pass'd the rest of the Summer pretty tolerably, but for these *periodical* Returns of that *Erisipelas*, which continued very regular, above two Years. About the *Michaelmas* of that Summer, I was seiz'd with such a perpetual *Sickness, Reaching, Lowness, Watchfulness, Eructation,* and *Melancholy*, continuing six or eight Months: that Life was no longer supportable to me, and my Misery was almost extreme.

§. XI. At last, my Sufferings were not to be expressed, and I can scarce describe, or reflect on them without *Horror*. A *perpetual Anxiety* and *Inquietude*, no *Sleep* nor Appetite, a constant *Reaching, Gulping,* and fruitless Endeavour to *pump* up *Flegm, Wind,* or *Choler* Day and Night: A *constant Colick,* and an ill Taste and Savour in my Mouth and Stomach, that overcame and *poisoned* every Thing I got down; a *melancholy Fright* and *Panick,* where my Reason was of no Use to me: So that I could scarce bear the Sight of my Patients, or Acquaintances, that had not been daily about me, and yet could not bear being a Moment

ment alone, every Inſtant expecting the Loſs of my *Faculties* or *Life*; and ſurely nothing but *Almighty Power* preſerved them both, ſuch as they are. I had a conſtant violent Pain in the *Neck* of my *Stomach*, and was obliged almoſt every Week to take a ſtrong *Emetick*, without which I could not enjoy a Moment's Eaſe, beſides daily urging with my Finger, or chewing *Tobacco*. I had Recourſe to my old Friend the *Quinquina* in ſeveral Shapes, but to no Purpoſe. I drank *Bath* Waters without ſenſible Relief. I went out in my Chariot, in the coldeſt Winter Weather, for four Hours every Day; but nothing mitigated my Sufferings. At laſt I tried the *Fœtids*, the *Gums*, the *Volatiles* and *Vipers* Powders (not indeed regularly and ſteadily) but all in vain. In fine, I had Recourſe to *Opiates*, which I knew were a ſlow *Poiſon*; but one will ſtick at nothing for even a Moment's Reſpite in ſuch Extremities. This, inſtead of relieving, aggravated my Miſeries; for ſo ſoon as the ſtupifying and confounding Effects of them were over, my Anxiety and Sinking was ſo extream after, that I was forced to repeat them ſo often, and in ſo large Doſes, that I was juſtly afraid, leſt by their becoming ſo familiar they would, at laſt, loſe even the poor, diſtracting, uncomfortable Relief they afforded me; yet all this Time, I attended indeed (in a Manner) the Buſineſs of my *Profeſſion*, and took *Air* and *Exerciſe* regularly in the Day-time; but in ſuch a wretched, dying Condition, as was evident to all that ſaw me. I had many different and contradictory Advices, from my Friends and Acquaintances, who obſerved my Miſery; but I neither could, from the Nature of my Diſtemper, nor from the ill Effects the ſmalleſt Tryals of any thing propoſed, were attended with, continue them any Time. I well knew my Caſe was the *Gouty* and

Eri-

Erisipelatous Matter retired, and drawn into my Stomach and Bowels: I likewise knew, that if I took hot and strong Medicines and *Cordials* to drive them out (as is usual) I should thereby lose all the Pains I had taken, and the Benefit of the Abstinence I had gone through, to thin and sweeten my Blood and Juices, to open the Obstructions, and to obtain an *Extirpative Cure*, if possible there might be Time enough remaining for it; but the worst was, my *Stomach* would not retain any Medicine, for they had a present ill Effect, by making my Sufferings more intense; however, I was persuaded then to take a little strong warm Wine made with *Spices*, and to have Bread and this Wine mixed for my Dinner: Continuing Tea, with boil'd Milk, and toasted Bread for Breakfast; but all this Time I had no sensible Relief. My *Family* and *Relations* pressed me extreamly to go for *London* (where I had not been for many Years) to pass the Dead of the Winter among my old Acquaintances and Friends, for Amusement and Diversion only: But to this I was extreamly averse, apprehending I might be teized to change my *Regimen*, and sneer'd at by the Freelivers; and being convinced, from former Experience, that if my Life was to be sav'd, it was only by this *Regimen*, at least, if my Time of *Dissolution* was come, I knew I should die under less Misery by it, than by any other Means.

§. XII. However, at last, to prevent *Friendly Teazing*, and the *Character* of Obstinacy, I promised to be *passive*, and to be governed by them; so in the Beginning of *December* 1725, I set out, and with great Difficulty got to *London*. Next Day after my Arrival, I sent to the very *learned*, *ingenious*, my very *worthy Friends*, Dr. *Arbuthnot*, and Dr. *Broxholm*, who, at my Desire, brought with them Dr. *Mead* and the *late* Dr. *Freind*, with
Dr.

Dr. *Douglas* and Dr. *Campbel*, all *Gentlemen* of great Learning, Worth and Experience. They unanimously advised me to try a warm *chalybeat* Electuary, with *Pyrmont* Waters, and by all Means to drop my *Opiates*; for as to *Cathartics*, which were mentioned, they so exceedingly sunk and ruffled me, that I was always dying under them. This *Method* being reasonable and just, I followed some Time, continuing tho' the same *Regimen of Diet*: And though some of those *Gentlemen* and others thought I might have then, with Safety, changed my *Diet*, very slowly, at least. Yet having passed through the same *Course* twenty Years before, and having suffered to such Extremity, and in a younger and more vigorous Part of my Life, and run the utmost Hazard, even by a very slow and gradual *Change*: And knowing the Danger others had undergone by the like *Change*; I was firmly resolved to continue my *Regimen*, happen what wou'd; and indeed when all this was represented to these *Gentlemen* and *my other Friends*, none had the Courage to press it; much less to urge it, in so *insolent* and *sneering* a *Manner* as some, who ridicule all *Shame* and *Truth*, have thought fit falsly to represent it. I have once or twice, in nine or ten Years, been tempted to eat an Ounce or two of young tender *animal* Food, but with such sensible Suffering and Oppression after, that I have resolved never more to make the Trial: And I have known others much younger than I, on whom a *potch'd Egg*, under so long and strict a *vegetable Diet*, for an *Epileptick Case*, has had a disagreeable Effect. As the Winter advanced, meeting with some true *Sylphium* to join with these other Medicines, I became somewhat easier and more chearful by the Spring, tho' almost every month I was forc'd to have Recourse to a strong *Vomit* to clear the *Glands*: But by these warm *chalybeat* Medicines, and the *vitriolick* Waters,

Waters, and drinking near half a Pint, or rather a Gill of *Port* a Day, I had, by the *May* following, forced out such a Fit of an *Erisipelas*, as the best and most experienced Surgeons (who then treated me) had never seen the like: the whole *Leg, Thigh,* and *Abdomen* being *tumified, incrusted,* and *burnt* almost like the Skin of a *roasted Pig:* And such a Quantity of *Ichor* issued from it, as was not to be expressed; at last it ended in a *sinuous Ulcer* in my Leg, which confined me near two Months, and the *sinking Effects* were not quite worn off in almost six; however I passed the next Winter again in *London* much better, and in the Spring was extreamly *easy, active* and *gay*; for from the Time of this last and most severe *erisipelatous Paroxysm,* I reckon I mended daily: For this had the same Effect upon my whole Constitution now, as the *depuratory Fever* before-mentioned had then, both being the *Crise* and *Period* of my Distemper, and the Beginning of my perfect Recovery. This was above six Years since, though I became not perfectly well till the Spring following, and indeed not absolutely so, till about four Years ago.

§. XIII. Upon the Whole, as in my *Nervous* and *Scorbutical* Disorder, I had continued my *Milk, Seed,* and *Vegetable* Diet, with proper Evacuations, for above two Years, before I obtain'd a compleat Recovery, so in this last Illness, I had observ'd the same Regimen near twice as long, before my Health was perfectly established; being in the first Case twenty Years younger than in the last; tho' my Excesses were much more violent in the Time preceding my first Illness, than between that and the last, having, during all that Interval, scarce once been heated with Wine, and never eating *Animal Food* but once a Day. But my exceeding Bulk and Want or Inability of necessary Exercise, and a continued, tho' temperate Fulness, with the Difference of twenty

Years

Years in my Age, concurred to make the *Paroxysms* even more distracting and painful, as well as more durable in this last *Case*. And after all I have said of my Excesses, especially in Liquor, if it be considered, that I was near *thirty* Years old before I drank scarce any thing strong, at least, for a Continuance: and that for near one half of the Time since, *viz.* from *Thirty to Sixty*, I scarce drank any strong Liquor at all: it will be found, that upon the Whole, I drank very little above a Pint of Wine, or at most, not a Quart one Day with another, since I was near thirty: And I was never six times in my Life overtaken with Wine, and scarce ever tasted any distilled Liquors, but as a Medicine, however mix'd or brew'd; always believing them to be actual *Cauteries*, and almost direct *Poison* to an animal Habit, from their Nature, and the Delicacy of the *animal Machine*: And during that whole Time, I scarce ever ate *Animal* Food above once a Day. But Temperance is a mere *relative* Thing; and by much Observation I find, that notwithstanding my *large Size*, I was not made to bear *Animal Food* and fermented Liquors in any Quantity, without suffering to the last Degree. But I believe none will ever be brought to such a *Regimen* as mine is now, without having been first extremely miserable; and I think common Life, with Temperance, is best for the Generality, else it would not be common. But extreme Cases require extraordinary Remedies.

§. XIV. I found I never began to recover fully and lastingly, either first or last, till my Blood had entirely lost its *Size* (which I came to know by an accidental Occasion for opening a Vein) and all the former Habit (except the mere *Organical Membranes and Solids*) was wasted, wore away, and discharged by *Evacuations*, Diet and Exercise; for I had wasted and lost of my former Size and Bulk, in this last Illness, almost one third in Weight and Measure: and had pass'd through a State of entire bodily *Purification*,

rification, and a true *Cyclus Metasyncriticus*, both first and last, before I began to recover and fill up again. *Vomits* were the first Evacuations that with any Relief, or without infinite *Ruffling*, I could bear: and so soon as I could endure gentle Stomach *Cathartics*, I began already to mend; but no sooner had I recovered any Degree of Ease and Freedom, but my Appetite and Digestion returned to their usual Stint towards my new Food, and *Vomits* were no longer necessary, nor indeed useful, they being only required to squeeze the internal *Glands*, open *Obstructions*, and pump up the *Wind*, *Choler*, and *Phlegm* from the *Alimentary Tube* when lodged there.

§. XV. Upon any Accident, Disorder, or any greater Oppression or Anxiety than ordinary, arising naturally in the Course of the Cure, I found that living even much *lower* under my *Milk* and *Vegetable Diet* for two or three Days at least, would always help me out again, and restore me to my usual *Serenity* and *Freedom*, (for I found Temperance necessary even in this, as well as a higher Diet, tho' Excesses were not attended with such *extreme Suffering*) and scarce any Time less than three Days would do it; for though all my Symptoms were less severe under it, yet I found by indulging a *false Appetite*, or a *liquorish Palate* even in it, that I exasperated these *milder Symptoms*, at least to such a Degree, as was sufficient to convince me, that the *Stomach* and *digestive Organs* were the primary and principal *Delinquents*, *Sufferers*, and *Patients*, in most, if not in all *nervous* Symptoms, though this was not always sensible and manifest: and that by using them tenderly, and abstemiously, all the rest of the *Animal Functions* were proportionably reliev'd. And, I think, I never once departed from the *Simplicity* of the *Alimentary Gospel*, and indulged in *Onions* and *Garlick*, *viz.* the *poignant, hard, spicy,* or *unctuous*
Vege-

Vegetables, with much Butter or Oil, or in a greater Quantity than usual, even of the common ones for any Time, but that I suffered Pains and Penalties in Proportion.

§. XVI. I found all my *Restlesness*, *Watchings*, and want of Tranquility or sound Sleep, to be owing entirely to *Inflation*, stored up *Wind* and *Flatulence*, constantly urging and stimulating as it were with its *Spring*, *Elasticity* and *Points*, the tender sensible *Membranes* of the *Stomach* and *Guts*, and the whole *Glands* and *Membranes* of the *Abdomen*; for upon *Fasting* some Time, *Eating* very little, or very thin, light and soft Food, or on using a great deal of more *Exercise*, to urge the *Perspiration*, and to throw off and discharge this *Wind*, *Vapour*, or *sharp Steams*, I found my Sleep return in a greater Degree; and I am bold to say, where no manifest *Fever*, *acute Pain*, *interrupted Circulation*, or *spoil'd Organ* is the Case, that want of Sleep and natural Rest proceeds from the Disorders of the *Alimentary Tube*, continually, tho' perhaps not sensibly, stimulated by this *Vapour*. And hence it is, that *Assa fœtida*, *Volatiles*, *Fœtid Gums*, gentle *Diaphoreticks* and *Opiates*, procure Sleep; merely by encreasing and promoting *Perspiration*, and expelling this twitching *Vapour* or *Steam*, for which they ought chiefly to be used; and this serves to shew the Necessity, and infinite Preference of Exercise to all *Anodyne* Medicines whatsoever, and even to *Cordials*, *Diaphoreticks* and *Volatiles*, except as a present Relief, *Whip* or *Spur* only.

§. XVII. Want of Appetite and Digestion mostly proceeds from the Thickness, Grossness, and Viscidity of the Juices and of the whole Mass of Blood; every *Vein* and *Artery* thereby becoming like so many *Black-Puddings*, or leathern Pipes, stuff'd with a *glewy* or tenacious Fluid: by which all the *Secretions* being more scanty, and less being expended by them, less can be receiv'd thro' the *Lacteals* into the Blood;

Blood; which shews the Necessity and Preference of the *ponderous* and deobstruent Medicines to procure an Appetite and Digestion, even to *Bitters*, *Cordials* or *Chalybeats* themselves: whose Efficacy principally lies in strengthening the Solids, and winding up and contracting the *Fibres*, to make them play, and compress with greater Force the circulating Fluids, which can never solidly answer the Intention of *Digestion* and *Appetite*. And accordingly, by *Quicksilver*, *Æthiops*, *Cinnabar*, but especially by *Mercurius Alcalisatus*, and other *mercurial* Preparations, I have been always able to cure the Disorders of the *Alimentary Tube*, Inappetency, and even *Colicks*, when scarce any other Method or Medicine could effect it. And seeing, by a thin, cool *Milk* and *Vegetable Diet* long continued, I found my Appetite full as good as before, and likewise my *Strength*, *Activity*, *Flesh*, and *Complexion*, and every *Power*, *Organ* and *Faculty* restor'd to as great a Degree as I could justly expect at my Time of Life, had no such Disorder ever happen'd; it appears that the *Fluids* are chiefly and primarily the Seat of Disorders: and that when they are sufficiently *sweetened* and *diluted*, they generally leave the *Solids* with a sufficient Force and Spring to play such Fluids off, and circulate them fully and freely; and then all the *Animal Functions*, and the Exercise of the Faculties will again be pleasantly and regularly performed, as in perfect Health; for good Health supposes this State. which does not depend on the Kind of the *Diet*, though *mechanical* Strength does. So that such a *Diet* is only proper for the *thinking*, *speculative*, and *sedentary* Part of Mankind, and not for the *active*, *laborious*, and *mechanical*.

§ XVIII. After I began to recover, I found little Alteration from *Cold* or *Heat*, *Wet* or *Dry*, *Summer*
or

or *Winter* Seasons, especially as to my *Appetite, Spirits* or *Sleep*; at least not near so much as I usually found in my best Health on these Occasions, under a full *animal* and *fermented* Liquor *Diet*; so that I can sit, and walk, and be abroad in all Weathers, Seasons or Times of the Year, Day or Night, without much Dread or Hazard of Cold, and with little Difference of Cloathing, providing I keep my *Stomach* and *chiliferous Tube* clear and clean; which often put me in mind of the Saying of a *Roman Emperor*, who affirmed, that *Spitting, Coughing, Excretion, Eructation, Yawning*, and the like, were Symptoms and Effects of mere *Laziness* and *Luxury*.

§. XIX. After I had perfectly recovered, observing, that still, on *liquid, slippery* Stools, from cramming I was somewhat less lively and chearful, and rather more *grip'd* and *inflated*, I resolved to change my *half Pint* or *Gill* of *Port* at Dinner, into the same Quantity of *Florence*, thinking it more binding and *astringent*. I ate at the same Time a good deal of more *Butter* with my Vegetables, and Plenty of *old rich Cheese*; and liking *Nuts* extremely, I procur'd from abroad and at home, great Plenty of all Kinds as *Filberts, Walnuts, Chesnuts, Almonds*, &c. eating them in great Quantities after Dinner, by way of *Desert*. I went on all Winter, and for eight or ten Months in this *Regimen* extremely well; and out of *Wantonness*, to try what my Constitution could now bear, I indulged freely (though in these only) together with my usual *Milk* and *Vegetable Diet*. But after my common, slight, vegetable Fit of the *Gout*, (which I still have in the *Spring*, without necessary Confinement, though for an Hour, or altering either *Regimen* or *Cloathing*, or any other Circumstance, but a Lameness for a few Days) I had first a Touch of my *Erisipelas* on my Leg; after that I seemingly catch'd Cold, and began to be sick at my Stomach,

Stomach, *Reaching, Inflated, Low-spirited,* and *Colick'd,* with restless Nights, and almost all those dismal *Symptoms* I had gone through in my late long Illness. I soon found my *Error,* and that my Constitution could not bear even that slight *Alteration* without severe Sufferings. I had a violent humourous Cough, and threw up great Quantities of gross viscid Flegm, which I knew to be the *Nuts,* not so sufficiently digested and attenuated, as to become thin enough to circulate freely through the small Vessels: but were thrown off and despumated upon the larger *Emunctory* and open *Glands.* In a Word, I suffer'd all the Kind of Misery I had formerly, tho' not with quite so much Violence and Duration. I went through the former lesser *Purgation* again: Repeated *Vomits,* took frequent Stomach *Purges,* chew'd *Bark,* return'd to the Simplicity of my former *Regimen,* lessening their Quantities, and drinking no Wine (which I now have dropped for ever, but as others use *Spirits,* for a *Cordial,* if wanted) and drinking first *Bristol* and then *Bath,* and after *Pyrmont* Water, as the Defluxion abated; by these Means I got quite well in about three Months, *viz.* in the *August* after; and since that Time, I thank GOD, I have gone on in one constant *Tenor* of Diet, and enjoy as good Health, as, at my Time of Life (being now *Sixty*) I, or any Man, can reasonably expect; and have learned, that young, tender, animal Food is less dangerous, in a small Quantity, than *hard, hot, spicy,* and *oily* Vegetables.

§. XX. I know not if it be worth the mentioning, that during my *Recovery,* about four Years ago, I was thrown, or rather threw myself, out of my *Chariot* (upon the Fore-Horses being frighted, and the Coachman being thrown off his Box) and falling on my Head, was taken up dead and senseless, being wounded in my *Temple,* and the Wheels of the Chariot having entirely

shav'd

The Author's Case.

shav'd my *Eye-Brow*. But on being blooded, I found my Spirits and Stomach mostly affected with it. I grew, for some short Time, low, feeble, and lost my Appetite; but in two or three Months recovered to a *Miracle*, from what would have kill'd another with bad Juices, and have continued perfectly well ever since.

§. XXI. My *Regimen*, at present, is Milk, with *Tea*, *Coffee*, *Bread* and *Butter*, *mild Cheese*, *Salladin*, *Fruits*, and *Seeds* of all Kinds, with tender *Roots* (as *Potatoes*, *Turneps*, *Carrots*) and, in short, every Thing that has not *Life*, dress'd, or not, as I like it; (in which there is as much, or a greater Variety than in *animal* Foods:) so that the Stomach need never be cloyed. I drink no *Wine*, nor any *fermented* Liquors, and am rarely dry, most of my Food being liquid, moist, or juicy; only, after Dinner, I drink either *Coffee* or *green Tea*, but seldom both in the same Day, and sometimes a Glass of soft small *Cyder*. The thinner my *Diet* is, the easier, more cheerful and lightsome I find myself; my Sleep is also the sounder, tho' perhaps somewhat shorter than formerly under my full *animal* Diet: But then I am more alive than ever I was, as soon as I awake and get up. I rise commonly at *Six*, and go to Bed at *Ten*. The Order I find in this *Diet*, from much Experience, is, that *Milk* is the lightest and best of all Foods, being a *Medium* between *animal* Substances and *Vegetables*; dress'd *Vegetables*, less *windy* and griping, than *raw*; ripe Fruit than *unripe*; the *mealy* Roots more than the *fibrous*; and the *dry* than the *crude Vegetables*. I find much *Butter*, *Cream*, *fat* and oily Vegetables, and especially *Nuts* both hard of Digestion, stuffing and *inflating*. When I am dry (which is rarely) I drink *Bath*, *Bristol* or *Pyrmont* Water.

§. XXII.

§. XXII. I am heartily ashamed, and humbly beg Pardon of my *polite* and *delicate* Readers (if any such should deign to look into this low *Tattle*, contrary to my Intention.) I know how *indecent* and *shocking Egotism* is, and for an *Author* to make himself the Subject of his Words or Works, especially in so tedious and circumstantiated a *Detail*: But so various and contradictory have been the Reports of, and sneers on my *Regimen*, *Case* and *Sentiments*, that I thought thus much was due to Truth, and necessary for my own Vindication; and perhaps it may not be quite useless to some *low, desponding, valetudinary, overgrown Person*, whose Case may have some Resemblance to mine: which every one's has in some Degree, that has a *mortal Tabernacle*, subject to, and afflicted with *nervous* Disorders, by a mistaken *Regimen*, or hereditary Misfortune: and I have, on that Account, written *this* in a plain *narrative* Stile, with the fewest Terms of Art possible, without supposing my *Reader*, or shewing *myself*, to have look'd ever into a *physical* Book before; thinking this *Manner* and *Stile* might be most instructive and beneficial to common *valetudinary* Readers: and tho' some may not have quite my *Bulk* and natural Strength, or have run into such *Excesses*, or have not begun to manage so early in Life as I did first, yet they will only for that require lesser or greater *Doses* of the same *Method*, *Medicines* and Management; and if it have not quite so full and perfect an Effect, as, *under God*, it has had with me, (tho', perhaps, the worst Subject and the most difficult *Case* possible, for so absolute a *Cure*) yet it may, and will always have a better than any other Method (I mean only in so deplorable and *excruciating* a *Case* as mine was) and if it cannot *cure*, it will certainly *reprieve*, and make the Sufferings of all such miserable

able Persons more tolerable: as I have experienced once and again, in the most eminent Degrees: who, from the most *extreme Misery*, do now enjoy as *perfect Health*, as much *Activity* and *Cheerfulness*, with the full, free and perfect Use of my *Faculties*: a Facility of *Study*, and of going about the Business of my *Profession*; and, in short, of every *rational Function of Life*, as I was ever capable of in my best Days: and indeed of every Thing worth living for as a *free and rational Intelligence*; every Thing, I say, except that I cannot *eat* and *drink* so highly and voluptuously as I have formerly; and, if I know my Heart (which I am sure I do not fully) tho' I were to be *eternal* and *unaccountable*, I should live (at least wish to live in the Main and as to *Diet*) as I now do, and would not willingly and deliberately go thro' the same *Misery*, for the mere Gratification of my *Senses* only; no, not to obtain the Dominion of our *System*, and all the *Glories* and *Pleasures* in it. What I may happen to do, *God only knows*; I am too old, I hope, to make any new Tryals and Changes in this my *bodily Regimen*; and indeed to what Purpose? being as well as any, and much better than most are at my Time of Day: And therefore, with *God's Grace*, if my *Health*, *Senses* and *Love of Virtue* continue with me the same, I shall, I hope, go on in the Method now described, and *live*, and, I hope, *die* in continual Gratitude to the *Best of Beings*, who, by an overruling *Providence*, and, as it were, by meer *casual Hints*, far beyond the Reach of my *Penetration*, has irresistibly (as I should almost say, if I felt not my own *Liberty*) directed the great Steps of my *Life* and *Health* hitherto.

Misericordias Domini in æternum cantabo.

The CONCLUSION.

AFTER all the Pains I have taken, I have not yet got so large a Share of *Enthusiasm*, as to hope by these my poor *Labours*, to do Good to any, except perhaps, to a few poor low, *valetudinary*, *dying*, *miserable* Creatures, who have not the Courage *magnanimously and gloriously* to suffer, pine, and putrify. The *Brave*, the *Bold*, the *Intrepid*, the *Heroic*, who value not *Pain*, who can suffer for *Diversion*, and who prefer *Death* with a *Bounce*, to Life, on such Conditions as I propose: and chuse rather to *extinguish* now, than *forty* or *fifty* Years hence, will heartily despise and pity me and my *Lucubrations*. *Nunquam persuadebis etiamsi persuaseris*. You shall never convince tho' you convict me. I have heard of a great *modern Philosopher*, celebrated for his *Wit*, *Wealth*, and *high Living*, who used, in the *Sun-shine* of his Days, to boast, that if *Temperance* and *Abstinence* could make a Man live half a *Century* longer, in Gaiety and Mirth, it were worth the While then to *deny* one's Appetites; but for *Ten* or a *Dozen* of Years more, it was but a poor *Purchase*; and yet I have been told, that the same *Hero*, when his *Time came*, would have parted with his great Estate for a *Reprieve* of a few Years. I own I am one of those poor *mean-spirited Wretches*, who am contented to live as long as *Nature* design'd me to last, and desire to submit with the utmost *Peace and Resignation* I can arrive at when that *Period* is expired; but for *Pain*, *Sickness*, and especially for *Oppression*, *Anxiety* and *Lowness* avoidable, they are my *mortal Aver-*

Aversion, and no Means would I refuse to avoid them, but those, which, I am convinced, would infallibly bring me into greater *Misery and Suffering*; and yet, if I mistake not my own Nature, I have the *Appetites, Passions*, and *Feelings* common to other Men; and I usually ask myself the Question, and look into my own *Heart* for an *Answer*, to any thing proposed concerning human *Appetites, Passions* and *Feelings* that are *natural* and not forced: and give little Credit to what others say contrary to such *Sentiments*. It is true indeed, there are as many and as different Degrees of *Sensibility* or of *Feeling* as there are Degrees of *Intelligence* and Perception in *human* Creatures; and the *Principle* of both may be perhaps one and the same. One shall suffer more from the Prick of a *Pin*, or *Needle*, from their extreme Sensibility, than others from being run thro' the Body; and the *first* sort, seem to be of the *Class* of these *Quick-Thinkers* I have formerly mentioned; and as none have it in their *Option* to choose for themselves their own particular *Frame* of Mind, nor *Constitution* of Body; so none can choose his own Degree of *Sensibility*. That is given him by the *Author* of his *Nature*, and is already determined; and both are as various as the *Faces* and *Forms* of Mankind are. I imagine therefore, there must be required a *particular Make* and *Frame*, both of *Mind* and *Body*, to determine any one to receive heartily and pursue steadily this (as it were) material *Metaphysicks* of a *Regimen*. There seems to be necessary, previous to a Conviction of the Benefit and Necessity of such a State of *Purification, a Je ne sçai quoi*, to make Men comprehend, embrace, and prosecute this *Self-denying* Doctrine, for the sake of such insensible *Trifles*, as *Health, clear Faculties, Cheerfulness, Activity*, and *Length of Days*, when they are in Danger. If this *corporal Sensibility*, as well as *intellectual Delicacy* is wanting, they will prove but short-liv'd, diffident

fident and dastardly *material Spiritualists*, and fall away in the Time of *Trial*; tho' he that hath *Ears to hear will hear*: and good and sound *Threshing*, great and extream *Misery*, *Pain*, *Lowness*, and *Anxiety*, will go a great Way to beget this *Sensibility*, and *Conviction*; for the Means us'd by *infinite Wisdom* and *Goodness* towards reclaiming his *wandering Creatures*, seem only to be either *Love* or *Punishment*: that those whom *Love* will not draw and allure, *Punishment* may drive and force; but neither *Frame*, *Disposition*, *Organ*, nor *Faculty* can make their Objects, or alter their Nature, which are *Things given* and determined. The immutable *Laws of Nature*, and the *Relations of Things* are *constant*, and will subsist in their Order, notwithstanding our *Errors*, *Mistakes*, or *Prejudices*. And it will be *eternally* true, so long as we have such Bodies, that only *Temperance* and *Abstinence*, *Air*, *Exercise*, *Diet*, and proper *Evacuations* can preserve *Life*, *Health*, and *Gayety*, or cure *Chronical* Diseases: I mean in general and in the main; and the *contrary* will always destroy them; and that they will ever mutually expel one another, like *Fire* and *Water*. Even *Homer*, three thousand Years ago, could observe, that the *Homolgians* (these *Pythagoreans*, these Milk and Vegetable Eaters) were the *longest liv'd, and honestest of Men*. *Milk* and *Honey* was the Complexion of the *Land of Promise*, and *Vegetables* the *Diet* of the *Paradisiacal State*: And since such a *Diet* will (if any thing) certainly cure, by the Confession of all *Physicians*, learned and unlearned, ancient or modern, *High* or *Low-livers*, the *Gout*, the *Consumption*, and the *Scurvy*, and such like atrocious, otherwise incureable and mortal Distempers; it will be eternally true also, *quod potest majus potest minus*, or that, what will do to the greater, will do the less of the same Kind: And let the *Brave* and *Bold*, the *Free-living* and *Free-thinking Professors* sneer or rail

rail as they pleale, there muſt be an *eaſier*, *ſimpler*, and *more natural* Way of preſerving *Health* and *Cheerfulneſs*, of *lengthening Life* and *curing Diſtempers*, than that founded on deep *Reſearches*, tedious *Details*, *ſtudy'd Ingenuity*, and *Fineſſing*, elſe the *Poor*, the *Illiterate*, the *Laborious*, and the *Solitary* (the far moſt, if not the leaſt corrupted Part of our *Species*) would be of all Men, the moſt miſerable when ſick. And accordingly it is obſervable, that *Hippocrates*, *Gallen*, *Celſus*, and others of the *primitive Fathers of Phyſick* cured by *Air*, *Exerciſe*, *Diet*, and *Evacuation* moſtly, if not only, even as ſucceſsfully, (tho' not quite ſo ſoon perhaps) as we by all our *Mathematicks*, *Natural Philoſophy*, *Chymiſtry*, *Anatomy*, *Knowledge of the Materia Medica*, and *Animal Oeconomy*. Far be it from me, to leſſen the Value and Neceſſity *now*, of thoſe *Divine Sciences*; for ſince our *Luxury* has kept Pace with our *Knowledge*: the *Obſtinacy* and *Violence*, the *Number* and *Degrees* of our *Diſeaſes* have increaſed proportionally; and therefore *He* that would honeſtly and ſucceſsfully practiſe *Phyſick*, on the *Patients* and *Diſeaſes now* as they are, ought to know all theſe mentioned *Sciences*, to the greateſt Degree he can poſſibly, to enable him even to *alleviate*, *mitigate*, *leſſen* or *cure* theſe *unnatural* and *infernal* Diſtempers *now extant*; and *that Phyſician* will never arrive at true, natural and beautiful *Simplicity*, either of the *Theory* or *Practice of Phyſick*, who has not paſſed thro' endleſs *Multiplicity* in Study, Obſervation, and Experiment in theſe *Sciences*; ſuch a *Simplicity* is the greateſt Contradiction to *Lazineſs*, foreign Studies, *Negligence*, *Incurioſity* and *Ignorance* in the Profeſſion; but ſuch a *Simplicity* (produced by rejecting *Need-not's*) when (if ever) attained, is worth a *Million* of theſe little *falſe* and *foreign Arts* ſometimes us'd to riſe in it; for it is,

in

in Truth and Reality, an *Eminence* of *Light* and *Tranquility*.

*Despicere, unde queas alios passimque videre,
Errare atque viam palantes quærere vitæ.*
                                                            Lucret.

F I N I S.